Emerging Technologies for Recruitment Strategy and Practice

Mohamed Badouch
Ibn Zohr University, Morocco

Mehdi Boutaounte
Ibn Zohr University, Morocco

IGI Global
Scientific Publishing
Publishing Tomorrow's Research Today

Vice President of Editorial Melissa Wagner
Director of Acquisitions Mikaela Felty
Director of Book Development Jocelynn Hessler
Production Manager Mike Brehm
Cover Design Jose Rosado

Published in the United States of America by
IGI Global Scientific Publishing
701 East Chocolate Avenue
Hershey, PA, 17033, USA
Tel: 717-533-8845
Fax: 717-533-7115
Website: https://www.igi-global.com E-mail: cust@igi-global.com

Library of Congress Cataloging-in-Publication Data

Names: Badouch, Mohamed, 1994- editor | Boutaounte, Mehdi, 1987- editor
Title: Emerging technologies for recruitment strategy and practice / edited by Mohamed Badouch, Mehdi Boutaounte.
Description: Hershey, PA : IGI Global Scientific Publishing, 2026. | Includes bibliographical references and index. | Summary: "This book explores how emerging technologies are reshaping recruitment strategy across industries. It offers critical insights into the opportunities and ethical challenges these technologies present for HR professionals and organizational leaders"-- Provided by publisher.
Identifiers: LCCN 2025035576 (print) | LCCN 2025035577 (ebook) | ISBN 9798337365169 hardcover | ISBN 9798337365176 paperback | ISBN 9798337365183 ebook
Subjects: LCSH: Employees--Recruiting | Leadership
Classification: LCC HF5549.5.R44 E69 2025 (print) | LCC HF5549.5.R44 (ebook)
LC record available at https://lccn.loc.gov/2025035576
LC ebook record available at https://lccn.loc.gov/2025035577

British Cataloguing in Publication Data
A Cataloguing in Publication record for this book is available from the British Library.

Table of Contents

Detailed Table of Contents

This chapter presents a data-driven framework for modernizing recruitment through the utilisation of artificial intelligence and e-learning analytics. The proposed 7-stage methodology leverages behavioral data from online learning platforms to assess candidate skills, motivation, and adaptability more objectively than traditional methods. Key components include automated candidate profiling, multi-source data integration, AI-powered interviews, and continuous improvement mechanisms. The approach addresses critical limitations of conventional recruitment, including human bias, inefficiency in evaluating soft skills, and information overload. While offering benefits such as improved candidate-job matching and reduced subjectivity, the chapter also examines implementation challenges, including the issue of algorithmic bias, data privacy concerns, and ethical considerations. The framework contributes to emerging research at the intersection of HR technology, educational data mining, and responsible AI

Artificial Intelligence (AI) and Big Data are transforming recruitment by enabling adaptive, data-driven hiring. Traditional methods like manual resume screening struggle with dynamic labor markets. Using the MAPE-K model, AI systems automate candidate sourcing, enhance job matching, and predict turnover via real-time analytics and Virtual Reality simulations. Case studies, like Big Data for SMEs and AI in smart cities, show improved efficiency. Ethical challenges, including bias

Using Artificial Intelligence (AI) in Human Resources (HR) has completely changed HR work. Now, decisions about managing workers are smarter and based on data. AI uses tools like machine learning, predictive analysis, and natural language processing, and these are key for recruitment, keeping employees satisfied, managing talent, and organizational planning. So, how we teach HR professionals also needs to change. This chapter talks about new teaching methods focused on AI in HR. It highlights learning from different areas, hands-on learning, and thinking about ethics. It offers a detailed plan for what should go into teaching materials, the key skills needed, and includes practical tools, real-world examples, and ways to test understanding. The goal is to help teachers and students create and run programs that fit the changing HR field. By doing this, future HR leaders will be well-prepared for a workplace driven by data and digital technology.

The chapter discusses techniques for integrating sentiment and emotion analysis in video interviews using state-of-the-art deep learning approaches. Integrating multiple forms of data, including facial expressions, speech and text, automates and improves the evaluation of job candidates during the recruitment process. Deep learning models including CNNs, RNNs and transformers allow for precise analysis of emotions and provide a better understanding of the context in video interviews. Medium provides information on renowned datasets, key preprocessing steps, powerful deep learning models, real-world examples and significant ethical challenges. The chapter highlights emerging advancements in federated learning, explainable AI and multimodal fusion as important areas for future research, emphasizing the importance of responsible application in AI-involved recruitment.

Virtual Reality (VR) is transforming recruitment by offering immersive, interactive simulations that replicate real job scenarios. Unlike traditional interviews, VR enables recruiters to assess behavioral traits, decision-making, communication, and cultural fit with greater precision. Powered by Artificial Intelligence (AI) and Big Data, VR systems analyze verbal and non-verbal cues to predict job performance, reduce bias, and improve hiring outcomes. Industries such as emergency medicine, software engineering, and retail have successfully adopted VR, resulting in better employee retention and reduced training costs. Gamified and AI-driven environments enhance candidate engagement through avatar-based interactions, real-time feedback, and collaborative problem-solving. VR can simulate high-pressure scenarios to evaluate emotional intelligence, adaptability, and leadership—traits often overlooked in conventional interviews. This Chapter deals with how Virtual Reality helps for Interview simulations in conduction a smooth and efficient interview virtually.

This chapter, Future Trends and Innovations in Data-Driven Workforce Analytics, examines how Artificial Intelligence (AI), Big Data, and advanced analytics are revolutionizing Human Resource Management (HRM). It traces the shift from traditional HR metrics to predictive and prescriptive analytics, showcasing how these tools enhance talent acquisition, retention, and employee engagement. The chapter highlights emerging innovations such as real-time analytics, Natural Language Processing, wearable tech, blockchain, and gamification. It also addresses the integration of workforce analytics into broader business strategies and critically explores ethical concerns including data privacy and algorithmic bias. Supported by real-world case studies, the chapter offers strategic guidance for building a future-ready, data-driven HR culture that aligns with organizational goals.

Preface

Recruitment practices across industries are undergoing a fundamental shift, shaped by rapid advances in artificial intelligence, big data, and immersive technologies. Traditional models of hiring—once reliant on intuition, static resumes, and human judgment—are increasingly giving way to systems that are data-driven, algorithmically assisted, and designed for real-time adaptability. With these changes comes the necessity to reevaluate foundational assumptions about talent acquisition and to develop a new language of recruitment strategy that accounts for both innovation and ethical responsibility. This book was conceived in response to that very need.

Emerging Technologies for Recruitment Strategy and Practice brings together scholars, practitioners, and technologists from across the globe to explore the intersections between modern recruitment methods and cutting-edge technologies. The chapters span a range of topics including AI-driven candidate assessment, e-learning analytics, predictive workforce intelligence, virtual reality simulations, and sentiment analysis in video interviews. By combining theoretical foundations with practical case studies and methodological innovations, this volume offers a comprehensive look at how recruitment is being reshaped in the digital age.

We view this work not merely as a reference book, but as a collaborative roadmap for those seeking to align recruitment practices with the demands of a dynamic and data-rich labor market. Whether you are an academic researcher, an HR professional, a technology developer, or a policy strategist, this collection provides a foundation for understanding both the promises and challenges of technologically mediated hiring. Our goal as editors was to curate a volume that reflects the global, interdisciplinary, and rapidly evolving nature of recruitment today.

CHAPTER 1: ENHANCING HIRING PROCESSES WITH E-LEARNING AND RECOMMENDATION SYSTEMS

This chapter presents a seven-stage, AI-driven framework that leverages behavioral data from e-learning platforms to modernize recruitment. By integrating automated candidate profiling, multi-source data analysis, and AI-powered interviews, the authors propose a system that objectively assesses candidate skills, motivation, and adaptability while reducing human bias and inefficiencies. The framework addresses critical limitations of traditional recruitment and emphasizes ethical considerations, including algorithmic bias and data privacy, offering a path toward more transparent and data-informed hiring practices.

CHAPTER 2: SELF-ADAPTIVE SYSTEMS: REDEFINING BEST PRACTICES IN AI AND BIG DATA IN RECRUITMENT

Focusing on the MAPE-K model, this chapter explores how self-adaptive AI systems and Big Data technologies are redefining recruitment best practices. The authors demonstrate how adaptive platforms automate sourcing, enhance job matching, and predict employee turnover using real-time analytics and simulations. Supported by case studies in SMEs and smart cities, the chapter also highlights the need for ethical governance and fairness-aware algorithms, while forecasting future trends such as federated learning that promote responsible collaboration between HR, data science, and technology domains.

CHAPTER 3: TRADITIONAL VS. MODERN RECRUITMENT METHODS

This chapter contrasts conventional recruitment strategies with modern, tech-enabled approaches, examining the rise of online platforms, AI tools, and social media campaigns in today's hiring landscape. The authors analyze how these evolving methods impact various industries, offering insights into the advantages and drawbacks of each. They also address key barriers to adoption—such as resistance to change and concerns over data use—while underscoring the need for structured, inclusive, and future-ready recruitment practices grounded in analytics and automation.

CHAPTER 4: THE IMPACT OF ARTIFICIAL INTELLIGENCE ON MODERN HIRING

Exploring the role of AI in reshaping human resource management, this chapter delves into its application across resume screening, chatbots, interview scheduling, and predictive candidate evaluation. Technologies such as NLP, machine learning, RPA, and facial recognition are discussed within global and local (Sri Lankan) contexts, emphasizing both operational gains and ethical risks. By applying theoretical models like TAM, UTAUT, and DOI, the chapter provides a framework for understanding AI adoption and its implications for the future of digital hiring.

CHAPTER 5: TEACHING METHODS FOR AI-DRIVEN HR PRACTICES

This chapter addresses the evolving needs of HR education in response to the increasing use of AI in workforce management. It advocates for interdisciplinary, hands-on teaching strategies that cover machine learning, predictive analytics, and NLP, while also emphasizing the importance of ethics in AI applications. The authors propose a practical teaching framework with real-world tools and assessment methods to ensure that future HR professionals are equipped to lead in data-driven, technology-enabled workplaces.

CHAPTER 6: SENTIMENT AND EMOTION ANALYSIS IN VIDEO INTERVIEWS USING DEEP LEARNING TECHNIQUES

Focusing on the integration of deep learning into video interviews, this chapter explores how AI can analyze facial expressions, speech, and text to assess candidates' emotional states and communication styles. Utilizing models such as CNNs, RNNs, and transformers, the approach enhances the objectivity and precision of interview evaluations. The chapter also addresses ethical concerns and highlights emerging research in explainable AI, multimodal fusion, and federated learning for more transparent and responsible use of emotional analytics in recruitment.

CHAPTER 7: VIRTUAL REALITY FOR INTERVIEW SIMULATIONS

This chapter examines how virtual reality, combined with AI and Big Data, enables realistic, immersive interview simulations that assess communication, decision-making, and cultural fit. Through avatar-based interactions and gamified environments, VR helps recruiters evaluate candidates in high-pressure scenarios that reveal emotional intelligence and leadership potential. The authors highlight successful applications in industries like medicine and retail, showcasing VR's potential to reduce bias, enhance engagement, and improve long-term hiring outcomes.

CHAPTER 8: SHAPING TOMORROW'S TALENT STRATEGIES WITH PREDICTIVE WORKFORCE INTELLIGENCE

Focusing on the shift from traditional HR metrics to predictive and prescriptive analytics, this chapter explores how advanced technologies—such as real-time analytics, wearable tech, and blockchain—are reshaping talent acquisition, retention, and engagement. The author presents strategic frameworks and case studies that illustrate how data-driven insights can be integrated into broader business objectives. Ethical concerns surrounding privacy and bias are critically examined, reinforcing the need for responsible innovation in workforce intelligence.

As editors, we are grateful to the authors whose research and perspectives shape this volume. Their commitment to exploring both the innovative and responsible uses of technology in recruitment has made this book possible. The diversity of viewpoints—from different institutions, disciplines, and national contexts—reflects the multifaceted nature of hiring in today's global economy. Each chapter contributes a unique lens, but together they form a unified call for forward-thinking, inclusive, and evidence-based hiring strategies.

We also recognize that emerging technologies are not without risk. Issues of algorithmic bias, data privacy, and fairness are recurring themes across chapters, and rightly so. Our intention in highlighting these challenges is not to discourage innovation, but to ensure that technological progress in recruitment remains aligned with human values. In doing so, we hope to contribute to a more equitable and transparent hiring landscape.

It is our sincere hope that this book serves as a catalyst for new conversations, collaborations, and innovations in the recruitment space. As the tools at our disposal become more sophisticated, so too must our strategies for deploying them thoughtfully. We invite readers to engage with these ideas critically and constructively—because the future of recruitment is not just being predicted, it is being built.

Chapter 1

Enhancing Hiring Processes With E-Learning and Recommendation Systems

Boulmane Es-said
https://orcid.org/0009-0007-7477-522X
Ibn Zohr University, Morocco

Mohamed Badouch
https://orcid.org/0000-0003-0495-3784
Ibn Zohr University, Morocco

Hasna Mahmoud
https://orcid.org/0009-0006-5457-3594
Ibn Zohr University, Morocco

Mehdi Boutaounte
https://orcid.org/0009-0001-0459-7532
Ibn Zohr University, Morocco

ABSTRACT

This chapter presents a data-driven framework for modernizing recruitment through the utilisation of artificial intelligence and e-learning analytics. The proposed 7-stage methodology leverages behavioral data from online learning platforms to assess candidate skills, motivation, and adaptability more objectively than traditional methods. Key components include automated candidate profiling, multi-source

DOI: 10.4018/979-8-3373-6516-9.ch001

data integration, AI-powered interviews, and continuous improvement mechanisms. The approach addresses critical limitations of conventional recruitment, including human bias, inefficiency in evaluating soft skills, and information overload. While offering benefits such as improved candidate-job matching and reduced subjectivity, the chapter also examines implementation challenges, including the issue of algorithmic bias, data privacy concerns, and ethical considerations. The framework contributes to emerging research at the intersection of HR technology, educational data mining, and responsible AI

1. INTRODUCTION

The digital transformation of recruitment mirrors the revolution that AI-powered recommendation systems brought to education and tourism (Badouch & Boutaounte, 2024), where personalized learning pathways have demonstrated significant improvements in outcomes (Mahmoud et al., 2025 ; Zioudi et al., 2025).

Just as these systems transformed educational experiences, a similar paradigm shift is now occurring in talent acquisition through e-recruitment technologies. The technological revolution has given rise to new disciplines, such as e-recruitment. Originally, recruitment was mainly done through newspaper advertisements. Today, it is predominantly done online. This new method allows job offers to be published on various online platforms. Furthermore, the emergence of specialized networks, such as LinkedIn, has transformed the way companies and candidates interact.

This emergence presents advantages for several stakeholders: both companies and job seekers who have successfully capitalized on this opportunity. E-recruitment allows candidates to be matched with suitable job offers based on massive amounts of data (Gilch & Sieweke, 2021). Therefore, making the right decision in online recruitment is not easy; it begins with carefully selecting the profile characteristics of the desired candidates. The choice of this new approach is justified by the limitations of traditional approaches, which use analysis methods such as CVs and traditional interviews, which do not comprehensively assess candidates' skills and ignore soft skills, as well as soft skills such as adaptability, teamwork, and collaboration, which are highly sought-after qualities in a professional workplace. Furthermore, the high number of applications makes candidate selection less accurate and a tiring process for recruiters faced with information overload, which directly affects the quality of their assessments.

Among these, e-learning platforms are among the tools that generate a significant amount of data, which are not only used for e-learning but can also be seen as a new source of data (M.r.m. & Ramesh, 2022).

In this context, our chapter follows the same vision by emphasizing this digital transformation that will accelerate human resources practices, exploring this innovative approach to recruitment based on the analysis of user engagement in e-learning platforms (Fenech et al., 2019). The main objective is to clarify how candidate engagement in online learning environments can be identified, measured, and leveraged to significantly improve recruitment decisions.

This innovative approach leverages behavioral and analytical data generated by user interactions with e-learning platforms. This data offers a unique perspective on candidates' actual skills, intrinsic motivation, learning capacity, and adaptability dimensions that are often difficult to assess using conventional recruitment methods (Staubitz et al., 2022; Chassignol et al., 2022).

The integration of Artificial Intelligence (AI) and Big Data into this approach transforms digital traces of engagement into reliable predictive indicators for candidate assessment (Albassam, 2023). This data-driven methodology represents a major shift toward more objective, personalized, and efficient recruitment.

This chapter contributes to the ongoing exploration of AI in recruitment by presenting a structured, data-driven framework and examining its implications for the future of talent acquisition. The proposed methodology is distinguished by its systematic and reproducible nature, simultaneously integrating the technological, organizational, and experiential dimensions of digital recruitment.

This chapter follows a logical progression in six sections: the literature review examines existing work on AI and Big Data applied to recruitment and identifies research gaps; the methodology details the seven steps of the proposed automated recruitment process, along with ethical considerations; the results present an analysis of the benefits in terms of efficiency, bias reduction, and improved candidate experience; the discussion analyzes the practical implications and implementation challenges; Finally, future perspectives synthesize the contributions and propose directions for the evolution of recruitment practices in the digital age.

2. LITERATURE REVIEW:

In this section, we begin by placing our work in the scientific literature and attempt to present the general context of our research.

1.2 limitations of traditional recruitment methods:

Traditional recruitment methods are characterized by a number of significant limitations that compromise their efficacy. Consequently, there is a necessity to optimize the recruitment process as shown in table 1.

Table 1. limitations of the tradional recruitment methods

Recruitment Limitation	Description	Key References
Limited Access to Diverse Talent Pools	Marginalized groups are frequently subjected to discrimination, a factor which serves to limit their employment opportunities.	(Speed & Kulichyova, 2021)
Inefficiency and Delays	These approaches consume resource-intensive compared to online methods, reducing efficiency.	(Nwokwu,2020)
Potential for Bias Subjectivity	It is important to note that recruiters may unconsciously apply biases during review and interview processes, thereby impacting the selection of candidates in a manner that may not be aligned with principles of fairness and impartiality.	(Benedict et al., 2019) (Portillo & Mancera-Valencia, 2021)
Low-quality hire and Time-Consuming Processes	Methods such as manual screening, referrals, advertisements, and eligibility checks are often time-consuming and costly. These inefficiencies can delay the recruitment process, prolonging project timelines such as clinical trials or organizational hiring cycles.	(Yassine & Said, 2024)
Lack of Real-Time Analytics and Personalization	Traditional methods do not leverage advanced data analytics or AI, resulting in less personalized candidate evaluation and slower decision-making. This limits the ability to optimize recruitment strategies dynamically	(Saouabe et al., 2024)

According to this study, traditional recruitment methods are ineffective due to the evolution of the process. In addition, the lack of integration with recent technologies, such as artificial intelligence, automation and big data analysis, is preventing organizations from extracting and exploiting information to improve candidate selection and strategic planning. As a result of these findings, it is more important than ever for organizations to adopt data-driven and adaptive recruitment practices that are aligned with the digital transformation trends.

1.2 Digital Transformation in Recruitment:

At its inception, the job search process primarily involved browsing newspaper advertisements and mailing physical résumés. Over time, this procedure has undergone several transformations, culminating in its current form: digital recruitment.

This evolution cannot be reduced to a mere digitization of existing practices; rather, it constitutes a paradigmatic shift in the way organizations identify, evaluate, and select talent. This transformation has unfolded in three distinct phases, each characterized by increasing complexity and technological integration.

In the late 1990s, several platforms—such as Monster and CareerBuilder—began offering online job listings. These platforms enabled companies to publish job vacancies and allowed candidates to consult them easily via virtual bulletin boards. Furthermore, the exponential growth of the internet encouraged companies to establish their own online recruitment portals. These websites centralized essential information such as corporate profiles, available positions, and the application process. This innovation simplified job searching for applicants while optimizing profile selection for employers.

This developmental trajectory continued, as illustrated by the emergence of Applicant Tracking Systems (ATS) in the mid-2000s. These systems aim to enhance the efficiency of the recruitment pipeline—from job posting to final hiring—by facilitating candidate tracking and communication. Automating repetitive tasks enables recruiters to focus on more strategic dimensions of talent acquisition. Subsequently, professional social networks such as LinkedIn, as well as mainstream platforms like Facebook and Twitter, expanded recruitment capabilities. Organizations could now target passive candidates, promote their employer brand, and engage with applicants in real time. The rise of smartphones further accelerated this transformation, making mobile job applications an essential feature. Companies were compelled to optimize their interfaces for mobile usage to remain competitive in talent acquisition.

Today, Artificial Intelligence (AI) continues to redefine the recruitment landscape. Leveraging advanced algorithms, AI-driven systems can shortlist résumés, match candidate skills with job requirements, and even conduct preliminary interviews via chatbots. This enables faster, more accurate, and data-driven hiring processes.

This evolution initiated more than two decades ago highlights how digital technologies have profoundly reshaped recruitment practices, equipping both recruiters and candidates with increasingly sophisticated tools. Having followed the progression from traditional to digital recruitment, the comparison between two models across multiple dimensions shown in table 2.:

Table 2. Comparison of the recruitment types

Aspect	Traditional Recruitment	E-Recruitment (Electronic)
Method	In-person, phone, paper ads	Email, social media, job portals, AI tools
Speed	Slower	Faster
Cost	Higher per candidate	Lower per candidate
Geographic reach	Limited	Broader, global
Diversity of candidates	Often less diverse	More diverse
Conversion rate	Higher (more likely to enroll)	Lower conversion but higher volume
Efficiency	Lower	Higher
Use of technology	Minimal	Extensive (including AI and big data)

1.3 E-Recruitment Advantages

As demonstrated in the previous section, digital recruitment has emerged as a strategic alternative to traditional recruitment methods. As a first benefit, this approach significantly reduces recruitment costs, saving up to 80% compared to conventional recruitment methods (Gulomkodirova, 2022). Among the benefits of this reduction are the reduced need for physical advertising, travel, and in-person interviews.

Concurrently, E-recruitment facilitates substantially more extensive reach. Online platforms allow job offers to be shared with an international audience, thus increasing the chances of attracting diverse and highly qualified candidates (Agarwal and Sinha, 2024). This increased visibility also promotes and facilitates access to rare and specialized talent profiles.

Beyond geographical reach, automation is another key pillar of e-recruitment, enabling operational optimization. Several studies have confirmed the feasibility of outsourcing repetitive and time-consuming tasks to automated systems (Dhamija, 2012). This research highlights the potential of automation to streamline screening and interview processes, thus reducing the time spent on manual tasks. As a result, recruiter productivity improves, and administrative burdens decrease.

E-recruitment therefore stands out as a modern, efficient, and cost-effective solution, well-aligned with the evolving demands of the digital labor market.

1.4 E-Learning Platforms as Talent Indicators

Currently, training platforms are not limited to skills acquisition and learning. Online platforms generate large volumes of data within their platforms.

The data generated comes from users' interactions with the platform, both with the educational content and with the learners. This provides a valuable new source of information that can be used for recruitment purposes.

The data collected on these platforms goes well beyond simple academic results. It includes, as shown in the figure below *(see Fig.1.1):*

Figure 1. Taxonomy of E-Learning Data

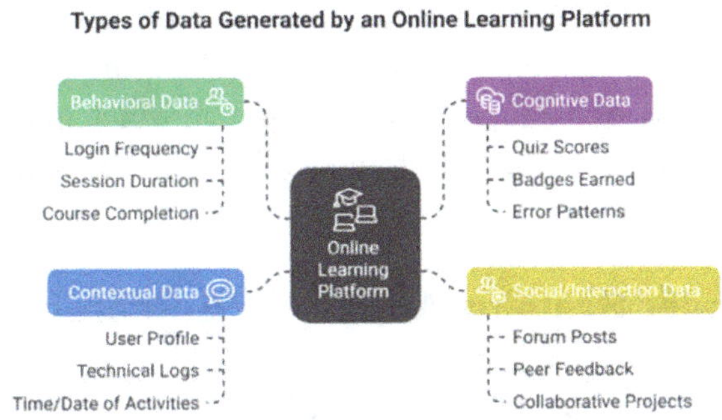

The nature of the information collected is indicative of the type of data that is subsequently collated. It is important to acknowledge the possibility of the existence of additional types that fall outside the confines of this classification.

In the context of human resources management, the utilization of digital data from application processing constitutes a strategic imperative. Indeed, preliminary analysis of this information, utilizing a data analyst's methodology, facilitates the identification of indirect indicators of so-called "non-technical" or "soft" skills, which are challenging to assess using conventional methods. These competencies, which have garnered heightened attention from recruiters, encompass personal attributes such as autonomy, perseverance, self-directed learning, adaptability, and collaborative skills. Once this data has been processed, it can be used as a relevant tool in recruitment processes, allowing the selection of the most suitable candidates for the positions offered.

For instance, a learner who successfully completes multiple certifications programmed within a relatively short timeframe may exhibit strong intrinsic motivation and effective time management skills. These are two essential qualities in a dynamic professional environment. By leveraging this data, recruiters can gain a rich, contextual view of the candidate profile, thus going beyond the limitations of traditional CVs. The analysis of engagement on e-learning platforms has the potential to predict performance in real-life situations, particularly for roles that necessitate continuous learning and autonomy in developing skills.

Recent research in Learning Analytics (Johar et al., 2023) has shown that these indicators are correlated with future performance attributes. In addition, some companies are now incorporating results from platforms such as LinkedIn Learning or Google Career Certificates into their selection process, particularly to identify self-trained candidates in technical fields such as web development, data science or cybersecurity.

In this way, e-learning platforms are no longer simply training spaces, but are also becoming sensors for predictive indicators that are useful in recruitment decision-making. Exploiting them represents a step towards more objective, individualized recruitment, in line with the demands of a rapidly changing labor market.

This wealth of behavioral data is the foundation on which intelligent recommendation systems are built, capable of automatically matching learning profiles with the specific needs of companies.

1.5 Recommender Systems Applied to E-Recruitment

1.5.1 Definition and Typology of Recommender Systems

Recommender Systems (RS) are intelligent tools designed to assist decision-making by suggesting relevant content, products, or services based on user preferences, behavioral history, or similarities with other users. Initially popularized in commercial contexts (e.g., Netflix, Amazon, Spotify), these systems have expanded to other domains, including education and human resource management.

There are three main types of recommender systems:

Collaborative Filtering: This approach recommends items based on similarities in user behavior. If two users completed the same courses or liked the same content, the system may recommend to one user what the other enjoyed.

Content-Based Filtering: This method focuses on analyzing item characteristics (e.g., courses, job requirements, skill sets) and matching them with the individual's preferences or profile.

Hybrid Systems: These combine both collaborative and content-based methods to enhance accuracy and personalization.

In recruitment contexts, recommender systems can intelligently match candidate profiles with job requirements, going beyond traditional metrics (CVs, diplomas) to incorporate behavioral and learning data derived from online learning platforms, as previously discussed.

1.5.2 Integrating Recommender Systems in E-Recruitment

As recruiters face increasingly large applicant pools, recommender systems serve as powerful tools to automate, personalize, and enhance the accuracy of candidate selection. These systems not only match applicants to job positions, but also:

Rank candidates based on a relevance score tied to job criteria.

Identify high-potential profiles that may be overlooked by traditional methods.

Suggest alternative job roles to candidates based on their learning history and inferred competencies.

Recommend personalized learning paths to help candidates bridge skill gaps and reach target profiles.

Such systems become especially powerful when fueled by rich, multidimensional data from e-learning platforms. For example:

A candidate who recently completed a MOOC on agile project management could be recommended for project management roles, even if this is not explicitly mentioned in their CV.

Recruiters can assess engagement patterns such as course completion rates, forum participation, and consistency—to evaluate soft skills like perseverance and motivation.

1.5.3 Toward Ethical and Personalized Recommendations

The adoption of recommender systems in recruitment presents a unique opportunity to enhance the candidate experience while optimizing recruiter efficiency. However, this transformation must be carefully managed to address several key risks:

- **Algorithmic Bias:** If training data is biased, recommendations may reproduce or reinforce discriminatory patterns.
- **Transparency and Explainability:** Candidates and recruiters should be able to understand how and why recommendations are made.
- **Privacy and Data Protection:** Behavioral learning data must be handled in compliance with data protection laws and user consent frameworks.

To address these concerns, emerging approaches such as responsible AI and fair recommender systems are being developed. These models integrate ethical principles like diversity, equity, and interpretability into the core algorithms.

Ultimately, recommender systems represent a paradigm shift in talent acquisition, enabling a deeper and more dynamic understanding of candidate potential. By leveraging e-learning data, recruitment becomes more data-informed, inclusive, and future-ready, bridging the gap between learning behavior and employability in the digital era.

1.5.4 Challenges

Recommender systems (RS) have emerged as valuable tools in the recruitment domain, aiming to enhance the efficiency and fairness of the hiring process. These systems help match candidates with job opportunities by analyzing large volumes of data such as resumes, job descriptions, candidate preferences, and historical hiring patterns.

Two main approaches dominate the field: content-based filtering and collaborative filtering. Content-based methods recommend jobs to applicants (or applicants to recruiters) based on similarities between profiles and job requirements (Goda et al., 2024). In contrast, collaborative filtering leverages the behavior and preferences of similar users to suggest potential matches, even when explicit skill overlaps are limited (Zbib et al., 2022).

More recently, hybrid systems combining both approaches have shown promising results, particularly when enhanced with natural language processing (NLP) techniques for semantic analysis of job descriptions and CVs (Fenech et al., 2019). Additionally, context-aware RS incorporate factors like location, salary expectations, and company culture to refine recommendations (Staubitz et al., 2022).

Despite their potential, recruitment RS face key challenges(Table1), such as bias mitigation, cold-start problems (for new users or jobs), and data privacy concerns (Chassignol et al., 2022). Addressing these issues is critical for building transparent, inclusive, and effective recruitment tools.

Table 3. Key Challenges in Recruitment Recommender Systems

Challenge	Description	Potential Impact	Possible Solutions
Algorithmic Bias	Historical data may favor certain groups	Unfair or discriminatory recommendations	Fairness audits, diverse training data (Mahmoud et al., 2025)
Heterogeneous and Unstructured Data	CVs and job descriptions vary in format and content	Inaccurate matching	NLP preprocessing and standardization (Zioudi et al., 2025)
Cold Start Problem (Kuanr & Mohapatra, 2021)	Lack of data for new users or new job postings	Poor quality recommendations	Hybrid or contextual models
Lack of Explainability (Mashayekhi et al., 2024)	Users may not understand why a candidate or job is recommended	Reduced trust in the system	Use explainable models (LIME, SHAP)
Data Privacy Concerns	Sensitive information used in recommendation pipelines	Legal and ethical risks (e.g., GDPR)	Anonymization, compliance mechanisms (Ogunseyi et al., 2023)

These challenges require interdisciplinary solutions *as shown in table 3* combining machine learning, ethics, and human-computer interaction. Overcoming them is key to ensuring adoption and trust in AI-driven recruitment systems.

1.6 Summary and Identified Research Gaps

The literature reviewed in this chapter highlights a significant shift from conventional recruitment methods to technology-enhanced, data-driven hiring processes. Traditional approaches—centered around résumé screening, unstructured interviews, and manual decision-making—have been shown to suffer from inefficiencies, subjectivity, and limited capacity to assess soft skills or dynamic candidate potential. In contrast, e-recruitment strategies powered by artificial intelligence (AI), automation, and digital platforms offer a more scalable, inclusive, and cost-effective alternative.

The digital transformation of recruitment has introduced various technological tools, including applicant tracking systems, social recruiting platforms, and chatbots. These tools streamline administrative tasks and broaden candidate reach. However, most current systems still rely primarily on static indicators (e.g., job titles, degrees, or keywords), which fail to capture behavioral nuances or contextual skills critical for long-term performance.

While recommender systems have been extensively deployed in domains such as e-commerce and entertainment, their integration into human resource management—particularly in recruitment—remains underdeveloped. Existing work has explored job matching algorithms, but few studies have examined hybrid recommendation models that incorporate behavioral learning data.

Moreover, the field of learning analytics has primarily focused on improving educational outcomes, with limited application in recruitment contexts. The potential of e-learning engagement data—such as completion rates, persistence metrics, or peer collaboration—as predictive indicators of workplace performance has been largely overlooked in the recruitment literature.

Therefore, this chapter addresses three critical research gaps:

1. **Lack of behavioral-based recruitment models:** Existing recruitment systems underutilize dynamic learning behaviors that reflect adaptability, intrinsic motivation, and self-directed learning capacity.
2. **Limited integration of recommender systems with HR analytics:** Few frameworks combine content-based, collaborative, and learning-derived data for personalized candidate-job matching.
3. **Absence of structured methodologies linking e-learning data with AI-driven talent acquisition:**

There is a need for reproducible, ethically grounded, and operationally feasible models that bridge educational data mining and recruitment decision-making.

By proposing a structured, seven-stage data-driven recruitment framework, this chapter contributes to the emerging intersection of learning analytics, AI, and talent acquisition. It offers a novel perspective on how engagement with digital learning platforms can serve as a reliable, multidimensional input for candidate evaluation in modern hiring systems.

3. PROPOSED METHODOLOGY

The recruitment field is undergoing a major transformation, moving away from the limitations of traditional recruitment to the adoption of data-driven approaches. In this context, the recent chapter presents a structured seven-step framework designed to enhance recruitment process, building on the identified constraints and the growing relevance of behavioral data from online learning platforms.

The proposed methodology developed to evaluate candidates by integrating recent technologies in artificial intelligence, data analytics, and predictive modeling.

Recent research indicates a strong association between digital learning engagement patterns and future job performance, positioning these behavioral indicators as reliable predictors of career success. In addition, AI-powered assessment tools have demonstrated their potential to reduce implicit bias and improve the accuracy and objectivity of talent selection processes.

The following sections provide a description of each component; detailing objectives and the data sources used at each step.

3.1 Data-Driven Candidate Profiling

The initial step of the framework focus on creating a comprehensive candidate profile from data generated by digital platforms, thus identifying candidates' learning behaviors. This approach explores how candidates interact with training materials, manage their time, and collaborate with others in digital environments. In contrast to the traditional approach, which offers a static view of candidates' learning journey, this novel method provides a more dynamic and comprehensive understanding of candidate performance and progress.

To support the analysis, data is collected from various online sources, including popular MOOCs like Coursera, edX, and Udemy, as well as institutional learning platforms like Moodle. These raw activity traces are then translated into relevant indicators that allow for a more complete profile of each candidate's potential (see Figure 1.2).

Figure 2. phase1

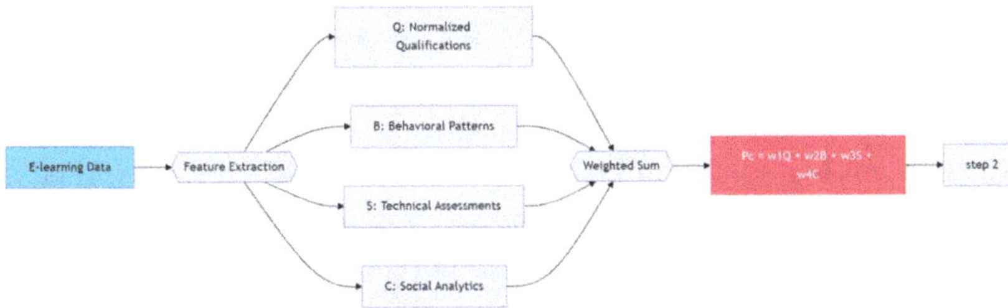

The profiling is structured around four key dimensions:

- **Q: Standardized Qualifications** – including course completion rates, grades, and certifications.
- **B: Behavioral Engagement** – such as regularity of participation, time management, and persistence.
- **S: Skills and Technical Assessments** – including quiz scores, coding challenges, and project performance.
- **C: Collaborative and Social Interaction** – such as forum discussions, peer feedback, and group activity.

To synthesize these components into a unified candidate profile score, we use the following weighted aggregation model:

$$Pc = \sum_{i=4}^{4} wi \cdot fi(X)$$

Where:

- Pc : The overall candidate profile score.
- wi : The weight assigned to dimension i, with $\sum wi = 1$
- $fi(Xi)$: A normalization function applied to the raw input data Xi of each dimension.
- Specifically, $fQQ(XQ), fB(XB), fS(XS), fC(XC)$ reflect the normalized contributions from qualifications, behavior, skills, and collaboration, respectively.

3.2 Multi-Source Data Analysis and Integration

After establishing an initial behavioral profile, the second step deepens the analysis by combining data from multiple sources to refine and enrich the understanding of each candidate (see Fig. 1.3).

Rather than relying solely on resumes or interview impressions, this step integrates diverse information streams, ranging from official documents to digital engagement traces, allowing for a more comprehensive and nuanced view of a candidate's strengths and learning patterns.

Figure 3. phase2

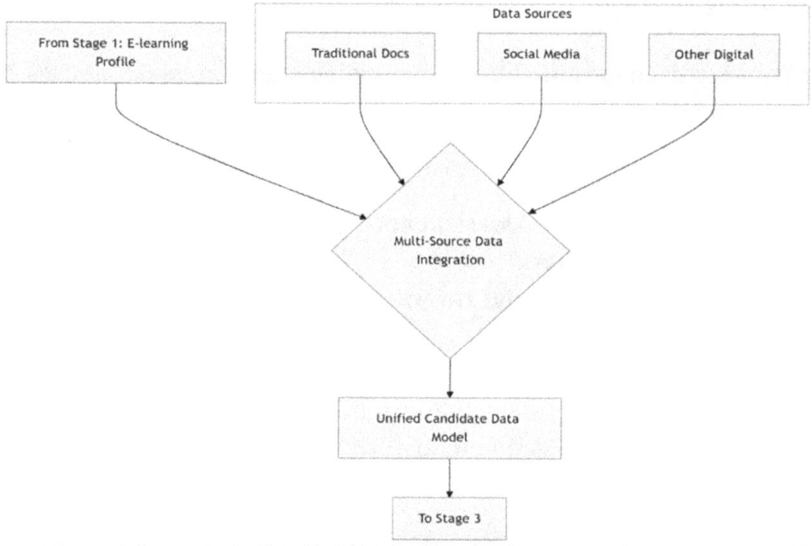

This phase leverages multiple data sources to optimize candidate analysis. Traditional documents, such as resumes and cover letters, are analyzed using natural language processing techniques to extract relevant skills and qualifications.

In addition, social media activity and digital engagement patterns are also analyzed to provide additional information about the candidate.

The data integration process brings together formal application content and behavioral traces from online learning platforms. By analyzing these layers simultaneously, the system reveals correlations that might not be visible in a single data source. Advanced algorithms help identify consistent skill indicators, while anomaly detection flags discrepancies between reported and observed behaviors.

This enriched dataset sets the stage for the next phase, where automated systems begin interacting with candidates based on these multidimensional profiles. This data integrity is essential to ensure candidate authenticity. Machine learning algorithms are computational tools that analyze data and extract patterns or schemas. They offer the ability to perform sophisticated correlation analyses between different behavioral indicators, facilitating the recognition of these patterns across various types of data. This comprehensive database establishes the necessary foundation for automated interaction systems, ensuring that subsequent stages operate with substantial and duly validated candidate information.

3.3 Intelligent Automated Interactions

After defining the candidate model, step 3 involves sharing electronic communications and resumes. The objective of the present study is to minimize the involvement of human resources in the recruitment process, thereby optimizing the allocation of time and effort. This will be achieved by replacing human resources with advanced tools of artificial intelligence (AI) such as chatbots inspired form the (Badouch et al., 2025) that enhance the e-tourism also automatic scoring systems, which possess the capacity to learn and extract data from the preceding step *(see Fig.1.4).*

Figure 4. phase2

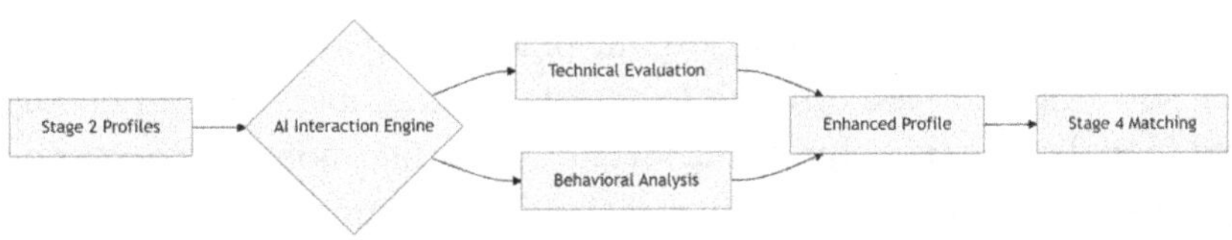

These chatbots are designed to conduct sophisticated candidate assessments, thereby facilitating the selection process. The chatbot implementation incorporates adaptive questioning strategies, whereby interaction complexity is adjusted based on candidate responses and behavioral patterns.

Conversational analytics provides additional dimensionality to candidate evaluation through communication style analysis, response latency patterns, and engagement depth measurement. A dynamic representation of candidates can be created by combining static candidate profile information with behavioral data generated during the interaction. The system analyses linguistic patterns, emotional indicators and problem-solving approaches to better understand the candidate's personality traits and potential cultural fit. The automated interaction acts as an intermediary between data collection and full assessment, preparing candidates for a more intensive assessment while refining their profile. This transition enables the subsequent assessment stages to optimize the efficiency and accuracy of the assessment thanks to a more in-depth understanding of the candidates.

3.4 Comprehensive Skills Assessment Through E-learning Analytics

The current phase examines the way candidates learn and act in digital environments, providing a more holistic assessment of technical and non-technical skills. Rather than relying on traditional tests, it uses engagement data to better reflect how individuals assimilate knowledge, solve problems and collaborate.

For technical skills, the system uses adaptive testing, where the difficulty of the questions is adjusted according to the candidate's previous answers. This personalized approach ensures that the evaluation remains sufficiently stimulating, enabling skills to be measured more accurately.

Additionally, candidates submit projects such as coding tasks, case simulations, and digital portfolios, which are automatically assessed by the system. This practice-based strategy captures applied knowledge and offers a more authentic view of technical skills than standardized tests alone. (Mislevy et al., 2020) confirms that adaptive testing improves predictive validity by approximately 23% compared to traditional static formats.

Behavioral data collected from digital platforms plays an important role in assessing soft skills that are difficult to detect. For example, regularly completing advanced modules can be a sign of perseverance. Furthermore, active participation in discussion forums or collaborative tasks often demonstrates communication and teamwork skills. These behavioral indicators, often overlooked in traditional recruitment, offer valuable insights into the personality traits that influence professional performance.

The system applies machine learning techniques to analyze this multidimensional data. K-means and DBSCAN identify common engagement patterns among candidates, while regression models estimate job performance based on behavioral indicators. The result is a detailed, data-driven profile of each candidate, highlighting their strengths and areas for development. This enriched profile feeds into the next stage: the structured interview, where human assessors can explore high-potential signals, clarify uncertainties, or validate behaviors flagged by the system. Thus, the learning phase creates a crucial bridge between algorithmic analysis and human expertise, improving the fairness and efficiency of the selection process.

3.5 Structured Interviews Enhanced by Predictive Intelligence

The fifth step leverages the results of the previous steps to create tailored interview experiences. This reduces cognitive bias and improves assessment consistency, enabling human assessment guided by predictive data.

The system generates interview guides that include points for clarification, potential concerns identified through data analysis, and strengths worth exploring further. This allows recruiters to optimize their time and ensure each profile has been properly assessed.

During the interview, candidates' responses are analyzed by real-time interviewing tools, including emotional tone and assessing the quality of responses. These tools can also flag potential biases in interviewer behavior and suggest follow-up questions based on the candidate's responses. A study by Kothari et al. (2024) suggests that AI-assisted interviews improve fairness and significantly increase inter-rater reliability.

To ensure consistency in interviews, a structured assessment grid is used. It contains standardized criteria aligned with organizational performance indicators and a behavioral anchor to base judgments on observable behaviors. This not only improves the reliability of interview results, but also their trustworthiness.

Finally, data from the interview phase is added to each candidate's profile to complete the overall profile view for decision-making. As the process moves from individual assessment to comparative analysis, the structured interview stage sets the stage for multi-criteria assessments in the final selection phase.

3.6 Multi-Criteria Decision Analysis for Final Selection

The sixth step involves making hiring decisions using advanced algorithms that integrate all previously collected assessment data. The system translates complex candidate profiles into clear and actionable recommendations, balancing multiple assessment criteria and prioritizing fairness, consistency, and organizational relevance.

Multi-criteria decision analysis is at the heart of this process. The system evaluates each candidate along several dimensions using weighted scoring models, aligned with organizational objectives and job requirements. These weights are not fixed: they adapt according to internal priorities, market trends or strategic changes. The algorithms also take into account the interactions between different skills; for example, good performance in collaboration can compensate for a lower score in technical expertise (Pourkhodabakhsh et al., 2023).

To guide selection, predictive models estimate future job performance based on trends observed in high-performing employees. Machine learning techniques (Smelyakov et al., 2023) can identify combinations of skills, behaviors, and learning traits that correlate with high performance, high retention, and cultural fit. Empirical studies show, for example, that incorporating behavioral data from online learning analytics improves prediction accuracy by 34% compared to traditional assessment methods.

The system detects all potential issues, such as cultural fit, and also performs risk assessments. This information can help recruiters set realistic expectations and plan onboarding and support accordingly.

Finally, the platform generates decision reports documenting the reasons for each choice. These reports improve transparency, facilitate communication with stakeholders, and contribute to continuous improvement by feeding the system with new data. Ultimately, this phase ensures that final hiring decisions are data-driven, balanced, and aligned with broader organizational objectives.

3.7 Continuous Improvement Through Post-Hire Analytics

The final step is to provide feedback to continually refine the system, transforming recruitment from a discrete process into a continuous learning system that improves accuracy and efficiency over time.

Performance monitoring systems track new hire onboarding, productivity growth, and retention over multiple time horizons. These indicators validate the accuracy of the predictive model while identifying areas for system improvement. Longitudinal analysis reveals the behavioral indicators most correlated with long-term success, allowing for continuous refinement of evaluation criteria and their weighting.

Feedback integration considers the perspectives of multiple stakeholders, including hiring managers, peers, and new hire evaluations. This multi-source feedback approach enables comprehensive validation of selection decisions while identifying systematic biases or assessment gaps. Regular calibration ensures the adequacy of predictive models in response to evolving organizational needs and market conditions.

The continuous improvement framework integrates advanced analytics to identify emerging trends in candidate success, enabling proactive adaptation to changing skill needs and organizational priorities. Machine learning algorithms automatically adjust assessment parameters based on outcome data, ensuring the system evolves without manual intervention. This adaptive capability represents a significant advancement over static recruitment approaches, delivering a sustainable competitive advantage through improved talent acquisition efficiency.

4. ANTICIPATED OUTCOMES AND ANALYTICAL DISCUSSION

4.1 Projected Benefits of the Proposed Framework

Although the proposed framework has not yet been deployed in an operational environment, it is grounded in validated approaches from artificial intelligence, behavioral analytics, and educational data mining. Based on this foundation, the framework is expected to offer several key advantages:

- **Enhanced Alignment Between Candidate Profiles and Job Requirements**: The analysis of e-learning engagement traces provides access to behavioral indicators such as regularity, perseverance, and adaptability—dimensions often overlooked in traditional recruitment. These factors are likely to improve the predictive accuracy of candidate-job matching.
- **Reduction of Human Bias in Evaluation Processes**: Automated assessment tools based on machine learning enable the replacement of subjective judgment with consistent, quantifiable criteria, contributing to fairer candidate selection.
- **Improved Evaluation Reliability Through Multisource Data:** Integrating data from various sources—certifications, behavioral analytics, and technical tests—enhances the overall quality of recruitment decisions while reducing the administrative burden on human resource departments.

4.2. Methodological Scope and Practical Implications

- **Scientific Perspective**: This framework redefines talent profiling by incorporating metrics derived from online learning environments. It contributes to bridging the gap between learning analytics and recruitment science by providing a replicable model for data-driven talent evaluation.
- **Organizational Perspective:** The approach supports a shift from static documentation (CVs, cover letters) to dynamic, behavior-based assessment, enabling organizations to better capture candidates' potential and adaptability in real-world professional contexts.

4.3. Methodological Limitations

Several limitations must be acknowledged at the current stage:

- **Lack of Experimental Validation:** The proposed framework has not yet been tested in real-world scenarios. The expected results remain theoretical and require empirical verification.
- **Data Heterogeneity and Standardization Challenges**: Data from e-learning platforms vary significantly in format, granularity, and reliability, posing integration challenges across systems.
- **Ethical and Legal Considerations** Leveraging learning analytics for recruitment raises important ethical questions related to data privacy, informed consent, and transparency in candidate evaluation processes.

5. FUTURE DIRECTIONS

5.1. Experimental Implementation

A critical next step involves testing the framework in pilot environments. These may include academic institutions, training centers, or organizations with access to e-learning platforms. Pilot studies would aim to:

- Calibrate the weighting of behavioral indicators in the candidate profiling model;
- Validate the statistical correlations between learning behavior and professional performance;
- Evaluate candidate and recruiter perceptions regarding the fairness and transparency of the system.

5.2. Technical Enhancements and AI Optimization

To further refine the framework, future development should explore:

- Adaptive algorithms for personalized recruitment pathways;
- Integration with real-time learning analytics dashboards;
- Expansion to informal learning ecosystems, such as GitHub activity, Stack Overflow contributions, and open-source collaborations.

5.3. Ethical Governance and Legal Compliance

Future research should also address:

- Frameworks for ethical AI usage in recruitment, ensuring alignment with data protection laws (e.g., GDPR);
- Transparent consent mechanisms for learners whose data may be analyzed;
- Mechanisms for human oversight and auditability of AI-driven decisions.

6. CONCLUSION

This chapter has introduced a data-driven framework for modernizing recruitment practices through the integration of artificial intelligence, learning analytics, and recommendation systems. By leveraging behavioral data extracted from e-learning platforms, this approach goes beyond traditional CV-based assessments to uncover latent skills, engagement patterns, and professional potential. Each stage of the proposed methodology—from data-driven profiling to intelligent interviews has been designed to reduce human bias, enhance prediction accuracy, and provide a holistic candidate evaluation grounded in empirical evidence.

By using adaptive testing, behavioral clustering, and recommendation systems, organizations can not only assess candidate skills but also gain detailed insights into their learning, collaboration, and retention behaviors. This approach marks a broader shift in HR practices toward more personalized, ethical, and scalable recruitment solutions. Integrating these technologies offers the potential to significantly improve recruiting efficiency, diversity, and employee skill matching over time.

REFERENCES

Agarwal, P., & Sinha, J. (2024). Digitizing talent acquisition: A comprehensive analysis of e-recruitment practices and trends.

Albassam, W. A. (2023). The power of artificial intelligence in recruitment: An analytical review of current AI-based recruitment strategies. International Journal of Professional Business Review: Int. *J. Prof. Bus. Rev.*, *8*(6), 4.

Badouch, M., Boulmane, E. S., Mahmoud, H., Zioudi, O., & Boutaounte, M. (2024, December). Smart Tourism: How AI is Reimagining the Travel Experience. In International Conference on Electrical Systems and Smart Technologies (pp. 187-198). Cham: Springer Nature Switzerland.

Badouch, M. Boutaounte, M. (2025). Smart E-commerce Recommendations with Semantic AI. Fusion: Practice and Applications, (), 264-271. DOI: 10.54216/FPA.170120

Badouch, M., Boutaounte, M., Zioudi, O., & Mahmoud, H. (2025). The Future of Travel: A Review of Chatbot Recommender Systems in E-Tourism and Smart Tourism. In *International Conference on Electrical Systems and Smart Technologies* (pp. 103-115). Springer, Cham. DOI: 10.1007/978-3-031-86705-7_10

Benedict, C., Hahn, A. L., Diefenbach, M. A., & Ford, J. S. (2019). Recruitment via social media: Advantages and potential biases. *Digital Health*, *5*, 2055207619867223. DOI: 10.1177/2055207619867223 PMID: 31431827

Biased Performance Results of Commercial AI Products (2019 Jan) in Proceedings of the 2019 AAAI/ACM Conference on AI, Ethics, and Society, Honolulu HI USA: ACM, pp. 429–435. DOI: 10.1145/3306618.3314244

Carrico, C., Matusovich, H. M., & Paretti, M. C. (2019). A qualitative analysis of career choice pathways of college-oriented rural central Appalachian high school students. *Journal of Career Development*, *46*(2), 94–111. DOI: 10.1177/0894845317725603

Chassignol, M., Khoroshavin, A., Klimova, A., & Bilyatdinova, A. (2022). AI-driven skill mapping via e-learning engagement patterns. *Computers in Human Behavior*, *128*, 107075. DOI: 10.1016/j.chb.2021.107075

Deshmukh, A., & Raut, A. (2025). Applying BERT-based NLP for automated resume screening and candidate ranking. *Annals of Data Science*, *12*(2), 591–603. DOI: 10.1007/s40745-024-00524-5

Dhamija, P. (2012). E-recruitment: A roadmap towards e-human resource management. *Research World*, *3*(3), 33.

Fenech, R., Baguant, P., & Ivanov, D. (2019). The changing role of human resource management in an era of digital transformation. *Journal of Management Information & Decision Sciences*, *22*(2).

Gilch, P. M., & Sieweke, J. (2021). Recruiting digital talent: The strategic role of recruitment in organisations' digital transformation. *German Journal of Human Resource Management*, *35*(1), 53–82. DOI: 10.1177/2397002220952734

Gizi Gulomkodirova, M. S. (2024). A STUDY ON VARIOUS E-RECRUITMENT TOOLS AND ITS EFFECTIVENESS FOR RECRUITMENT. QO 'QON UNIVERSITETI XABARNOMASI, 10, 32-34.

Goda, S., Hayashi, Y., & Saito, Y. (2024). A Best-of-Both Approach to Improve Match Predictions and Reciprocal Recommendations for Job Search. arXiv preprint arXiv:2409.10992.

Jin, D., Wang, L., Zhang, H., Zheng, Y., Ding, W., Xia, F., & Pan, S. (2023). A survey on fairness-aware recommender systems. *Information Fusion*, *100*, 101906. DOI: 10.1016/j.inffus.2023.101906

Johar, N. A., Kew, S. N., Tasir, Z., & Koh, E. (2023). Learning analytics on student engagement to enhance students' learning performance: A systematic review. *Sustainability (Basel)*, *15*(10), 7849. DOI: 10.3390/su15107849

Kothari, P., Mehta, P., Patil, S., & Hole, V. (2024). InterviewEase: AI-powered interview assistance.

Kumari, S. (2023). Job Recommendation System Using NLP. *International Journal for Research in Applied Science and Engineering Technology*, *11*(5), 2721–2728. DOI: 10.22214/ijraset.2023.52183

Mahmoud, H., Zioudi, O., Boulmane, E.-S., Badouch, M., & Boutaounte, M. (2025). Recommendation system in the educational context: Experience in Morocco. In Benabid, A., El Imadi, I., & Chemsi, G. (Eds.), *Personalized learning through adaptive systems and intelligent tutoring* (pp. 167–188). IGI Global., DOI: 10.4018/979-8-3373-0740-4.ch006

Mashayekhi, Y., Li, N., Kang, B., Lijffijt, J., & De Bie, T. (2024). A challenge-based survey of e-recruitment recommendation systems. *ACM Computing Surveys*, *56*(10), 1–33. DOI: 10.1145/3659942

Mislevy, R. J., Yan, D., Gobert, J., & Sao Pedro, M. (2020). Automated scoring in intelligent tutoring systems. In *Handbook of automated scoring* (pp. 403–422). Chapman and Hall/CRC. DOI: 10.1201/9781351264808-22

Mohapatra, R. B., & Li, K.-C. (Eds.). (2021). *Advances in Intelligent Systems and Computing* (Vol. 1199, pp. 353–365). Springer Singapore., DOI: 10.1007/978-981-15-6353-9_32

M.r.m., V., & Ramesh, P. (2022). Analysis on quality of learning in e-Learning platforms. Advances in Engineering Software (Barking, London, England: 1992), 172(103168), 103168. DOI: 10.1016/j.advengsoft.2022.103168

Nwokwu, T. C. (2020). Delay in Recruitment: Evidence from a Developing Country. NWOKWU, TC (2020). Delay in Recruitment: Evidence from a Developing Country. *International Journal of Business and Economic Affairs*, *5*(1), 9–22. DOI: 10.24088/IJBEA-2020-51002

Ogunseyi, T. B., Avoussoukpo, C. B., & Jiang, Y. (2023). A systematic review of privacy techniques in recommendation systems. *International Journal of Information Security*, *22*(6), 1651–1664. DOI: 10.1007/s10207-023-00710-1

Portillo, A. E., & Mancera-Valencia, F. J. (2021). The processes of recruitment and selection of personnel: Between objectivity and subjectivity. *International Journal of Social Sciences Perspectives*, *9*(1), 1–8. DOI: 10.33094/7.2017.2021.91.1.8

Pourkhodabakhsh, N., Mamoudan, M. M., & Bozorgi-Amiri, A. (2023). Effective machine learning, Meta-heuristic algorithms and multi-criteria decision making to minimizing human resource turnover. *Applied Intelligence*, *53*(12), 16309–16331. DOI: 10.1007/s10489-022-04294-6 PMID: 36531972

Raji, I. D., & Buolamwini, J. (2019, Jan). Actionable auditing: Investigating the impact of publicly naming biased performance results of commercial ai products. In Proceedings of the 2019 AAAI/ACM Conference on AI, Ethics, and Society (pp. 429-435).

Saouabe, A., Oualla, H., Mazar, M., & Messadia, M. (2024, Dec). Evolution of Human Resources Management Methods: From Traditional Approaches to Generative Artificial Intelligence. In *2024 International Conference on Decision Aid Sciences and Applications (DASA)* (pp. 1-5). IEEE. DOI: 10.1109/DASA63652.2024.10836655

Smelyakov, K., Hurova, Y., & Osiievskyi, S. (2023). Analysis of the effectiveness of using machine learning algorithms to make hiring decisions. *Proceedings of CEUR Workshop*, 1613, 0073.

Speed, F., & Kulichyova, A. (2021). The role of talent intermediaries in accessing and developing refugee talent pools. *Journal of Organizational Effectiveness: People and Performance*, *8*(4), 407–426. DOI: 10.1108/JOEPP-01-2021-0023

Staubitz, J., Renz, J., Meinel, C., & Teusner, R. (2022). Using MOOC analytics to evaluate digital learning behaviors and predict professional competencies. *IEEE Transactions on Learning Technologies*, *15*(2), 210–223. DOI: 10.1109/TLT.2022.3160012

Yassine, T. K., & Said, A. (2024). Predictive Hiring and AI: Elevating Recruitment with Optimized Neural Networks and Gradient Descent. *International Journal of Intelligent Information Systems*, *13*(6), 117–127. DOI: 10.11648/j.ijiis.20241306.11

Zbib, R., Lacasa, L. A., Retyk, F., Poves, R., Aizpuru, J., Fabregat, H., & García-Casademont, E. (2022). Learning job titles similarity from noisy skill labels. arXiv preprint arXiv:2207.00494.

Zioudi, O., Mahmoud, H., Badouch, M., Boulmane, E., & Boutaounte, M. (2025). AI-powered predictions transforming the future of brand management. In Aboudrar, I., Ilahi Bakhsh, F., Nayyar, A., & Ouachtouk, I. (Eds.), *Innovative technologies on electrical power systems for smart cities infrastructure* (pp. 177–186). Springer Nature Switzerland., DOI: 10.1007/978-3-031-86705-7_17

Chapter 2
Self-Adaptive Systems: Redefining Best Practices in AI and Big Data in Recruitment

Sri Rizqi Wahyuningrum
https://orcid.org/0000-0003-1094-0277
IAIN Madura, Pamekasan, Indonesia

Abd Ghofur
https://orcid.org/0000-0002-5714-1635
IAIN Madura, Pamekasan, Indonesia

Arina Mufrihah
https://orcid.org/0000-0001-6589-5018
IAIN Madura, Pamekasan, Indonesia

Iswatun Hasanah
https://orcid.org/0009-0009-3149-289X
IAIN Madura, Pamekasan, Indonesia

Anna Aisa
IAIN Madura, Pamekasan, Indonesia

ABSTRACT

Artificial Intelligence (AI) and Big Data are transforming recruitment by enabling adaptive, data-driven hiring. Traditional methods like manual resume screening struggle with dynamic labor markets. Using the MAPE-K model, AI systems automate candidate sourcing, enhance job matching, and predict turnover via real-time analytics and Virtual Reality simulations. Case studies, like Big Data for SMEs and AI in smart cities, show improved efficiency. Ethical challenges, including bias and privacy, demand fairness-aware learning and human oversight. This chapter

DOI: 10.4018/979-8-3373-6516-9.ch002

explores these advancements, proposes ethical governance, and forecasts trends like federated learning, fostering collaboration across computer science, HR, and data science to optimize talent acquisition.

1. INTRODUCTION

The digital age has brought about unprecedented growth in the volume, velocity, and variety of data, marking a paradigm shift from traditional data storage and retrieval models to dynamic, real-time data environments. These environments are characterized by continuous data streams, high-frequency updates, and context-aware fluctuations. As a result, they necessitate equally responsive analytics systems capable of adjusting to rapid shifts in input data patterns, a demand traditional batch-processing systems struggle to meet.

The theoretical underpinning of this phenomenon draws heavily from system theory and the principles of cybernetics, where feedback loops and adaptive behavior are crucial for resilience. This aligns with the "velocity" dimension of the three Vs of Big Data. As noted by (Han et al., 2025), emerging environments such as the Internet of Vehicles (IoV) and adaptive healthcare platforms operate under conditions where data is not only high-volume but contextually volatile, requiring systems that can learn and adapt in real time (Han et al., 2025).

Scholars have also highlighted the need for AI models that can incrementally learn and unlearn, effectively managing concept drift and seasonal variability. For example, Wang et al. (2025) propose an ensemble-based online learning architecture for IoV systems that dynamically adjusts model weights based on incoming data stream properties (Wang et al., 2025). Digital Transformation in the Business World. More and more companies are adopting cloud-based technology, big data, and artificial intelligence (AI). This will further increase the demand for reliable and quality telecommunication services and digital infrastructure (*StaticData_IDX*, n.d.).

Beyond technical requirements, dynamic environments demand new governance models. Data lineage, traceability, and ethical handling must also evolve to reflect changing data contexts and ownership models in federated learning ecosystems. This reflects the growing convergence between technical adaptivity and socio-ethical responsiveness.

Critically, the shift to dynamic data environments signals a broader evolution in how we conceptualize intelligence in systems—not as static knowledge repositories, but as continuously updating, interacting agents. This reconceptualization supports the development of systems that are not only reactive but anticipatory. In summary, the proliferation of dynamic data environments challenges traditional paradigms of system design, necessitating architectures that are scalable, responsive, and ethically aligned. The ability to dynamically adapt to ever-changing data streams has become a defining capability for next-generation AI and Big Data systems.

1.1 Limitations of Static AI–Big Data Systems

Despite significant advances in artificial intelligence and data analytics, many AI systems remain fundamentally static in their core architecture. These systems are trained on historical datasets and deployed with fixed model parameters, assuming the operational environment remains stable over time. However, in practice, most environments exhibit substantial temporal and contextual variability. Static models are particularly vulnerable to concept drift, where the statistical properties of the target variable change over time. As a result, models that initially perform well can quickly degrade, becoming obsolete. Jean (2025) observes this phenomenon in security systems, where threat patterns evolve rapidly, and models not designed for continuous updates fail to detect novel attacks (Jean, 2025).

Moreover, the process of retraining static models is resource-intensive, requiring significant computational power, retraining datasets, and manual supervision. This leads to operational bottlenecks, especially in real-time or mission-critical settings, such as autonomous navigation or adaptive clinical diagnostics (Ulfah et al., 2022). Static architectures also struggle with data sparsity and generalization in non-stationary contexts. Architecturally, batch-processing pipelines are ill-equipped to deal with continuously arriving data. These systems often require manual scheduling, re-ingestion, and retraining cycles that are incompatible with the fluid nature of dynamic systems. The lack of feedback-driven learning renders them inflexible and reactive, rather than proactive.

The issue extends to ethical and legal dimensions as well. Static models risk perpetuating biases embedded in training data, with no mechanism to learn from newer, more representative samples. As Abdul Karim et al. (2025) point out, systems deployed in healthcare settings that fail to update their models risk systemic inequities and diagnostic errors (Abdul-Karim et al., 2025). Ultimately, the rigidity of static AI–Big Data systems hinders their scalability, adaptability, and trustworthiness in today's data-driven ecosystems. There is a clear and urgent need for transitioning to architectures that can evolve alongside their operational contexts.

1.2 Emergence and Significance of Self-Adaptive Systems

In response to the shortcomings of static systems and the rise of dynamic data contexts, self-adaptive systems have emerged as a transformative paradigm. These systems are designed to autonomously monitor, Analysis, and respond to changes in their internal state or external environment, thereby sustaining performance and alignment with evolving objectives.

The conceptual basis of self-adaptive systems lies in the MAPE-K loop—Monitor, Analysis, Plan, Execute, over a shared Knowledge base. As Fan et al. (2025) describe, this architectural model enables systems to engage in a form of continuous self-management, reducing reliance on external interventions while enhancing responsiveness to environmental volatility (Fan et al., 2025).

Nevertheless, challenges remain. These include maintaining system stability during adaptation, preventing negative feedback loops, and ensuring that adaptive behaviors do not conflict with human goals. The development of safe adaptation policies is therefore an active area of research. In conclusion, the emergence of self-adaptive systems represents a crucial evolution in AI and Big Data practices. These systems hold the potential to deliver robustness, flexibility, and accountability—qualities that are indispensable for next-generation intelligent infrastructure.

2. THEORETICAL FOUNDATIONS

2.1 Foundations of Adaptive and Autonomic Systems

The foundational concepts of adaptive and autonomic systems stem from interdisciplinary advances in control theory, cybernetics, and systems engineering. Originally inspired by biological systems' capacity to self-regulate, adaptive systems in computing are defined as those capable of adjusting their behavior in response to internal and external stimuli without direct human intervention. Autonomic systems extend this paradigm by encompassing self-management features across dimensions such as self-configuration, self-healing, self-optimization, and self-protection (IBM's autonomic computing blueprint, 2001) (Wahyuningrum & Damayanti, 2024). In modern intelligent infrastructures, this framework serves as a cornerstone for building resilient, context-aware systems that evolve over time (Wahyuningrum & Fransiska, 2023).

A key theoretical anchor in these systems is the feedback loop—a construct central to both control theory and cybernetics. Feedback loops provide the structural and operational underpinning for continuous monitoring, evaluation, and adjustment of system behavior. In autonomic computing, these loops are operationalized through the MAPE-K model, which enables systems to iteratively monitor their state, Analysis deviations, plan corrective strategies, and execute modifications, all governed by a shared knowledge base. As documented by Ghadekar et al. (2024), real-time robotic systems integrating reinforcement learning with sensor-driven feedback loops exemplify such adaptive navigation models that dynamically update operational strategies based on the environment (Ghadekar et al., 2024).

Another theoretical underpinning comes from systems theory, which emphasizes modularity, scalability, and interoperability—crucial properties for modern adaptive systems operating in distributed AI environments. According to (Weyns et al., 2022), this theoretical lens supports the design of systems that not only react to changes but also learn and optimize based on long-term objectives and system-wide performance metrics. These systems can thus be seen as *goal-oriented agents*, capable of negotiating trade-offs under uncertainty and partial observability—capabilities increasingly crucial in edge-cloud hybrid systems.

The transition from static to adaptive systems is also driven by the demands of AI-integrated ecosystems, where pre-programmed logic is insufficient to handle the variability and complexity of modern data streams. This evolution necessitates embedding *decision-making autonomy* and *situational awareness* into system components. For instance, the growing adoption of AI of Things (AIoT) in sectors like autonomous vehicles and smart energy grids highlights how adaptive control models must integrate with real-time AI analytics and distributed sensor networks, ensuring operational integrity amidst environmental volatility (Zhou et al., 2024).

Critically, the implementation of adaptive and autonomic systems is not without challenges. The calibration of feedback loops, the definition of optimal adaptation policies, and the assurance of stability during transitions remain open research questions. Moreover, the ability to balance autonomy with explainability and trust—especially in safety-critical systems—requires the integration of ethical frameworks and human-in-the-loop design principles. These aspects underscore the continuing need for theoretical rigor and practical innovation in evolving the foundations of self-adaptive systems in AI and Big Data contexts.

2.2 The MAPE-K Model: Monitor, Analysis, Plan, Execute + Knowledge

The MAPE-K model is a foundational architectural pattern introduced in autonomic computing to facilitate self-management in complex systems. MAPE-K stands for Monitor, Analysis, Plan, and Execute, orchestrated through a centralized Knowledge component that stores goals, rules, historical data, and environmental models. It provides a modular feedback control loop that enables systems to sense changes, reason about them, devise solutions, and act autonomously. Its conceptual elegance and modular decomposition make it particularly suited to managing system complexity, heterogeneity, and real-time adaptivity.

At its core, each phase of the MAPE-K loop plays a distinct but interdependent role. Monitoring collects data from sensors and system logs; Analysis evaluates this data to detect anomalies or trends; Planning devises responses using AI models, and Execution implements these strategies. The Knowledge repository enhances adaptivity by storing context-aware data and supporting learning from experience. As documented by Sanwouo et al. (2024), MAPE-K is increasingly being augmented with AI capabilities such as generative modeling and reinforcement learning to support reasoning under uncertainty (Sanwouo et al., 2024).

In dynamic environments such as cyber-physical systems (CPS), the MAPE-K model serves as a vital structure for managing feedback loops across distributed components. For instance, Romero-Garcés et al. (2022) implemented a graph-based runtime model to structure knowledge sharing within robotic systems, enabling adaptive spatial planning through hierarchical feedback mechanisms. This demonstrates how MAPE-K can be operationalized not only in logical architectures but also in real-time embodied systems (Romero Garces, 2022).

Furthermore, the MAPE-K model is gaining attention for its flexibility in integrating with machine learning (ML) components. Highlights how generative AI models and large language models (LLMs) can be embedded within the Analysis and Plan stages to improve prediction accuracy, scenario simulation, and context-aware decision making. This cross-pollination of AI with self-adaptive architecture illustrates a path toward more intelligent, proactive, and even self-optimizing systems (Li et al., 2024).

Despite its broad applicability, MAPE-K implementations face challenges such as managing the latency between loop components, ensuring consistent knowledge representation across modules, and preventing adaptation oscillations or feedback instability. Current research seeks to overcome these challenges through hybrid architectures, multi-loop coordination strategies (Wahyuningrum, 2022), and runtime assurance techniques. Extending MAPE-K with history-aware explanations and human-in-the-loop mechanisms enhances transparency and accountability—an increasingly critical factor in ethically sensitive applications like healthcare or autonomous defense systems (Parra-Ullauri et al., 2022).

Figure 1. MAPE-K Loop Implementation in Adaptive AI System

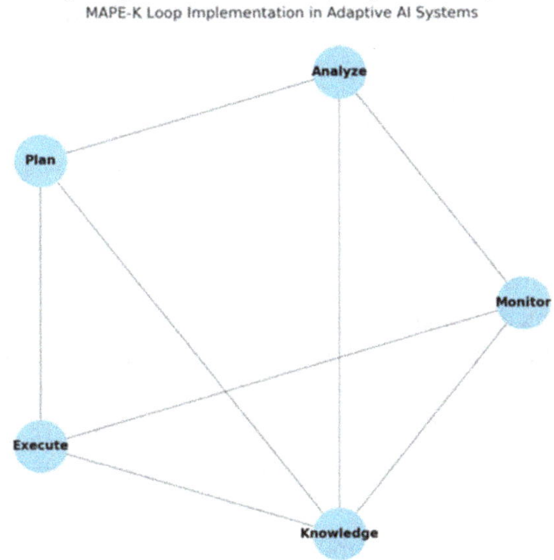

Core Components:

- **Monitor**: Continuously observes data from sensors, logs, system metrics, or user inputs. It translates low-level system events into structured information.
- **Analysis**: Identifies trends, anomalies, or deviations using techniques like statistical analysis, clustering, or ML-based prediction.
- **Plan**: Decides on a set of actions to correct or optimize the system. AI planning algorithms, reinforcement learning, or heuristic search are commonly used here.
- **Execute**: Applies planned changes to the system, often via effectors, actuators, or control APIs.
- **Knowledge**: A central repository containing models, goals, rules, system states, and historical logs that inform the other components.

2.3 Theories of Complex Systems and Self-Organization

Self-organization is a key emergent property of complex systems, where global order arises from local interactions without centralized control. This phenomenon is commonly observed in natural ecosystems, neural systems, and social networks. In AI systems, self-organization manifests in decentralized decision-making, dynamic task allocation, and evolving system architectures. The context of computational social science, adaptive intelligence emerges when simple agents interact under local rules, resulting in sophisticated global behavior without external orchestration (Sun, 2025).

The application of complexity theory to AI is also reflected in swarm intelligence and multi-agent reinforcement learning, where self-organizing principles are embedded in agent coordination protocols. For instance, swarm robotics utilizes evolutionary algorithms and decentralized learning to adaptively navigate uncertain terrains—highlighting the practical implementation of complexity theory in real-world adaptive systems (Acharya et al., 2024).

Moreover, framing digital infrastructures (like smart cities) as complex adaptive systems (CAS) enables designers to integrate adaptive governance and feedback-rich architectures. This allows for flexible responses to urban phenomena like traffic, energy consumption, or social behavior. The ability of CAS to reorganize and evolve based on feedback aligns closely with the goals of adaptive AI systems (Ochoa et al., 2024).

However, the inherent unpredictability of complex systems introduces challenges. Emergent behaviors can be beneficial or detrimental depending on context, and predicting the outcomes of adaptive interactions is often computationally intractable. Therefore, the need for hybrid models that blend deterministic planning with stochastic simulations to account for dynamic emergent phenomena in human-augmented ecosystems, advancing planetary-scale self-organizing systems (Funabashi, 2024).

The study of complex systems focuses on how heterogeneous, interconnected components interact in nonlinear, adaptive, and often unpredictable ways (Wahyuningrum & Fitriyah, 2023). A fundamental property of such systems is emergence—the rise of global behavior that cannot be directly deduced from the properties of individual parts. In AI and Big Data, complexity theory provides a vital lens through which adaptive behavior can be understood, especially in domains where rigid programming cannot account for environmental uncertainty or evolving objectives.

Figure 2. Comparison Traditional Rule Based Systems vs Complex Adaptive Systems

Criteria	Traditional Rule-Based Systems	Complex Systems & Self-Organization
Control Structure	Centralized, top-down logic	Decentralized, bottom-up emergence
Adaptation	Manual updates or retraining	Dynamic adaptation via local interactions
Scalability	Limited by predefined rules	Scales with system complexity
Learning Mechanism	No learning, static rules	Adaptive, emergent learning
Response to Environment	Reactive (predefined)	Proactive and co-evolving
Robustness	Fragile to unexpected input	Resilient through redundancy and feedback
Predictability	Highly predictable	Unpredictable but stable patterns emerge

The mathematical basis of self-organization often includes nonlinear differential equations, stochastic processes, and cellular automata, who models chaotic dynamics in biological and cyber-physical systems to uncover attractor states and phase transitions—key concepts in understanding system stability or collapse. These models are essential in simulating how self-organization emerges in artificial ecosystems, particularly in areas like adaptive logistics or digital twinning (Demopoulos, 2025).

2.4 Relationship to Artificial Intelligence and Machine Learning

The evolution from static, rule-based computing to adaptive, learning-based architectures marks one of the most transformative shifts in artificial intelligence. Rule-based systems, once dominant in expert systems and early decision-support tools, operate by encoding domain knowledge into explicit *if-then* logic (Suhartono et al., 2016). While they perform well in constrained environments, their rigidity limits adaptability, especially in non-deterministic or data-intensive scenarios. This limitation led to the widespread adoption of machine learning (ML), which learns rules from data rather than relying on human-crafted logic (Wahyuningrum & Akbar, 2016).

Modern self-adaptive systems integrate machine learning not as a peripheral component but as a core engine of adaptation. Algorithms such as reinforcement learning (RL), meta-learning, and continual learning are used not just for model optimization but to guide system-level decisions—what to monitor, when to retrain, how to allocate resources, and how to manage uncertainty. These ML techniques now power the Analysis and Plan components of MAPE-K architectures, transforming adaptive systems into semi-autonomous agents capable of strategic reasoning (Li et al., 2024).

Figure 3. Integration of Machine Learning in the MAPE-K Loop

Finally, the application of AI in adaptive systems raises significant questions around transparency, interpretability, and governance. While machine learning offers powerful generalization, its often black-box nature makes adaptation difficult to audit. This has spurred interest in Explainable AI (XAI) techniques, which aim to render ML decisions interpretable at runtime. Such tools are now critical in safety-sensitive domains like finance, healthcare, and critical infrastructure, where adaptation must be both effective and accountable (Qomariyah & Wahyuningrum, 2023).

3. METHODS

3.1 Adaptive Machine Learning Techniques

Adaptive machine learning (ML) lies at the heart of self-adaptive systems, allowing models to evolve as new information is introduced. One of the foundational techniques is online learning, which enables continuous model updates with each incoming data point. This approach is crucial in dynamic contexts such as real-time fraud detection, streaming analytics, or sensor-driven systems, where the data distribution is non-stationary and requires immediate response.

A closely related concept is continual learning, which addresses the challenge of maintaining past knowledge while acquiring new patterns, avoiding what is known as *catastrophic forgetting*. In edge-cloud systems, where data contexts vary frequently, continual learning ensures that models remain accurate without constant re-training. As emphasized by Gheibi and Weyns (2024), systems that support *lifelong self-adaptation* are more efficient and resilient when handling distributed, evolving data sources (Gheibi & Weyns, 2024).

AutoML (Automated Machine Learning) further enhances adaptivity by automating model selection, feature engineering, and hyperparameter tuning. This reduces reliance on manual intervention, enabling more responsive and scalable AI systems, especially in settings with limited data science expertise. AutoML tools are increasingly embedded into pipelines for adaptive control and optimization.

3.2 Reinforcement Learning for Policy Adaptation

In self-adaptive systems, RL is often embedded in the Plan and Execute phases of the MAPE-K loop. It allows for iterative policy refinement based on exploration and exploitation strategies. Techniques such as Deep Q-Networks (DQNs), Actor-Critic Methods, and Policy Gradient Algorithms have been successfully used in domains such as cloud orchestration, autonomous vehicles, and robotic motion planning (Ahmed et al., 2023).

RL is used in cloud computing to perform self-healing operations. By monitoring environmental states and applying corrective actions through learned policies, cloud systems can autonomously recover from faults and dynamically reallocate resources based on load. What distinguishes RL in adaptive systems is its ability to function without complete environmental models. Instead, it learns behavior from experience, which is ideal for partially observable, high-dimensional spaces. However, this strength also introduces complexity in ensuring stable convergence and safe exploration in critical systems. To mitigate these challenges, modern adaptive architectures often combine RL with simulation-based pre-training or model-based planning to reduce training times and ensure safe deployment. This hybridization of RL with other adaptive strategies has significantly improved system robustness in real-world applications.

3.3 Runtime Model-Based Adaptation

Runtime models are a key enabling technology for reflective and adaptive system behavior. These models represent the system's current state and environment, and are actively maintained during execution. By serving as an interface between monitoring and control, runtime models empower systems to reason about their condition and enact adaptations accordingly. The central idea is that adaptation should be context-aware, not merely reactive. Runtime models allow the system to simulate or predict outcomes before executing changes, enhancing both stability and performance. This is especially vital in mission-critical applications, such as autonomous drones or surgical robots, where wrong adaptations can have severe consequences (Aljohani et al., 2025).

Despite their promise, runtime models also pose challenges, including computational overhead, the need for precise synchronization, and runtime validation. However, ongoing advances in lightweight modeling frameworks and declarative adaptation rules are helping address these limitations, making runtime models increasingly viable in real-world deployments.

3.4 Data Processing Frameworks in Adaptive Contexts

Adaptive systems handling high-throughput data streams often rely on frameworks such as Apache Flink, Kafka Streams, and Spark Streaming. These platforms provide the infrastructure for stateful stream processing, windowing, and low-latency analytics. When integrated with ML pipelines, they enable near-instantaneous feedback loops essential for self-adaptation. The backbone of large-scale adaptive AI systems lies in their ability to process and respond to continuous data streams. Technologies like Apache Flink, Kafka Streams, and Spark Streaming provide real-time processing engines that support stateful stream analytics, essential for time-sensitive decision-making.

These frameworks are designed for event-time processing, windowing, and exactly-once semantics, enabling accurate and reliable computation even when data arrives out of order or late. This is particularly useful in environments like IoT, financial services, and adaptive cybersecurity. Cloud systems use these frameworks for auto-scaling, dynamically adjusting computational resources in response to workload fluctuations. Combined with real-time ML pipelines, these systems can detect anomalies and respond before performance degrades, enhancing both system reliability and user experience (Dogani et al., 2023).

Furthermore, these frameworks support seamless integration with AI models, enabling feedback loops that continuously refine decision policies. For example, anomaly detection models can be retrained based on flagged events, creating a closed adaptive loop that improves over time.

In sum, modern stream-processing frameworks serve not only as data engines but also as adaptation enablers. They bridge the gap between raw input and intelligent action, allowing systems to learn and evolve in tandem with their operational data environments.

Figure 4. Mapping Methodological Approaches to the MAPE-K Loop

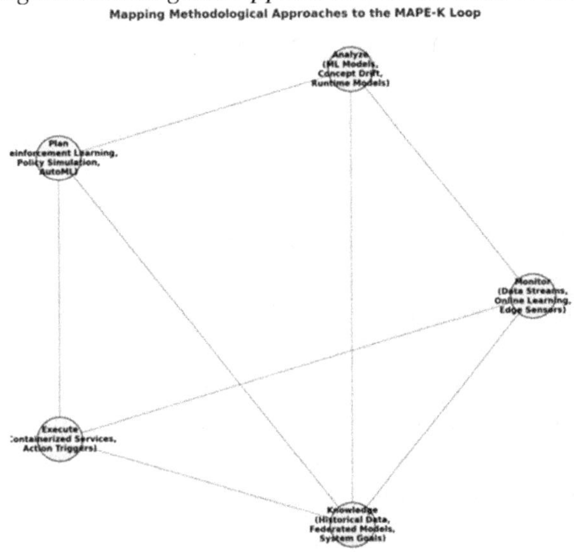

The diagram above presents a conceptual mapping of methodological approaches to the MAPE-K loop, illustrating how each methodological pillar supports specific phases in self-adaptive systems:

- **Monitor**: Linked to *online learning* and *sensor-driven edge inputs*, enabling continuous data intake and context sensing.
- **Analysis**: Powered by *machine learning models*, *concept drift detection*, and *runtime models* for real-time reasoning and diagnostics.
- **Plan**: Supported by *reinforcement learning*, *policy simulation*, and *AutoML* to generate adaptive strategies.
- **Execute**: Implemented using *containerized services* (e.g., Docker, Kubernetes) and action orchestration layers.
- **Knowledge**: Serves as a dynamic repository of *historical data*, *federated models*, and *adaptive policies*, informing the entire loop.

4. RESULTS

4.1 Adaptive Cloud Computing Platforms

Adaptive AI systems rely heavily on cloud computing for scalability, elasticity, and orchestration of AI services across global infrastructures. Leading platforms such as Amazon Web Services (AWS), Microsoft Azure, and Google Cloud Platform (GCP) offer tools like auto-scaling groups, event-driven functions, and managed Kubernetes services that are pivotal in enabling system adaptivity. These services dynamically allocate resources, respond to fluctuating workloads, and support fault-tolerance through redundancy mechanisms.

Modern adaptive AI systems are critically dependent on cloud platforms for dynamic scaling, resource pooling, and orchestration of intelligent services. Platforms such as Amazon Web Services (AWS), Microsoft Azure, and Google Cloud Platform (GCP) offer a range of elastic computing services—such as auto-scaling, serverless functions (e.g., AWS Lambda), and infrastructure-as-code tools (e.g., Terraform)—that are integral to supporting runtime adaptivity. These tools allow systems to dynamically respond to shifts in user demand, operational context, or environmental conditions.

Cloud-native tools also facilitate continuous integration and deployment (CI/CD), enabling real-time updates to AI models and system configurations. Through managed services like SageMaker, Vertex AI, or Azure ML, cloud providers now offer end-to-end ML lifecycle management. These environments are not only programmable but also increasingly self-optimizing, thereby reducing human intervention in adaptive control processes. As discussed in the ISC High Performance 2024 Workshops, cloud-enabled adaptive systems demonstrate significantly better resilience under volatile load conditions than their on-premises counterparts (Weiland, 2024).

Moreover, adaptive AI systems benefit from cloud platforms' ability to distribute workloads across multiple regions, ensuring fault tolerance and data redundancy. The geographical elasticity of the cloud enhances responsiveness and compliance with data sovereignty regulations. When integrated with observability stacks and intelligent control mechanisms, adaptive cloud platforms become foundational enablers of resilient, scalable, and intelligent infrastructure.

One of the critical features of cloud platforms in this context is elastic computing. Elasticity allows systems to adjust compute and storage resources on demand, supporting AI model training, inference, and deployment without manual intervention. Adaptive systems embedded in cloud infrastructures outperform traditional static deployments in both efficiency and resilience across variable workloads (Weiland et al., 2024).

4.2 Integration of Edge and Fog Computing Architectures

While cloud provides centralized power, edge and fog computing introduce decentralization critical for latency-sensitive applications. These architectures extend computing to the "edge" of the network—closer to data sources—thereby reducing latency, enabling local decision-making, and easing bandwidth demands. Edge computing is essential in autonomous vehicles, wearable health systems, and smart manufacturing.

Fog computing, which acts as an intermediate layer between the edge and the cloud, adds contextual awareness and supports distributed decision-making across heterogeneous nodes. It enables workload partitioning based on latency tolerance and data sensitivity. By embedding intelligence into routers, switches, and local data centers, fog computing enhances the system's ability to orchestrate adaptive behavior without compromising on privacy or real-time responsiveness.

Together, edge and fog architectures form a hierarchical adaptive ecosystem. At the edge, lightweight ML models manage local anomalies and short-term decisions. In the fog, coordination algorithms manage shared tasks and security. The cloud, in turn, orchestrates long-term learning, policy enforcement, and centralized analytics. This architecture is particularly effective in domains requiring situational responsiveness and robustness under infrastructure constraints.

Adaptive AI systems deployed at the edge utilize lightweight models and runtime monitors to make decisions in real time. Fog computing complements this by offering intermediate layers between the cloud and edge, providing context-aware processing and system-wide coordination. Studies show that combining cloud-edge-fog paradigms enhances not only responsiveness but also the system's robustness to failure and connectivity loss. These architectures support hierarchical adaptation, where edge nodes handle local anomalies, while the cloud refines global strategies. This distributed model is becoming essential in sectors like disaster response, energy management, and defense logistics.

4.3 Containerization and Orchestration Tools

Containerization, primarily through Docker, provides encapsulation of services with their dependencies, ensuring environment consistency across deployments. Kubernetes, as the dominant orchestration platform, manages clusters of containers, automating deployment, scaling, and healing of adaptive services. These technologies enable rapid iteration and rollout of AI updates without system downtime.

Containerization has revolutionized software deployment in adaptive systems by encapsulating applications along with their dependencies into portable, isolated units. Docker is the most widely adopted platform for creating and managing containers, allowing adaptive systems to ensure reproducibility, portability, and isolation across various runtime environments. This is crucial in adaptive settings where frequent redeployments are needed without compromising stability.

Kubernetes, the dominant container orchestration framework, automates deployment, scaling, and management of containerized applications. It supports features like self-healing, automatic rollbacks, and horizontal scaling, which are essential for dynamic adaptation. Kubernetes operators and custom resource definitions (CRDs) further allow for domain-specific adaptation logic to be embedded directly into the orchestration layer.

Additionally, service mesh architectures such as Istio or Linkerd provide observability, secure communication, and fine-grained traffic control among services. These capabilities support real-time behavioral changes in adaptive systems without modifying the application logic. In combination, these orchestration tools form the infrastructural backbone for resilient and modular self-adaptive software ecosystems, where services evolve independently but operate coherently.

Adaptive systems benefit from orchestration tools by enabling self-healing, load balancing, and policy-based automation. For instance, Kubernetes Horizontal Pod Autoscaler adjusts the number of running pods based on CPU or memory usage, supporting dynamic system scaling. Helm charts, Istio mesh, and CRDs (Custom Resource Definitions) further enhance orchestration granularity and observability. The microservices pattern, when implemented with container orchestration, allows each system module to evolve independently. This is crucial for adaptive systems operating in heterogeneous environments where localized updates are frequent and system-wide coherence must be maintained.

4.4 Monitoring and Observability Frameworks

Effective adaptation is not possible without continuous monitoring and observability. Monitoring tools like Prometheus, Grafana, and Elastic Stack track system metrics, resource usage, anomaly rates, and performance trends in real time. These insights feed into the MAPE-K loop, informing the Monitor and Analysis components.

Observability extends beyond traditional monitoring by incorporating distributed tracing, structured logging, and telemetry, which collectively offer a comprehensive understanding of system state and behavior. This is especially critical in debugging emergent behaviors or diagnosing cascade failures in adaptive systems.

The ability to adapt presupposes the ability to observe and interpret. Monitoring and observability frameworks provide the sensory and analytical capabilities necessary for adaptive systems to detect, interpret, and respond to change. Tools like Prometheus, Grafana, and the Elastic Stack (ELK) offer powerful real-time telemetry, metric collection, and visualization capabilities that feed into the Monitor and Analysis phases of the MAPE-K loop.

Observability goes beyond monitoring by integrating tracing, structured logging, and time-series analytics into a cohesive system of insight. Distributed tracing (e.g., with Jaeger or OpenTelemetry) enables visibility into the interactions of microservices and edge nodes, which is vital for diagnosing errors, latency bottlenecks, and emergent behaviors in adaptive AI pipelines. This detailed observability supports fine-tuned adaptation strategies, such as shifting traffic from degraded services or rebalancing load across nodes. AI-enhanced monitoring tools now employ predictive analytics and anomaly detection to preempt failures before they impact users. This proactive layer forms the foundation for predictive maintenance, dynamic provisioning, and real-time feedback integration within adaptive infrastructures.

4.5 Security, Governance, and Compliance Layers

As adaptive systems become more autonomous, the need for robust security, data governance, and compliance grows. Adaptive infrastructures must comply with evolving regulations such as GDPR, HIPAA, and ISO/IEC 27001, while also responding in real time to emerging security threats.

AI systems operating in cloud-edge ecosystems must integrate zero-trust architectures, dynamic access control, and continuous risk assessment to mitigate vulnerabilities arising from autonomous decision-making. Additionally, auditable logs, explainable decision trails, and policy-aware adaptation rules are essential for ensuring legal accountability and ethical AI deployment.

Security strategies in adaptive infrastructures include zero-trust architecture, dynamic role-based access control (RBAC), and real-time threat detection. These mechanisms must function at both the software and infrastructure levels. Adaptivity must also be auditable: mechanisms such as versioned model registries, explainable AI tools, and decision provenance logging allow for post-hoc investigation and policy review.

From a governance perspective, adaptive AI requires runtime policy enforcement, where decisions must be filtered through ethical and legal lenses dynamically. Policy engines like OPA (Open Policy Agent) or Kyverno integrate with Kubernetes to enforce adaptive behavior that aligns with governance requirements. As the complexity of AI infrastructures grows, so too does the importance of embedding compliance logic into the very foundation of system adaptivity.

5. DISCUSSION

Self-adaptive systems in healthcare are transforming traditional clinical decision-making into real-time, responsive, and context-aware processes. These systems can modify their behavior dynamically based on continuous feedback from medical sensors, electronic health records, and external variables like patient movement or environmental conditions. The deployment of **clinical decision support systems (CDSS)** with adaptive learning mechanisms helps tailor treatments and monitor patient conditions more effectively.

In smart hospitals, self-adaptive platforms integrate Internet of Medical Things (IoMT) devices and AI analytics to detect early warning signs and trigger interventions. For example, adaptive early warning systems for sepsis and cardiac events learn from historical data while adjusting thresholds in real time to improve predictive accuracy. These systems outperform static models in detecting deteriorations in high-dependency wards by up to 27% in accuracy (Chen et al., 2021). In the 2016 Higher Competitive Grants Research (Hibah Bersaing Dikti), we have been successfully developed models, infrastructure and modules of Hadoop-based big data analysis application. It has also successfully developed a virtual private network (VPN) network that allows integration and access to the infrastructure from outside the FTIS Computer Lab. Infrastructure and application modules of analysis are then wanted to be presented as services to small and medium enterprises (SMEs) in Indonesia. This research aims to develop application of big data analysis service interface integrated with Hadoop-Cluster. The research begins with finding appropriate methods and techniques for scheduling jobs, calling for ready-made Java Map-Reduce (MR) application modules, and techniques for tunneling input / output and meta-data construction of service request (input) and service output. The above methods and techniques are then developed into a web-based service application, as well as an executable module that runs on Java and J2EE based programming environment and can access Hadoop-Cluster in the FTIS Computer Lab. The resulting application can be accessed by the public through the site http://bigdata.unpar.ac.id. Based on the test results, the application has functioned well in accordance with the specifications and can be used to perform big data analysis (Karya & Moertini, 2017).

Furthermore, the pandemic accelerated the adoption of adaptive telemedicine platforms. These systems adapt to varying patient contexts—connectivity constraints, comorbidities, and personalized health goals. Integration of federated learning in edge-based smart health applications ensures that sensitive patient data remains localized while still benefiting from global learning improvements (Liu et al., 2022).

Cybersecurity is one of the most critical application areas for self-adaptive systems due to the highly dynamic and adversarial nature of cyber threats. Traditional signature-based detection models are no longer sufficient to handle polymorphic and zero-day attacks. Adaptive systems, on the other hand, continuously learn from anomalous behaviors to evolve defense mechanisms in real time.

Self-adaptive **Intrusion Detection Systems (IDS)** leverage reinforcement learning and anomaly detection techniques to recalibrate thresholds and adapt rules without manual reprogramming. Nepomuceno et al. (2023) emphasized that these systems are vital in environments like 5G networks and smart grids, where fixed rules are easily bypassed by sophisticated attackers.

Adaptive systems also play a central role in cyber resilience, where rapid detection is followed by self-mitigation routines such as isolating compromised microservices or modifying access control policies. The integration of blockchain for immutable audit trails supports forensic analysis while adaptive access controls enforce dynamic zero-trust principles.

Smart cities are an ideal testing ground for self-adaptive systems due to their complexity, scale, and need for responsiveness across domains such as traffic, energy, public safety, and waste management. Self-adaptive infrastructure enables cities to respond to real-time fluctuations in resource usage, demand patterns, and environmental variables. A major use case is adaptive traffic control, where sensor networks and edge-based learning models dynamically adjust traffic light timings and route diversions. Cities implementing adaptive traffic systems saw a 35% reduction in congestion and a 22% reduction in vehicle emissions compared to fixed scheduling systems. Smart grids and energy management systems also benefit from adaptivity. These systems optimize electricity distribution and storage by learning consumption patterns and weather forecasts. This results in reduced energy waste and improved integration of renewable sources. Adaptive grid controllers enable autonomous decision-making to switch loads or reroute supply based on real-time constraints.

Urban safety systems, including surveillance and disaster alert platforms, use adaptive AI to recognize abnormal behaviors or conditions, such as crowd anomalies or air quality hazards. These systems dynamically adjust their operational sensitivity based on environmental data and historical patterns, enhancing responsiveness and reducing false alarms (Wahyuningrum & Ghofur, 2025).

A primary component is adaptive recommendation engines that employ hybrid filtering and reinforcement learning. These engines not only predict preferences but also adapt strategies in real time to maximize conversion rates. For instance, A/B testing platforms integrated with adaptive models autonomously determine the best-performing variants without requiring manual oversight. User segmentation and behavior prediction systems now incorporate AutoML and continual learning to adapt to evolving customer preferences. These systems are capable of detecting subtle changes in purchase intent, enabling more targeted messaging, bundling strategies, and inventory decisions.

Additionally, adaptive fraud detection systems are deployed to monitor transaction patterns and instantly flag suspicious behavior. Unlike traditional static rules, these systems evolve their detection thresholds based on live transaction histories, geographic anomalies, and behavioral fingerprints.

The evolution of e-commerce into immersive environments such as the AI-driven metaverse has further underscored the importance of adaptive interfaces. Systems that dynamically adjust layouts, avatars, and interaction modes based on user preferences or emotional states are setting new standards for personalization and engagement in digital retail.

Figure 5. Comparative of Adaptive Systems Across Domains

Domain	Key Adaptivity Feature	Core Technologies	Primary Benefit
Smart Healthcare	Clinical Decision Support, Remote Monitoring	IoMT, Federated ML, Edge AI	Personalized and Proactive Care
Cybersecurity	Self-adaptive IDS, Zero Trust Models, Dynamic	Reinforcement Learning, Blockchain, Anomaly	Resilient and Predictive Defense
Smart Cities	Traffic Management, Smart Grids, Public Safety	Sensor Networks, Edge Computing, GIS-based	Responsive and Efficient Infrastructure
E-Commerce	Real-time Personalization, Adaptive Recommen	AutoML, Reinforcement Learning, Behavior Mo	Optimized User Experience and Revenue

- **Smart Healthcare** focuses on personalization and safety using clinical intelligence and federated learning.
- **Cybersecurity** prioritizes resilience and responsiveness with real-time adaptive threat mitigation.
- **Smart Cities** emphasize efficiency and adaptability in managing critical urban systems.
- **E-Commerce** leverages personalization and continuous learning to enhance user engagement and revenue.

6. EMERGING ISSUES AND ETHICAL CONSIDERATIONS

6.1 Explainability and Transparency in Adaptive Behavior

Explainability is further complicated by the dynamic nature of these systems: their behavior changes over time in response to environmental shifts and learned experiences. A model that was once explainable in a static state may lose transparency after a series of adaptations. This creates a moving target for regulators and users alike, making it harder to track rationale or assign accountability.

Techniques such as local interpretable model-agnostic explanations (LIME), SHAP values, and counterfactual explanations are being incorporated to address this. However, these methods often assume static models and are still underdeveloped in streaming and reinforcement learning contexts, where state-action trajectories are highly temporal and interactive.

Adaptive systems must integrate explainability as a first-class design constraint, not as an afterthought. This involves developing self-documenting systems that maintain versioned decision logs, policy shifts, and explanatory trails through each stage of the MAPE-K loop. Such features are vital for ethical audits and regulatory compliance.

6.2 Bias Propagation and Adaptation to Biased Data

One major risk is bias amplification—a situation where feedback loops cause the system to reinforce skewed decision patterns over time. For instance, a biased recommendation engine may only suggest male candidates for technical roles if past data was skewed in that direction. Adaptive learning, while powerful, can compound these issues if not properly monitored.

Debiasing techniques such as fairness-aware learning, counterfactual data augmentation, and adversarial training offer partial solutions, but most assume static data or offline models. In adaptive systems that continuously retrain, bias can emerge dynamically and evolve with user interactions, necessitating ongoing fairness auditing.

It's crucial that adaptive systems be equipped with bias-detection modules that assess data sources and decision outcomes in real time. Integration with human-in-the-loop processes can also provide oversight, especially in sensitive applications where subjective judgment is needed.

6.3 Regulatory Challenges and System Accountability

As self-adaptive AI systems gain autonomy and real-time decision-making capabilities, they pose unique challenges to existing regulatory frameworks. Traditional regulatory models—based on static system specifications and predictable behavior—are insufficient to handle systems that learn and evolve after deployment. This gap necessitates a reevaluation of regulatory design principles that govern AI systems (Unver, 2023).

A major challenge is accountability attribution. When adaptive behavior results in unintended harm or bias, it becomes difficult to determine whether the fault lies with the original developers, the operational agents, the learning algorithm, or the data environment. The dynamic nature of these systems demands traceability mechanisms that can log and explain the sequence of adaptations and the rationale behind each decision, as emphasized (Macher et al., 2023).

6.4 Trust and Human Oversight in Adaptive Autonomy

Trust in self-adaptive systems hinges on users' ability to understand, predict, and influence system behavior. In critical domains such as healthcare, finance, and national security, human oversight is essential not only for technical reliability but also for societal legitimacy. Without this oversight, trust in AI may erode even if system performance remains high (Cabrero-Daniel et al., 2023) .

The concept of human-in-the-loop (HITL) and human-on-the-loop (HOTL) provides models for integrating oversight at different stages of the adaptive decision cycle. While HITL ensures active human participation in key decisions, HOTL involves supervisory roles that intervene only when anomalies or ethical conflicts are detected. The literature increasingly supports adaptive oversight, where the system itself adjusts the level of human intervention based on risk, uncertainty, and operational criticality.

A significant challenge is maintaining trust in black-box learning agents, especially those that adapt their behavior over time. Explainability techniques, while promising, are still maturing for adaptive and online learning systems. Researchers argue for collaborative interfaces that continuously engage human stakeholders, providing real-time summaries, alerts, and options for override (Simakina & Wang, 2024).

Moreover, cultural and psychological factors influence trust perception. A system may be mathematically robust but socially rejected due to perceived opaqueness or alien decision logic. Therefore, designing for trust means more than proving correctness—it requires aligning system behavior with user expectations and ethical values.

6.5 Closing Reflections on Ethical Design in Self-Adaptive Systems

The ethical design of self-adaptive systems goes beyond traditional engineering; it requires embedding normative values into algorithms that make decisions autonomously and evolve over time. One of the foremost challenges in ethical AI design is defining what "ethically appropriate behavior" entails in complex, dynamic environments. As Hauptman and Schelble (2022) argue, ethical frameworks for adaptive autonomy must consider not only individual decision-making but also collective, system-wide consequences across human-AI teams.

Ethical awareness must be instantiated at the architectural level. Adaptive systems should be designed to explicitly represent and reason about ethical goals—e.g., fairness, accountability, sustainability—alongside technical objectives like performance or reliability. Approaches such as value-sensitive design (VSD) and ethics-aware feedback loops enable such systems to integrate moral reasoning into their core MAPE-K processes, not as auxiliary features but as guiding constraints (Weyns et al., 2023).

Recent proposals advocate for dynamic ethical governance frameworks, where systems can learn and adjust ethical norms based on stakeholder feedback and cultural context. This is especially relevant in global deployments, where legal, social, and moral expectations vary significantly. Rahoman et al. (2023) suggest adaptive ethical engines that allow reconfiguration of ethical priorities in real time based on evolving environments and user inputs.

However, embedding ethics into software is not a purely technical endeavor. It demands cross-disciplinary collaboration—ethicists, cognitive scientists, engineers, and legal scholars must co-develop models that reflect both human values and computational tractability. Without such integration, self-adaptive systems risk operating in ethically ambiguous zones that undermine trust and legitimacy.

As adaptive systems continue to shape healthcare, finance, education, and governance, the urgency to develop ethically aligned AI grows stronger. Future research must address not only how these systems adapt, but why and to whom they remain accountable. Ethical AI is not just about rules—it is about purpose, perspective, and the human condition embedded within autonomous computation.

7. BEST PRACTICES AND STRATEGIC GUIDELINES

7.1 Designing for Runtime Uncertainty

One of the defining features of self-adaptive systems is their operation under dynamic and uncertain conditions. Designing for uncertainty requires not only robust monitoring and feedback but also architectures that can reason under incomplete or evolving information. Uncertainty modeling must be treated as a first-class design principle, integrated throughout the software lifecycle—from requirement elicitation to runtime verification (Weyns et al., 2022).

In addition, probabilistic reasoning and runtime models (e.g., Markov Decision Processes, Bayesian networks) allow systems to anticipate possible outcomes of actions and proactively adjust strategies. These models must be continuously updated, forming a loop where prediction, adaptation, and evaluation occur in tandem.

7.2 Balancing Autonomy and Human-in-the-Loop Design

An essential strategic guideline in the design of adaptive systems is determining the appropriate level of human oversight. Too much autonomy may compromise accountability and trust, while excessive intervention may hinder responsiveness. The optimal balance depends on application domain, system criticality, and user expertise (Simakina & Wang, 2024).

Human-in-the-loop (HITL) and human-on-the-loop (HOTL) paradigms are frequently employed to implement this balance. HITL places human users within the decision loop, often used in domains such as healthcare and aviation. HOTL, on the other hand, delegates control to the system but allows humans to intervene when anomalies or ethical concerns arise. A third, emerging model—human-in-command (HIC)—focuses on strategic oversight and periodic audits rather than continuous supervision. Effective interaction between humans and AI systems requires interpretable user interfaces, real-time status updates, and context-sensitive alerts. Adaptive visualization dashboards, audit trails, and explainability modules are critical enablers in fostering trust and ensuring that decisions can be challenged or refined.

7.3 Testing and Validating Adaptive Systems in Production

Contemporary strategies now include runtime verification, online testing, and A/B testing in live environments. These methods allow the system to be observed under real conditions while simultaneously applying formal checks or logging deviations from expected behavior. Techniques like model checking using tools like UPPAAL-SMC and probabilistic model validation have proven effective in safety-critical domains such as automotive systems and critical infrastructure (Gheibi et al., 2022).

One key concept is the oracle problem: How do we define the correct behavior for systems that are inherently changing? Researchers suggest using adaptive test oracles that adjust expected outputs based on updated goals and context. Additionally, simulation-in-the-loop and digital twins allow for system evolution to be mirrored in controlled environments for robust validation before release into production (Bolender et al., 2021).

7.4 Organizational and Operational Integration of Adaptive AI

The successful deployment of self-adaptive AI systems hinges not only on technical sophistication but also on effective organizational integration. Adaptive systems must align with an organization's strategic goals, risk appetite, IT infrastructure, and governance culture. Adaptive AI and DevOps, AI systems are most impactful when embedded into the workflows of continuous delivery and monitored across the software delivery lifecycle (Oluwagbade, 2024).

Finally, organizations must foster a culture of agile governance. This includes providing training for staff on adaptive system behavior, establishing ethical review boards, and ensuring adaptive audit trails are transparent. Governance models must evolve from prescriptive rule sets to dynamic oversight frameworks that allow AI systems to adapt within ethical and legal boundaries while ensuring stakeholder accountability.

Figure 6. Mindmap Summary Best Practice and Strategic Guidelines

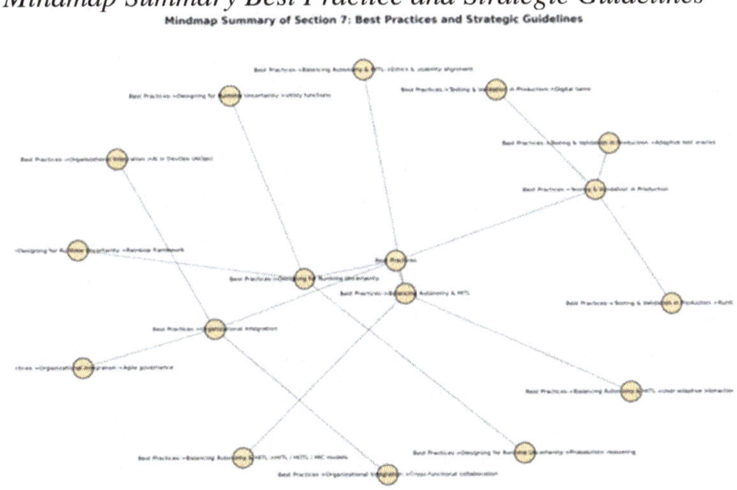

- **Designing for Runtime Uncertainty** — centered on dynamic models, adaptive utility, and probabilistic frameworks.
- **Balancing Autonomy and Human-in-the-Loop** — involving flexible oversight mechanisms like HITL, HOTL, and HIC.
- **Testing and Validation** — emphasizing runtime verification, adaptive test oracles, and digital twin environments.
- **Organizational Integration** — focusing on DevOps alignment, AIOps frameworks, and agile governance.

8. CONCLUSION

The evolution of self-adaptive systems marks a significant transformation in the landscape of artificial intelligence and big data integration. These systems are designed not just to operate in changing environments, but to thrive in them—by continuously monitoring, analyzing, planning, and executing adaptations with embedded knowledge structures (MAPE-K). Through this architectural shift, AI applications can now extend their relevance and reliability across diverse, dynamic, and unpredictable contexts. This comprehensive exploration has unpacked the theoretical underpinnings, technological methodologies, and operational strategies that define the self-adaptive paradigm. From system theory and cybernetics to runtime modeling and federated learning, adaptive systems reflect a convergence of computational intelligence and organizational resilience. They challenge conventional static models of automation by offering agility, fault tolerance, and optimized decision-making as built-in properties.

Moreover, their application across critical domains—from smart healthcare to cybersecurity and intelligent cities—demonstrates their transformative potential. As shown in case-specific studies, the ability to tailor behavior based on real-time feedback enables systems to enhance personalization, efficiency, and safety simultaneously. However, these benefits are coupled with increasing complexity in system testing, validation, and trust engineering, demanding new practices in software assurance and operational transparency. Ethical and governance challenges remain at the forefront. Trust in AI systems—particularly those capable of self-direction—must be actively cultivated through explainability, oversight, and adaptive regulatory frameworks. As adaptive autonomy grows more widespread, so too must our capacity to ensure its alignment with human values, legal norms, and societal expectations. Research has emphasized the role of "adaptive governance" as a socio-technical interface that allows regulation to evolve alongside the very systems it seeks to govern.

In closing, self-adaptive systems represent not just a technological innovation, but a paradigm shift in how we conceive intelligent infrastructure. They offer a vision of AI that is not only more responsive and robust, but also more ethically attuned and societally grounded. The future of intelligent systems, it seems, lies not in pre-programmed logic—but in the ability to learn, adapt, and collaborate with both machines and humans in increasingly sophisticated ways.

9. FUTURE RESEARCH

The evolution of self-adaptive systems is reaching a point of convergence with emerging technological paradigms such as federated learning, edge/cloud collaboration, and distributed policy governance. These trends are driving a research agenda focused on extending the scalability, explainability, and ethical robustness of adaptive AI. One key direction is the implementation of federated self-adaptation, where systems adapt across nodes without centralized data aggregation, enhancing privacy and reducing latency (Aljohani et al., 2025).

Edge-based adaptation introduces unique challenges and opportunities, especially in low-latency environments like IoT or autonomous systems. Collaborative frameworks between cloud and edge nodes—known as end-edge-cloud orchestration—are being explored to balance computational intensity and proximity to data sources (Wang et al., 2024). Research is focusing on enabling such systems to learn hierarchical decision models that delegate actions based on network state, energy availability, and task criticality.

Another crucial research trajectory involves adaptive governance: integrating legal and ethical oversight mechanisms directly into the operational logic of AI systems. Pioneering frameworks propose "governance-as-a-service" models that dynamically adjust constraints and permissions in response to contextual or policy changes. These models align with proposals for AI regulation in the EU and OECD frameworks, ensuring that AI remains socially accountable while technologically agile (Dazzi, 2025). The use of causal inference, scenario simulation, and symbolic planning is advancing this goal, as noted in recent IEEE reviews (Ashraf et al., 2023).

The integration of federated learning (FL) and distributed AI into self-adaptive systems represents a paradigm shift toward privacy-preserving, decentralized intelligence. Federated learning enables collaborative model training across edge devices or distributed nodes without requiring data to leave its origin. This addresses regulatory and ethical concerns around centralized data aggregation, particularly in sectors such as healthcare, finance, and personalized services. FL not only secures data locality but also introduces heterogeneity-aware optimization mechanisms, which are essential for self-adaptation across diverse environments (Smith & Md Rasel, 2025).

A critical advantage of FL lies in its compatibility with edge and fog architectures. These distributed environments demand models that can adapt to intermittent connectivity, device variability, and context shifts. To address this, researchers are exploring personalized FL, where the global model is dynamically adapted to individual node constraints and objectives. This ensures high performance and fairness across different user bases (Mai et al., 2025).

Despite these advances, FL integration into adaptive systems still grapples with resource constraints, system scalability, and trustability of decentralized decisions. Solutions such as blockchain-enhanced auditability, adaptive trust scoring, and adversarial robustness mechanisms are being developed to address these issues, as illustrated in the federated AI cybersecurity model (Ethan & Jack, 2025).

As AI systems increasingly exhibit adaptive and autonomous behavior, traditional regulatory mechanisms—designed for static, predictable technologies—are proving insufficient. The concept of adaptive governance has emerged as a response, offering a dynamic, flexible, and participatory model of oversight that evolves alongside the systems it aims to regulate. In their 2023 framework, Mäntymäki et al. propose meta-requirements for AI governance that incorporate responsiveness, cross-disciplinary participation, and continuous feedback (Mäntymäki et al., 2023).

One emerging technique in this area is the implementation of "governance-as-a-service" (GaaS), where cloud-based platforms deliver real-time regulatory updates, audit trails, and ethical rule sets directly to adaptive AI components. These services ensure compliance even when systems operate across multiple jurisdictions with differing legal standards (Kitsiou et al., 2025).

As the global landscape becomes increasingly interconnected and digitized, the future of intelligent infrastructure depends on its ability to respond to complexity, uncertainty, and constant change. Self-adaptive systems are poised to play a foundational role in this transformation. They serve not merely as tools for automation but as autonomous agents capable of runtime self-management, allowing infrastructures to evolve continuously based on internal states and external environmental stimuli. Their integration represents a shift from infrastructure that merely functions to infrastructure that thinks, learns, and heals.

Finally, the rise of infrastructure-as-a-service (IaaS) and edge computing further positions self-adaptive systems at the frontier of decentralized intelligence. These systems will coordinate between edge, fog, and cloud layers to ensure that infrastructure resources are provisioned dynamically, computationally optimized, and aligned with user demand at scale. In this vision, intelligent infrastructure becomes more than a utility—it becomes a living, adaptive ecosystem, continuously optimized and co-evolving with human society.

10. REFERENCES

Abdul-Karim, M., Aguilar, J., Ahlen, S., Alam, S., Allen, L., Prieto, C. A., Alves, O., Anand, A., Andrade, U., Armengaud, E., Aviles, A., Bailey, S., Baltay, C., Bansal, P., Bault, A., Behera, J., BenZvi, S., Bianchi, D., Blake, C., . . . Zou, H. (2025). *DESI DR2 Results II: Measurements of Baryon Acoustic Oscillations and Cosmological Constraints* (arXiv:2503.14738). arXiv. https://arxiv.org/abs/2503.14738

Acharya, S., Das, S., & Kitmo, D. (2024). Adaptive Learning and Self-Organization in Swarm Robotics. In *Bio-inspired Swarm Robotics and Control: Algorithms, Mechanisms, and Strategies* (pp. 116–139). IGI Global Scientific Publishing. https://www.igi-global.com/gateway/chapter/345311

Ahmed, M. I., Spooner, B., Isherwood, J., Lane, M., Orrock, E., & Dennison, A. (2023). A Systematic Review of the Barriers to the Implementation of Artificial Intelligence in Healthcare. *Cureus, 15*(10), e46454. DOI: 10.7759/cureus.46454 PMID: 37927664

Aljohani, A., Rana, O., & Perera, C. (2025). Self-adaptive Federated Learning in Internet of Things Systems: A Review. *ACM Comput. Surv., 57*(10), 252:1-252:36. https://dl.acm.org/doi/10.1145/3725527

Chen, H., Ma, Q., Lin, Z., & Yan, J. (2021). Hierarchy-aware Label Semantics Matching Network for Hierarchical Text Classification. In Zong, C., Xia, F., Li, W., & Navigli, R. (Eds.), *Proceedings of the 59th Annual Meeting of the Association for Computational Linguistics and the 11th International Joint Conference on Natural Language Processing (*Volume 1*: Long Papers)* (pp. 4370–4379). Association for Computational Linguistics. DOI: 10.18653/v1/2021.acl-long.337

Demopoulos, N. (2025). *From Chaos to Order: A Stochastic Approach to Self Organizing Systems* (2025021719). *Preprints*. DOI: 10.20944/preprints202502.1719.v1

Dogani, J., Namvar, R., & Khunjush, F. (2023). Auto-scaling techniques in container-based cloud and edge/fog computing: Taxonomy and survey. *Computer Communications, 209*, 120–150. DOI: 10.1016/j.comcom.2023.06.010

Fan, F. X., Tan, C., Wattenhofer, R., & Ong, Y.-S. (2025). *Position Paper: Rethinking Privacy in RL for Sequential Decision-making in the Age of LLMs* (arXiv:2504.11511). arXiv. https://doi.org//arXiv.2504.11511DOI: 10.2139/ssrn.5219045

Funabashi, M. (2024). Synecoculture experiments: Human augmentation of ecosystems and Planetary Health. *Science Talks, 12*, 100405. DOI: 10.1016/j.sctalk.2024.100405

Ghadekar, P., Shaligram, Y., Shimpi, V., Shingade, O., Singh, S., & Thakur, S. (2024). Simultaneous Localization and Mapping using object detection and Reinforcement Learning for automated Robot. *2024 IEEE Calcutta Conference (CALCON)*, 1–5. https://doi.org/DOI: 10.1109/CALCON63337.2024.10914203

Gheibi, O., & Weyns, D. (2024). Dealing with Drift of Adaptation Spaces in Learning-based Self-Adaptive Systems Using Lifelong Self-Adaptation. *ACM Transactions on Autonomous and Adaptive Systems*, *19*(1), 1–57. DOI: 10.1145/3636428

Golpayegani, F., Chen, N., Afraz, N., Gyamfi, E., Malekjafarian, A., Schäfer, D., & Krupitzer, C. (2024). Adaptation in Edge Computing: A Review on Design Principles and Research Challenges. *ACM Transactions on Autonomous and Adaptive Systems*, *19*(3), 1–43. DOI: 10.1145/3664200

Han, C., Yang, T., Sun, X., & Cui, Z. (2025). Secure Hierarchical Federated Learning for Large-Scale AI Models: Poisoning Attack Defense and Privacy Preservation in AIoT. *Electronics (Basel)*, *14*(8), 8. DOI: 10.3390/electronics14081611

Kitsiou, A., Pantelelis, M., Mazarakis, P.-A., Mavroeidi, A. G., Simou, S., Tzortzaki, E., Stavridis, S., Koutzamanis, G., & Kalloniatis, C. (2025). Self-Adaptive Privacy in Cloud Computing Environments: Developing an Integrated Framework and a Beta Tool for Social Media Platforms. *Electronics (Basel)*, *14*(7), 1412. DOI: 10.3390/electronics14071412

Li, J., Zhang, M., Li, N., Weyns, D., Jin, Z., & Tei, K. (2024). Generative AI for Self-Adaptive Systems: State of the Art and Research Roadmap. *ACM Trans. Auton. Adapt. Syst.*, *19*(3), 13:1-13:60. DOI: 10.1145/3686803

Liu, Q., Yang, M., Mohammadi, K., Song, D., Bi, J., & Wang, G. (2022). Machine Learning Crop Yield Models Based on Meteorological Features and Comparison with a Process-Based Model. *Artificial Intelligence for the Earth Systems*, *1*(4). DOI: 10.1175/AIES-D-22-0002.1

Macher, T.-H., Schütz, R., Yildiz, A., Beermann, A., & Leese, F. (2023). Evaluating five primer pairs for environmental DNA metabarcoding of Central European fish species based on mock communities. *Metabarcoding and Metagenomics*, *7*, e103856. DOI: 10.3897/mbmg.7.103856

Mai, J., Cao, K., & Wei, T. (2025). Personalized Federated Learning with State-Adaptive IoT Device Scheduling in Mobile Edge Computing. *IEEE Transactions on Computer-Aided Design of Integrated Circuits and Systems*, 1–1. DOI: 10.1109/TCAD.2025.3560221

Parra-Ullauri, J., García-Domínguez, A., Bencomo, N., & Garcia-Paucar, L. (2022). History-aware explanations: Towards enabling human-in-the-loop in self-adaptive systems. *Proceedings of the 25th International Conference on Model Driven Engineering Languages and Systems: Companion Proceedings*, 286–295. DOI: 10.1145/3550356.3561538

Romero Garces, A. (2022). *On Managing Knowledge for MAPE-K Loops in Self-Adaptive Robotics Using a Graph-Based Runtime Model.* Alejandro. https://www.mdpi.com/2076-3417/12/17/8583

StaticData_IDX. (n.d.). https://www.idx.co.id/StaticData/NewsAndAnnouncement/ANNOUNCEMENTSTOCK/From_EREP/202503/9a1083775c_cbda72f34a.pdf

Unver, M. B. (2023). Governing fiduciary relationships or building up a governance model for trust in AI? Review of healthcare as a socio-technical system. *International Review of Law Computers & Technology*, *37*(2), 198–226. DOI: 10.1080/13600869.2023.2192569

Wahyuningrum, S. R. (2022, Oct). *Analisis Penilaian Mahasiswa Terhadap Strategi Pembelaran Dosen Institut Agama Islam Periode Transisi Normal.* AICIS, UIN MATARAM. http://repository.iainmadura.ac.id/795/

Wahyuningrum, S. R., & Fitriyah. (2023). Pengaruh Penggunaan Gadget Terhadap Pola Belajar Siswa di SMPN 4 Pamekasan. *DA'WA: Jurnal Bimbingan Penyuluhan & Konseling Islam, 2*(2). https://doi.org/DOI: 10.36420/dawa.v2i2.217

Wahyuningrum, S. R., & Damayanti, M. C. O. (2024). *Self-Management: Peningkatan Konsentrasi Belajar Siswa SMPN 1 Galis* (SSRN Scholarly Paper 4932267). Social Science Research Network. DOI: 10.2139/ssrn.4932267

Wahyuningrum, S. R., & Fransiska, M. (2023). Pengaruh Efikasi Diri dan Kemandirian terhadap Pilihan Karier Siswa. *Edu Consilium : Jurnal Bimbingan dan Konseling Pendidikan Islam, 4*(1), Article 1. DOI: 10.19105/ec.v4i1.7713

Wahyuningrum, S. R., Putro, P. W., & Wulandari, D. R.Pera Wibowo PutroDian Ratri Wulandari. (2024). Analisis Potensi Ekonomi terhadap PAD Sektor Pariwisata Kabupaten Tulungagung di Masa Transisi Covid-19. *IQTISHADIA Jurnal Ekonomi & Perbankan Syariah, 11*(1), 1. DOI: 10.19105/iqtishadia.v11i1.10475

Wang, Y., Liang, Y., Huang, Y., & Qin, G. (2025). An automated data stream analysis framework for Internet of Vehicles based on online ensemble learning and two-dimensional fractal dimension. *The Journal of Supercomputing*, *81*(5), 744. DOI: 10.1007/s11227-025-07227-5

Wang, Y., Yang, C., Lan, S., Zhu, L., & Zhang, Y. (2024). End-Edge-Cloud Collaborative Computing for Deep Learning: A Comprehensive Survey. *IEEE Communications Surveys and Tutorials*, *26*(4), 2647–2683. DOI: 10.1109/COMST.2024.3393230

Weyns, D., Gerostathopoulos, I., Abbas, N., Andersson, J., Biffl, S., Brada, P., Bures, T., Di Salle, A., Lago, P., Musil, A., Musil, J., & Pelliccione, P. (2022). Preliminary results of a survey on the use of self-adaptation in industry. *Proceedings of the 17th Symposium on Software Engineering for Adaptive and Self-Managing Systems*, 70–76. DOI: 10.1145/3524844.3528077

Zhou, L., Cui, W., & Yang, F. (2024). Spatiotemporal variations and driving forces analysis of ecosystem water conservation in coastal areas of China. *Ecological Indicators*, *162*, 112019. DOI: 10.1016/j.ecolind.2024.112019

Chapter 3
Traditional vs. Modern Recruitment Methods

Saptarshi Kumar Sarkar
https://orcid.org/0009-0004-1786-8284
Brainware University, Sankrail, India

Anupama Sen
https://orcid.org/0009-0008-4806-0738
Brainware University, Sankrail, India

ABSTRACT

In the past, candidates would respond to newspaper ads or walk in to apply, but now, companies are using modern technology to hire new staff. This research examines how businesses now use online tools, social media campaigns and AI to recruit new employees. The analysis shows companies how to improve their hiring efforts by assessing the various pros and cons of each method. It is clear from examples that certain industries are evolving, using different approaches to reach more candidates. It's also part of the discussion to talk about frequent problems, including people not accepting change, technology difficulties and concerns about using data and AI. As automation, individual hiring and predictive analytics gain importance, recruitment will still move in the direction of being more structured and information-based. The assessment allows companies to understand the pros and cons of every approach and make their hiring progress better, more inclusive and relevant for future situations.

DOI: 10.4018/979-8-3373-6516-9.ch003

1. INTRODUCTION

From a human resource management standpoint, recruitment is a part of the human resource management and has played an important role in the success of any organization. Attracting, selecting and hiring the best talent has a direct bearing on the productivity, innovation and overall performance of an organization. From time to time, technological advances, changing societal expectations in addition to changing organizational needs have been allowing the recruitment methods to evolve. Whereas traditional recruitment relied on in-person meeting, manually guided process, and localized outreach, modern recruitments leverage technology, data investigation and digital platform to tap a more extensive and assorted pool of candidates. This chapter attempts to investigate the disparity between the old and new recruitment techniques and what advantages and disadvantages they hold and also attempt to contrast their efficiency in the modern organizational environment.

1.1 Overview of Recruitment

According to its basic essence, recruitment is the procedure by which organizations pick up, look into, and select qualified applicants to myriad jobs. Identifying need for new hire, sourcing, assessing, and selecting the most appropriate candidate for the job is a strategic process that takes several steps (Breaugh, 2013). In traditional times the recruitment process used to be through local newspapers, employee referrals and job fairs. In terms of feasibility, these methods worked where they were performed in the past but constrained most organizations to gather talent pools confined locally or within a specific region. In the realm of global economy expansion and technology advancement, recruitment practices adapted to fulfil the variance in the talent requirement of the changing and cast irregular workforce.

Over the past few years, technological advancement has impacted the recruitment schema. Online job boards, professional networking sites, social media platforms, and state of the art recruitment tools such as Applicant Tracking Systems (ATS) and Artificial Intelligence (AI) have all made it possible to bring coordination for identifying, engaging with and evaluating potential candidates in the same web. It is no longer the traditional way of recruiting as it has sped the pace of hiring while elevating the capacity of recruitment beyond the traditional tradition method of recruiting which has again facilitated recruitment among more diverse set of candidates. The core goal in recruitment practices as such is to find the best possible candidates that the organization's success can draw from. But the ways to accomplish this objective have become increasingly sophisticated and diverse and organisations have had to find a balance between traditional and current techniques in their own way to go towards meeting its own needs as well as the organisational goals.

1.2 Importance of Effective Hiring Strategies

The organization needs effective recruitment and hiring strategies. Hiring quality talent has a prevalent impact on the productivity, innovation and competitive advantage of any organization. The real value of the human resource function is in ensuring that the right candidates come in, and that has become more important I believe, especially as we are seeing competition for skilled workers, and this is competition — not just for employees but also in the knowledge-based industry. The end-result of a bad hiring decision: increased turnover, unforgivable low morale, and tremendous financial cost which can end up killing a business' opportunity to compete in a tough business climate (Chapman et al., 2005). Hiring strategy which is effective is that the organization is able to easily notice the candidates who have the skills needed and qualifications but also fit to the organization's culture and values. It is more cost effective to hire a right candidate who will help improve employee retention, team dynamics, and promote a positive organizational culture. In addition, as organizations are becoming more and more global and diverse, recruitment strategy must also respond to problems such as recruitment in large geography and culturally different pool of talent. In this respect, recruitment strategies have to dynamically flexible, and data driven. To deal with the complexities of hiring process, organizations have to combine modern and traditional recruiting approaches. Together the two approaches enable organizations to build a recruitment strategy that suits their own requirements and help attract top talent to get a stronger footing in the market.

1.3 Purpose and Scope of the Chapter

The objective of this chapter is to give an exhaustive analysis of the fire between classical and present-day recruitments. This paper aims at pointing out the strengths and weaknesses of the two approaches and suggests how organizations may make use of both methods in their recruitment pursuit. The chapter starts by describing certain basic characteristics associated with classic recruitment practice, with clear reference to the historical background of implementation of these practices and the reasons for their widespread. It then delves into the advent of the modern recruitment techniques that saw the move from traditional techniques that have been around for decades utilizing the role of technology and digital platforms in bringing forth contemporary recruitment techniques.

In the following pages, I carry out a comparative analysis between the traditional and modern methods, paying regard to cost effectiveness, speed, reach of major parameters and quality of candidates. In the process of this analysis, we will show the advantages and the disadvantages of each approach and help reader assess which methods will be most useful in particular organizations and recruitment requirements. Finally, the chapter features real life examples from different organizations that have been able to recruit using both traditional and modern methods to meet their recruitment objectives. The chapter ends with the discussion on challenges of shifting from traditional to modern recruitment processes. A few of these challenges are technological barriers, resistance to change, and Protection of privacy and ethical considerations involving the use of data. The chapter ends by looking at recruitment in the future, and what trends there are such as AI, automation, predictive hiring and what advice you as an employer should use to create the best process for you. The purpose of this chapter is to make a contribution to a better understanding regarding why recruitment practices develop as they are evolving and what is their place within the context of this dynamic activity, by describing and comparing various existing recruitment methods. It provides insights which are useful to HR professionals, organizational leaders and academic, who are interested in the future of recruitment and talent management.

2. TRADITIONAL RECRUITMENT METHODS

The term traditional refers to hiring procedures that mostly were used before widespread digital technology and online tools. However, these methods were widely used for decades and are still being used in some contexts, in particular in industries or areas where the access of the technology is limited or personal relationships and community bonds matter more on employment decisions. This part explores the details in the traditional recruitment methods, such as how it's classified and identified, the methods that are commonly used, advantages of such methods, challenges and predicators of such methods within current competitive and technology-controlled labour market.

2.1 Definition and Characteristics

Traditional recruitment is simply known as the work of bringing the candidates to the desired post, applying the non-digital, manual and most of the time face-to-face methods. On the other hand, these methods are based in familiar human resource practices, including personal interaction, printed communication, and outreach oriented towards a local audience. The mediums are commonly run-in newspapers advertisements, walk in interviews, employee referrals and campus recruitment. Also, the majority of the organizations have usually utilized 3rd party recruitment agencies or head-hunters to search for as well as attract candidates. Traditional recruitment methods characteristic of primary characteristics is use of physical materials (e.g. grinded resumes and job ads), slower communication channels and weakly supported by the algorithm. Also, these methods typically favour candidates from the geographically close or with social links to the organization, making the recruitment environment less geographically remote and more personal. Usually, the traditional hiring process runs in a linear and sequential way and begins with job postings, followed by in person interviews, and reference checks. Overall, they are somewhat more time consuming than modern digital approaches and tend to have fewer applications because they lack exposure. However, such limitations aside, many organisations respect traditional methods because of their familiarity, human touch and perceived reliability when their only criteria are the credentials of the candidate against the job description, but their time together, (Graham et al., 2008).

2.2 Common Traditional Methods

Under the traditional category, there are several well-established recruitment techniques. While modern technologies have in fact supplanted the use of these methods, several organisations — especially small businesses, public sector employer and companies based in regions where use of modern technologies is not as common—that use these methods solely or in addition to modern technologies. Newspaper advertisements constitute one of the most used traditional methods of recruitment. Companies post job advert in the classified sections of the regional or national newspapers which are read by many people. With this approach organizations would be able to reach local job seekers and available in ways that are good for cost for roles that are not asking for specific skills. Nevertheless, it only strikes those actively consuming print publications.

Employee refers are another longstanding means. In this approach, job openings are filled with people that current employees' professional or social networks could vouch for. Another reason to value employee referrals is that the hires that come from them are likely to be better quality hires because they know the culture of the organization in some ways. In addition, as the referral programs lead to shorter time to fill and lower costs (Zottoli & Wanous, 2000), the demand for these programs is significantly high. Traditional recruitment is another classic example of walk-in interview. Candidates apply, visit the organization, and submit their resumes in person and sometimes may be interviewed during various instances. This is common in the cases of retail, manufacturing and service sector where key input is in large numbers but is needed fast. It provides immediacy and allows recruiters to judge the candidates' interpersonal skills and their presentation real time.

Major traditional recruitment technique includes job fairs and campus placements. Career fairs on the part are of the organizations that participate, either of its own or with academic institutions, to interact with students and recent graduates. This is a common method used in order to form a talent pipeline to Entry level role and it can lend a helping hand to Companies improving their employer branding on campus. Recruitment agencies and head-hunters have been the last stop in assisting employers to recruit talent, especially for middle to senior level positions. Third party agents have candidate databases and drive their networks to seek talent for job opportunities while conducting initial screenings to weed out the bottom for their clients.

2.3 Advantages of Traditional Recruitment

While these traditional recruitment methods are being slowly replaced or substituted by digital ways, there are still some advantages of them that are so compelling to sustain their popularity in certain organizational situations. The advantages associated with these are primarily related to human centric and relationship-based nature of traditional approaches to the processes of hiring. The main plus is the personal interaction involved in traditional recruitment. Recruiters use face to face interviews and other walk-in meetings to assess soft skills, body language, emotions and overcome the difficulty of gauging such things using digital platforms. A direct interaction makes it possible for a more holistic evaluation of the candidate, which in turn improves the hiring decisions for positions that involve close work with people or in customer service roles.

One of the benefits is that referrals are something that the employee trusts and is considered reliable. When candidates are recommended by current employees this sense of trust is often built into the candidate and an assumption that whatever this person is don't necessarily mean he or she is qualified or has the same cultural fit as the person recommending. Additionally, referred candidates have more realistic expectations regarding the job and the organisation (Van Hoye & Lievens, 2009) and therefore may perform better at their job or have a lower turnover. Targeted outreach at the local or regional labour market also helps with traditional methods. Methods such as newspaper ads, community job boards, walk-in interviews are useful for companies that have a presence in a particular locale and may want to hire people already recognized in the neighbourhood. These methods enable the reduction of the relocation cost for candidates or international recruitment logistics cost.

Also, non-technology intensive processes are more traditional than what is used within the recruitment process, and this can benefit organizations that are not able to invest in the amount of technology or infrastructure that is needed to motivate this recruitment. For such companies, small or non-profits, manual methods are more practical and cost effective. In addition, certain types of roles are easier to manage with traditional methods while using traditional methods in general is easier to manage when turnover is high, or specialty is not high among those in a sector. For example, casual workers, entry level posts, and blue-collar ones are routinely hired through walk ins or local advertising with minimal digital screening.

2.4 Limitations and Challenges

Though they have historical significance and some current requirement, traditional recruitment methods are underutilized and subject to a number of limitations in the context of the modern global, digitized, and rapidly changing labour market. As limiting as these are, they only increasingly make it difficult for an organization to rely exclusively to traditional tactics to attract top talent. The major problem is that traditional methods of recruitment have a restricted range of people that can be accessed. Newspapers or physical job boards only extend to a tiny, sometimes localized, target market which significantly restricts companies from acquiring candidates from several geographic, educational or professional angles. Digital platforms, however, make global outreach possible with a few clicks and increase the employer's access to a much broader and more varied talent base (Stone et al., 2015).

Another major limitation of traditional process is that they are slow and inefficient. Long hiring cycles are provided by manual application handling, paper resumes, and interviews in person. This can be a huge disadvantage in such highly competitive industries where the bests may get multiple offers and expect quick decisions. Hiring long takes time and time lost can result to talent lost, reduced organizational agility and increased recruitment costs overtime. Traditional recruitment is also affected by the availability of little data and its poor tracking capabilities. Traditional features do not provide any actionable data and are usually textiles used with modern Applicant Tracking Systems (ATS) and analytics tools. However, for HR to be able to analyse such metrics as cost-per-hire, time-to-hire, source-of-hire and be able to optimize recruiting strategies in line with bigger organizational objectives may prove cumbersome.

Other traditional methods carry some parallels to equity and diversity concerns. For example, depending on employees' referrals is likely to create homogeneous workforces as employees find it easier to refer people similarly situated or from the same place. Without proactive outreach with New York University's diversity focused practices, there is an unintentional perpetuation of bias and reduction in potential opportunities for underrepresented groups. Cost considerations also pose challenges. Traditional methods may appear inexpensive (e.g., word of mouth, walk ins) but also more expensive methods (print advertisement, or third-party agencies) can cost a hefty amount but cannot promise great outcomes. Additionally, the current recruitment systems are not scalable in nature and hence large organizations experience difficulties in managing high demand hiring efficiently. Finally, traditional methods are not useful to remote work environment. Finally, the COVID 2019 pandemic massively accelerated the move to the remote and hybrid work model, and consequently demanded digital recruitment capabilities like video interviews, virtual assessments and they online on boding. These new norms for workplace are an ill fit for traditional methods and may hinder organizations striving to adjust to the new expectations of contemporary candidates.

3. MODERN RECRUITMENT METHODS

The methods of recruitment today are unique compared to the regular manual methods of recruitment that were used in the traditional ways. These methods use the progress in the digital platforms, artificial intelligence (AI), data analytics and in social media to find, engage and hire talent efficiently and effectively. These methods have risen in response to the growing demands of globally oriented organizations in a very competitive job market. This section consists of academic qualitative description of modern recruitment tools and trends, from its definitions and attributes to technological innovations, to common tools and platforms, their advantages, and drawbacks organizations consume when they implement the tools.

3.1 Definition and Key Features

Modern recruitment is a collection of practices and tools of modern era of recruiting where all parts of the hiring was covered via digital technology and online platform from searching for the job to selecting the job with the help of new technologies. Such a recruitment model is based on automation, efficiency, scalability and data driven decision making. Modern recruitment differs from what we traditionally think of as recruitment, which is overwhelmingly reliant on human intuition and local networks, in the fact that it is much faster, absolutely more accurate, and most of all — most people have access to a larger and more divergent candidate pool. Defining feature of modern recruitment is that it is digital. With applications for various occupations and applying through websites such as online job boards, applicant tracking systems (ATS), or AI powered screening tools, the process of recruitment has been streamlined for both the employer and the candidate. They can filter unqualified applicants automatically, and automate management of thousands of applications simultaneously, freeing up human resource professionals for trying to attract high quality applicants.

The other hallmark is that it is data-centric approach. The current distribution in hiring uses analytics and metrics to inform hiring decisions. These indicators are tracked by employers; time-to-hire, cost-per-hire, source of hire and candidate experience. It provides an analytical capability to continuously improve recruitment strategies in alignment with organization goals (Johnson et al.; 2016). Also, modern recruitment is for flexible and remote hiring. Virtual interviews, remote onboarding to full remote job interview can be done on cloud-based platforms. Particularly, given the climate post pandemic, many candidates liked hybrid or remote work options.

3.2 Technological Advancements in Hiring

Rapid progress in technology has had a major impact on the way we recruit now. These major ones are artificial intelligence, machine learning, big data analytics, mobile technology and cloud computing. Thanks to these new tools, companies are able to identify and reach out to future employees in new ways. Recruitment is now being supported by the use of Artificial Intelligence (AI). Examples of AI applications are resuming scanning, ranking job candidates, analysing results and chatbot (Badouch et al, 2025) support in communication. AI cuts out manual tasks and reduces bias by matching a person's skills in a CV to the position's job description. In addition, it helps evaluate candidates by looking at previous data and results of others (Artha et al., 2024). ATS is a key innovation when it comes to recruiting. ATS platforms let employers handle and manage the process of gathering, sorting and looking at candidate details. These solutions work with job boards, websites for careers and social media platforms to collect applications and make recruiter jobs more efficient. With big data analytics, recruiters can look into a candidate's qualities outside the things presented on a resume. Information collected through assessments, interviews and a person's work history is used to create models that guide where people are hired. By using analytics, organizations can see how people are being hired, if there are any diversity problems and where issues occur during the recruitment process. They also depend heavily on online communication and brand strategies. LinkedIn, Facebook and Twitter help companies introduce their brand as a good place to work, engage users outside the job market and assess what type of candidates are out there. Firms use social platforms to list job openings and to monitor how interested candidates are in their company. The COVID-19 pandemic has made using Zoom, HireVue and SparkHire platforms necessary in video interviews. Interviews can be organized for most times with asynchronous tools and for some moments with live video, also incorporating AI to understand and record the candidate's replies and mannerisms. Recruitment is changing because more people are using mobile-first strategies. Now that many people use smartphones, more candidates are applying to jobs on their mobile devices. Today, you can search for jobs, apply and message just as easily with your phone as you can on a PC.

3.3 Common Modern Methods (e.g., Online Job Portals, social media, AI Tools)

The way recruitment is done today depends on several tools and techniques. Every agency has skills that can help companies find and recruit excellent candidates during today's competitive recruitment landscape. Online Job Portals are popular with many job seekers. Indeed, Monster and Glassdoor feature millions of jobs and let you easily filter, view employer pages and search through resumes online. With these platforms, recruiters can connect with a wide group of job seekers quickly and candidates enjoy estimates for their potential salary, corporate reviews and tools to manage their applications. LinkedIn and other platforms have now become an important part of recruitment. Using LinkedIn, recruiters can search for workers by their work history, education or skills and connect with passive candidates. InMail messaging, ads for jobs and profiles of employers are the most important parts of LinkedIn's recruitment process (Nikolaou, 2014).

Adding profiles on Facebook, Twitter, Instagram and even TikTok lets companies reach out to youth. Firms display ads to specific people, make content that highlights their culture and have conversations to foster links with users that might help in the future. Roles in marketing, design and creative industries are best suited for social recruitment, since portfolio work and socializing matter. Candidates are assessed by Pymetrics and HireVue with machine learning to measure suitability using information from their cognition, emotions and actions. With these tools, video interviews, test results and psychometric data are used to predict how a person will perform in their next job. Also, they can help lower unconscious bias as they depend on gathered data rather than feelings. Attending job interviews online is becoming more popular. They create an online space that looks like a career fair, with digital booths, instant chat and online seminars. They save money and help organizations reach job candidates anywhere. TRM helps organizations gather and develop a collection of potential candidates. Thanks to these systems, recruiters can save people's data and keep in contact with those who might be well-suited for future job postings.

3.4 Benefits of Modern Recruitment Approaches

New approaches to recruitment increase effectiveness, improve efficiency and make the process better for candidates. These benefits attract companies that want to improve their talent acquisition processes in the digital and global market. The biggest advantage is that more people can easily use it. With digital tools, recruiters are able to announce openings worldwide and reach people interested or not, active or not. Because job listings reach many people, companies can hire a variety of experts for their specialized positions. It is also very beneficial that programming saves both time and money. Because automation handles a lot of the manual tasks, the process of hiring moves ahead more swiftly. If you hire new staff more quickly, it saves money and helps the company run smoothly with few interruptions. Also, digital advertising tools typically offer subscriptions at prices that are lower than what companies pay for print ads and other outsourced services. Hiring decisions are improved when data is used. Using current data and predictions, recruiters determine which sourcing channels bring in the best candidates, how fast each part of the recruitment process moves and what leads to bottlenecks. This information helps organizations grow stronger and better plan their workforce. Effective recruitment today ensures that jobseekers are well taken care of. When applications are simple, replies come quickly and personal communication is given, it benefits what the candidate sees in the organization. Having a good candidate experience greatly increases the chance of receiving an offer and it also helps the company look better to all jobseekers, regardless of the decision.

Employer branding can be improved a lot by using digital tools. Businesses can share their mission, office environment and achievements via posts on social media and their career website. Material that genuinely connects with readers leads to more people becoming interested in working with you. Thanks to modern hiring techniques, companies can now find excellent remote workers or hybrid staff from anywhere. Such flexibility is necessary because many professionals these days want balance between their work life and personal life and like to work remotely. In addition, modern recruitment efforts are designed today to emphasize diversity and inclusion on purpose. Using tools to hide identities, lower bias and keep an eye on diversity makes organizations more inclusive. As a result, the company gets more innovative, employees are happier, and the organization performs better.

3.5 Potential Drawbacks

While modern recruitment gives hiring professionals a faster way to recruit, it still brings several issues. Over-using technology in recruiting can make top candidates pass by ATS filters. There is a significant ethical issue when AI systems show bias. Because of biases found in the data used to train AI such technologies might result in unfair or discriminatory hiring practices. Recruitment via digital channels means collecting lots of data from candidates which increases privacy concerns and makes it necessary to obey laws like GDPR. Being cut off from technology or lacking digital literacy gives candidates from older or financially weaker groups an even greater disadvantage. With so many people applying online, recruiters face too much information, and it remains hard to efficiently screen candidates. Conducting interviews and evaluations online can make it harder to see whether a candidate fits with the company culture, as well as to develop a real rapport with them. Finally, because recruitment technologies are always changing, organizations with tight budgets find it very hard to keep up. Working to solve these issues helps us create fairer, ethical and more effective ways to hire in the modern era.

4. COMPARATIVE ANALYSIS

As recruitment methods have changed from classic to current ones, organizations now judge hiring strategies differently. Comparative analysis systematically explains the main points where these two paradigms vary. The section looks closely at the ways that traditional and modern recruitment styles differ with regard to budget, time spent, outcomes, job applicants, success of new staff and image as an employer. Each group of variables is assessed to advise organizations on how to match recruitment practices with their aims and working situations.

4.1 Cost-Effectiveness

A major focus in recruitment strategy is making sure the expenses are not more than the advantages gained when hiring qualified employees. Traditionally, using recruitment methods can be expensive up front. Ads placed in newspapers, trade magazines and at on-site job fairs take a lot of time and effort to organize and are very costly. Besides in-house sourcing, it is common to hire recruitment agencies whose fees are usually calculated on a percentage of the annual wage of the person hired from them. According to the Society for Human Resource Management, average hiring costs, as measured with conventional methods, are often greater than $4,000 for each available position, depending on where the job is located. By contrast, organizations now spend less money on hiring than they used to. You can post on Indeed and LinkedIn using methods that are either free or come with a budget-friendly, per-click fee. With digital channels, recruiters can reach the right people very accurately, thus spending less on ads. Besides, using ATS and AI resume screeners to process resumes helps lower how much time and money is needed to handle administrative tasks. Because you can do more with technology, companies are able to run different campaigns at the same time without a big increase in expenses. Still, it is necessary to think about the unseen costs of modern systems: joining paid digital services, investing in software and teaching staff about updates. Using the latest recruitment solutions may be too costly for smaller businesses. Modern methods produce greater long-term ROI than the old ways since they are both faster and more accurate. By comparing them, it's clear that the modern method for recruiting has better control, is more scalable and is flexible, saving money over time.

4.2 Speed and Efficiency

In industries with high demand, speed and efficiency matter a lot because top candidates are often taken by rivals. Going through standard recruitment is always a slow process. Putting together prints ads, allowing for publication cycles, receiving job applications by post and scheduling in-person interviews can make the process take longer. Resume reviews done manually and working with recruiters, often increase the journey from inviting candidates to their first day with the company. On the other hand, today's recruitment practices make it much faster to complete hiring processes with digital solutions and automation. Job portals on the internet make it very easy to publish openings that reach a broad range of candidates worldwide. ATS platforms quickly go through and filter a vast number of job applications with given criteria in a short time. Interview scheduling software allows conversations between recruiters and candidates to happen faster, making everything easier. With video interviews, both live and pre-recorded, the evaluation process is streamlined, and unnecessary trips and setup are removed. Deloitte's study found that businesses that introduced digital recruitment technologies could hire candidates 30% faster than those using only traditional ways. By using predictive analytics, AI recruitment tools make sure the best applicants are found which cuts down the time recruiters spend deciding. Even though automation is helpful, relying too heavily on it sometimes means we miss the importance of cultural fit and soft skills which are best noticed during face-to-face meetings. Modern tools, when used in combination with human judgment, guarantee both greater effectiveness and quicker responses. So, because modern recruitment is quicker and more efficient, it better matches the rapid demands in today's companies.

4.3 Candidate Reach and Diversity

Developing teams that succeed, and value diversity depends on a wide range of candidates being reached. Recruitment at this stage can't reach everyone and may not represent the entire country's population. Often, job seekers are found through newspaper ads, job fairs near the company or through friends. It's also possible that these methods favour some groups over others by favouring those with certain media or social networks. On the other hand, new approaches to hiring can bring in prospective candidates from a much wider area. Job recruiters can use LinkedIn, Glassdoor and other job boards to access talent from all around the globe. Younger people and those not currently looking for jobs can be reached on Facebook, Twitter and Instagram. When a program expands, it draws attention from people with different educational, cultural and professional experiences.

In addition, modern recruiting tools are built to help companies be more diverse and include everyone. When recruiting with this software, personal information about candidates is hidden, preventing bias based on name, gender or ethnicity. If trained correctly, these algorithms can put diversity metrics first and guarantee compliance with guidelines for fairness. In addition, the use of video and mobile platforms in recruiting lets applicants with disabilities or difficulties moving get more involved in the hiring process. Still, there are challenges with the new methods scientists use. Because digital skills are now so necessary, those who cannot use the internet can be at a disadvantage. The gap between digital skills can exclude many older and disadvantaged people, so their involvement in campaigns is only possible if steps are taken to avoid this problem. All in all, modern recruitment advantages include reach that is better and tools that support diversity more than traditional methods. Yet, in order to accomplish this, organizations must introduce digital inclusion programs to make sure all aspiring workers have equal opportunity.

4.4 Quality of Hire

One of the main effects of recruitment is how well new hires fit into the company which affects the organization's performance, reduces employee turnover and offers a good experience to workers. This area sees certain benefits from using old-fashioned techniques. You can recruit people who suit your workplace culture by interviewing them, getting recommendations from your network and relying on a recruiter's instinct. In many sectors that value close connections, using old-fashioned methods means having more in-depth understanding of a person. But the traditional method of recruiting doesn't always ensure that hiring is useful and fair in large teams. If a company relies on opinions, irregular interview approaches and little candidate data, the decisions may not be the best. Referrals lead to more people like that setting up a company who tend to agree which may limit new ideas. Actual hiring techniques today play a major role in making sure the right candidate is employed by using data and carefully assessing each person. Platforms powered by AI consider things like a person's employment background, the abilities they have, how they act and how smart they are. Assessments, tests and practice job sessions help show what candidates are good at and what they might bring to the company. Also, information about past achievements from developers' GitHub portfolios can be used in performance evaluations. According to a report by LinkedIn (2020), using structured digital assessments and predictive analytics helped organizations enjoy greater satisfaction with the new hires they made. Besides, HR teams can use post-hire analytics to monitor employees' performance and confirm whether previous hiring efforts worked well. Certain researchers are concerned that trusting technology alone could allow biases to persist if the data used was not properly checked (Raghavan et al., 2020). As a result, the best employees are most likely found by using both technology and human expertise. By comparison, the tools and analytics found in today's recruitment make it easier to get better results when used in partnership with human efforts.

4.5 Employer Branding

To attract great employees and ensure they stay, having a strong employer brand is very important. Organizational reputation covers the way job applicants, present employees and the general public perceive the company. Using traditional tools in recruitment limits the ways employers can show their brand. Company brochures, newspaper advertisements and career fair appearances tend to stay the same and only offer a single message. No interaction is possible with the traditional methods and their content is not easily updated. Currently, employer branding acts as a key, interactive and intentional part of how companies acquire talent. Firms use digital sources to communicate about their working culture, what workers say about the company, diversity campaigns and social responsibility efforts. As an example, LinkedIn company pages and Instagram accounts post content that lets job seekers learn about the company's working environment.

Review websites like Glassdoor exist so that employees can anonymously review the company's management, culture and what they earn. While open communication may harm a business's reputation, it also makes businesses more likely to resolve work-related problems in advance. Today's job candidates often visit these platforms prior to making an application and businesses with a good employer brand hope to attract passive talent. Employer branding today mostly depends on how businesses engage with social media. These forms of interactive content help the organization show its real side and build trust. Connections made during these meetings give potential candidates, especially young people, a good feel for how values and culture are upheld at the company. Today, employer branding in recruiting requires a constant and wide approach. Such tools equipped HR departments to track their brand's image and make the needed changes. By segmenting campaigns by demographics, roles and geography, personalization and their effects can be increased. All in all, regular recruitment provides little support for branding, though modern recruitment often includes branding from the very beginning of hiring. Companies that take advantage of these capabilities become more attractive in the effort to recruit top talent.

5. INDUSTRY TRENDS AND CASE EXAMPLES

Technology, globalization and new employer and candidate needs have propelled a major transformation in recent years within recruitment. The section covers how different fields have changed, spotlights companies that have introduced modern recruiting and provides valuable tips from old recruiting systems. They clearly demonstrate how companies in different fields are adapting and updating their hiring tactics.

5.1 Shifts in Recruitment Practices Across Sectors

In the past decade, recruitment has been transformed mainly because of needs for efficiency, diversity and technological innovations. Major tech firms such as Google use Ai to quickly screen and match candidates from all over the world, moving the whole industry forward very fast (Ebrahim & Rajab, 2025). With COVD-19 changing the way things are done; more healthcare organizations now rely on digital tools and video interviews. Cleveland Clinic and other institutions now turn to virtual recruitment to reach and hire candidates beyond the immediate area. Brands like Zara and Gucci now use Instagram and Facebook to attract applicants from a bigger and more varied group. Pre-screening and arranging interviews are becoming simpler for hiring teams, as AI chatbots play a role (Macchion et al., 2015). Classrooms are shifting their approach to digital tools which has brought noticeable but more subtle changes. Now, universities rely on recruitment sites for academics and ATS tools to help manage the hiring process and ensure compliance. The different techniques prove how technology and online tools make job recruitment faster, more efficient and reachable for businesses in different areas.

5.2 Case Studies of Organizations Adopting Modern Methods

Various industries are now using popular modern recruitment tools. These case studies point out how businesses are tackling hiring problems, improving diversity and improving how candidates feel.

Table 1. Case Studies of Organizations Using Modern Recruitment Methods

Sl No.	Organization	Sector	Modern Methods Used	Key Outcomes
1	Unilever	Consumer Goods	AI screening tools, gamified assessments	Reduced hiring time by 75%; improved diversity in new hires
2	Deloitte	Professional Services	Social media recruiting, AI-based chatbots	30% reduction in hiring cycle; improved global talent engagement
3	Accenture	Consulting	Virtual interviews, proprietary recruitment apps	20% increase in candidate pool; sustained hiring during pandemic disruptions
4	IBM	Technology	AI-based resume parsing, skill-based matching platforms	Improved quality of hire; automated early-stage screening
5	Amazon	E-commerce (Badouch & Boutaounte, 2025)	Internal job matching AI, virtual job fairs	Enhanced internal mobility and external candidate engagement
6	L'Oréal	Beauty and Cosmetics	Video interviewing platforms, social media hiring campaigns	Reduced geographic bias; improved candidate satisfaction
7	Siemens	Engineering/Manufacturing	Online assessment centers, employer branding via LinkedIn	Strengthened employer brand; streamlined graduate recruitment
8	Nestlé	Food and Beverage	Global recruitment portal, mobile application tracking	Enhanced user experience; centralized data for analytics

The variety of cases proves that these methods can be used in different sectors and adjusted to each organization's requirements. Every situation shows that improving KPIs in recruitment is made easier by introducing digital tools.

5.3 Lessons Learned from Traditional Approaches

Though conventional hiring methods were less effective at the time, they still taught valuable lessons that are still important. Many of the ideas found in the social psychology of work remain important in current recruitment strategies.

Table 2. Key Lessons from Traditional Recruitment Methods

Sl No.	Traditional Element	Lesson Learned	Application in Modern Practices
1	Personal Interaction	Assesses non-verbal cues and cultural fit	Final round video/in-person interviews remain critical
2	Employee Referrals	High-quality, lower-risk candidates from internal networks	Digital platforms now include structured referral systems
3	Structured Interviewing	Ensures fairness and repeatability across hiring cycles	Interview templates and scorecards still widely used
4	Campus Recruitment	Builds employer presence and early talent pipelines	Integrated with virtual campus drives and online career fairs
5	Print Advertising	Targeted reach in local or specific talent pools	Used selectively for regional and niche roles alongside online ads
6	Manual Background Checks	Personal and in-depth reference verification	Automated systems augmented by final manual checks for senior roles
7	Walk-in Interviews	Allows immediate screening of large volumes of candidates	Adapted into online open days and video screening tools
8	Job Fairs	Facilitates direct interaction between employers and candidates	Shifted to virtual job fairs and webinars to maintain large-scale reach

The research indicates that, even as technology changes how recruitment takes place, some traditional approaches are still integral to what recruiters do today when creating trust and fairness among applicants.

6. CHALLENGES IN TRANSITIONING FROM TRADITIONAL TO MODERN METHODS

Moving from old to new recruitment techniques is not always easy. There are many strong reasons to use digital tools, including increased efficiency and improved data management, yet many companies find it hard to introduce these technologies into recruitment. The roots of these difficulties include problems with technology, objections from company cultures and more complex questions about data privacy and ethics. In this section, we discuss how various aspects of these obstacles appear in the current market and in academic papers.

6.1 Technological Barriers

There is a major technology gap between traditional and modern methods of recruiting. Larger companies prefer to use Applicant Tracking Systems, AI and analytics, but smaller companies often don't have enough money or experience to set them up successfully (Johnson et al., 2021). It means that modern solutions cannot be widely used the same way in all regions. The use of old and mismatched systems makes progress even harder. If a business isn't integrated with digital tools, its employees end up re-entering data manually, making digital tools seem slow and less reliable. Unreliable internet, electricity and IT support in many developing locations are also challenges for online recruitment of talents (ILO, 2021). Modern recruitment tools are often so advanced that using them can be a challenge. Many HR professionals may avoid training because the process can be tricky and requires more effort for those with low digital fluency. If employees are not properly on-boarded, they won't use advanced tools very much. Also, since hiring algorithms do not disclose their reasoning, many might be suspicious and not fully use these tools. At the end of the day, many smaller companies and those facing financial problems cannot afford the expensive subscriptions, personal tailoring and support the technology used in recruitment calls for.

6.2 Resistance to Change

Many organizations hold back from trying new ways to hire employees simply because some people are afraid, mistaken or doubt their usefulness at different levels within the organization. Human resources teams may not embrace new technologies, since they think they might undermine their autonomy and prefer old-fashioned intuitive methods of judging candidates. Hiring professionals may worry that AI doesn't treat everyone objectively and, due to such concerns, engage in shallow adoption instead. The reason they resist is that clear ROI is needed before any budget is approved for technology. Adoption can be further delayed by difficulties caused by rules and the unwanted additions of different priorities. Despite adoption, a lack of support from above can keep hiring practices separate from the main company culture. The use of placement and personal contacts in some organizations is at odds with the objective information provided by digital recruiting tools. In many places, senior executives are often hesitant to accept new approaches. When there are mis-understandings between parties, this opposition is made stronger. Not explaining the purpose of new methods and ignoring employee opinions about these changes causes digital systems to be neglected, disliked and inefficient. Getting past this barrier is very important. Successful digital transformation in recruiting depends on clear messages, stakeholder input, proper training and a work culture focused on innovation and flexibility.

6.3 Data Privacy and Ethical Considerations

Moving to digital recruitment has raised many ethical and privacy questions. The collection of people's work histories, evaluations, online interviews and traits analysed by AI makes it much easier for companies to violate someone's personal data. AI and machine learning make things more serious because they rely on big collections of personal information. Protecting candidate data against improper dissemination is a major ethical issue. Because modern technology stores and processes much more data, the risk of an unauthorized breach has grown. A lack of protection for personal data can bring harm to a company's reputation, result in legal action and cause applicants to lose trust. Because of GDPR and similar laws, employees need strict consent, less data kept, clear notices and a right to erasure which adds extra steps to automated recruiting used around the world. Having an algorithm make biased decisions adds another ethical problem. Although claimed to be impartial, AI systems for hiring may actually pass on unfairness from past recruiting, hurting groups of people who are underrepresented in the workplace and leading to continued inequality at work. It is important that the system encourages transparency and allows complex learners to direct their own learning activities. Many applicants aren't sure that their resumes are reviewed by algorithms and that employers may look at what they share on social media, leading to concerns about knowing the exact reasons for their rejection. Firms should tell job seekers how they use data and create ways for people to examine their records. When organizations rely on predictive analytics, a person's many qualities might be bypassed, as they are often cared for as mere data entries after analysing their actions. For data and AI systems to be ethical as well as efficient, they must be governed well, audited often and watched by workers. A company must create an inclusive culture, respect every candidate's dignity and favour fairness throughout its recruitment. All of these reasons prove that address privacy matters and ethics is necessary for hiring that supports the needs of people and sustainability.

7. FUTURE OF RECRUITMENT

The way recruitment happens is being changed by fast technological progress, worker preferences and changes in world labour markets. Thanks to fierce competition for talent, changes in society and advances in technology, recruitment is becoming a strategic issue based on information, personal attention and automation. Using Artificial Intelligence (AI), automation, predictive analytics and big data together is changing the way talent is located and chosen, along with how businesses communicate with job seekers. In this section, we look at future changes in recruitment, considering the role of AI and automation, the introduction of targeted and predictive hiring plans and the increasing impact data analysis has on recruitment.

7.1 Integration of AI and Automation

Encompassing AI and automation in talent acquisition means that most resume reviews, interview setting and contacting candidates are streamlined. With AI progressing, it will probably participate in planning how the organization is staffed and more important business decisions (Artha et al., 2024). Using Natural Language Processing (NLP), AI can process a great deal of unorganized data found on resumes and other online pages. NLP helps uncover keywords, skill gaps and career paths, making it easier and quicker to evaluate candidates than completing the same process manually. Thanks to AI, chatbots now interact with job seekers in real-time, handling questions and getting basic information ready for the recruiters. With virtual assistants, almost every aspect of recruitment is streamlined, leaving less work for others to do. Artificial intelligence is very effective at matching candidates to jobs. Machine learning analyses Everyone's background and workplace compatibility to suggest suitable candidates and increase both hiring accuracy and employee retention. Tools for automation are used to actively find and manage potential employees found online. Even with all the advantages of automation, recruiting teams need to maintain a human element. The artificial intelligence used in the field can misunderstand the details and fail to react appropriately to emotions. The process for recruiting talented individuals will be based on both technology and human efforts in the years to come (Chamorro-Premuzic et al., 2017). AI integration in the workplace also makes us question if processes are visible and clear. Frequent biased threat assessment and safeguarding personal data should be important factors when working with such data. Using AI in recruitment requires making systems that everyone trusts and that do not take over from people in judgment.

7.2 Personalized and Predictive Hiring

Personalization is now recognized as a key factor in using recruitment technologies to attract talented individuals. Rather than following a common approach, personalized hiring matches the recruitment steps to a candidate's interests and hope for a career. Because of advances in AI and big data, organizations are now able to personalize communication, match people to jobs and involve candidates more fully. In order to provide personalized recruitment, companies first collect and organize data, follow online activity and act on this information by showing job alerts, ads and dynamic website material. A software developer could notice special roles and benefits within the field. Because of AI-assisted tools, employers can now send email, SMS or chat messages customized to each person and related to their particular interests. Doing so makes it easier for top talent to feel involved and have a rewarding experience in a tough job market. Another use is adaptive assessments which respond to a learner's answers right away by removing unhelpful questions and making the evaluation more accurate. In addition, predictive hiring makes use of past information and artificial intelligence to estimate a candidate's chances of fitting in. If organizations analyse education, work background, skills and interview performance, they have a better chance of finding candidates who will do well and remain on the job. IBM and Unilever apply predictive analytics to guess whether a product will be accepted, manage their resources well and select capable candidates. Personalized and predictive hiring face some difficulties. depending too much on algorithms can cut down the range of people looked at and support existing biases. The danger of violating a candidate's privacy is another concern because of personalization. Clear rules, proper consent and fairness are needed to properly make and run these systems. It is likely that top recruiters will combine personalizing the process with asking for predictions, all while making sure hiring is easy, effective and in line with the company's goals. Making sure automation is paired with empathy and privacy with personalization, will be very important.

7.3 Role of Data Analytics

Recruitment in the modern age depends on data analytics to help move decisions away from instincts and toward evidence in hiring. The use of descriptive, diagnostic, predictive and prescriptive analytics gives a full picture of the recruitment process and lets companies make it more efficient and likely successful. Using metrics like how long it takes to fill a position, the price per hire and where hires come from, descriptive analytics spots weak spots and helpful channels. If information shows that many high performers come from referrals, then giving priority to employee referrals. The purpose of diagnostic analytics is to find out why recruiters may see a lot of interview no-shows which may signal issues with the process or how staff communicate. Using existing and historical information from the labour market, predictive analytics predicts the future actions and needs of candidates. Because of this, businesses can prepare for upcoming skill gaps, decide which workforce programs to focus on and discover talent within the organization for future replacements. Prescriptive analytics is designed to share useful tips for action on the basis of what is predicted. An example would be changing job offers to include flexible work if the results show that it leads to better acceptance rates for preferred candidates. This allows companies to plan well and improve where they post their job ads. Analytic review of data in hiring practices may reveal where there is discrimination in how organizations identify and choose candidates which the company can then fix. By using CRM-like analytics, recruiters can keep track of candidates, how they interact with the company and personally connect with them for the long run.

Analysis of the labour market gives companies a big-picture perspective on hiring and competitors which helps with making key choices such as choosing a location and setting pay. As a result of COVID-19, recruiters found themselves handling remote interviews and figuring out what candidates want. To use data analytics well in recruitment, the data must be top quality, integrated and properly governed. When data and systems are separated, it becomes hard to see everything in one view. Platforms and data must be centralized and learning how data works is important. Careful ethical approaches need data use to be open and respected privacy regulations to be upheld. To earn trust and reputation, bias-reduction methods should be part of the company's practices. As AI, cloud computing and real-time processing become important in recruitment analytics, there will be more predictive dashboards and analysis from AI during interviews. Data analytics is helping organizations to move swiftly and build a position ahead of others.

8. CONCLUSION

Using technology to recruit has brought a major transformation to the process of attracting, selecting and hiring staff. Before, recruiters offered individual approaches with traditional methods, but today, AI, automation and data analysis help them improve how they conduct tasks. Using AI, data analytics and ethical AI in the future will help companies foster inclusiveness, increased adaptability and focus on candidates. Those organizations focused on change and individuals' well-being through innovation will handle talent changes better compared to others. Since technology is changing the way, we work and what organizations require, recruitment has to become forward-thinking, intelligent and able to adapt—matching both current and future needs of the workforce.

REFERENCES

Adam, A. K. (2020). Modern challenges of human resource management practice in job placement and recruitment within organisations in the African continent. *Journal of Human Resource Management*, *8*(2), 69–75. DOI: 10.11648/j.jhrm.201200802.14

Artha, B., Kurniyati, N. N., & Ratnawati, E. T. R. (2024). Artificial Intelligence: A New Paradigm in Human Resource Management. Jurnal Penelitian Pendidikan IPA, 10(SpecialIssue), 372-376.

Badouch, M., & Boutaounte, M. (2025). Smart E-commerce Recommendations with Semantic AI. Fusion. *Practice and Applications*, *17*(1), 264–271.

Badouch, M., Boutaounte, M., Zioudi, O., & Mahmoud, H. (2025). The Future of Travel: A Review of Chatbot Recommender Systems in E-Tourism and Smart Tourism. In Aboudrar, I., Ilahi Bakhsh, F., Nayyar, A., & Ouachtouk, I. (Eds.), *Innovative Technologies on Electrical Power Systems for Smart Cities Infrastructure. ICESST 2024*. Sustainable Civil Infrastructures. DOI: 10.1007/978-3-031-86705-7_10

Breaugh, J. A. (2013). Employee recruitment. *Annual Review of Psychology*, *64*(1), 389–416. DOI: 10.1146/annurev-psych-113011-143757 PMID: 23121331

Chamorro-Premuzic, T., Akhtar, R., Winsborough, D., & Sherman, R. A. (2017). The datafication of talent: How technology is advancing the science of human potential at work. *Current Opinion in Behavioral Sciences*, *18*, 13–16. DOI: 10.1016/j.cobeha.2017.04.007

Chapman, D. S., Uggerslev, K. L., Carroll, S. A., Piasentin, K. A., & Jones, D. A. (2005). Applicant attraction to organizations and job choice: A meta-analytic review of the correlates of recruiting outcomes. *The Journal of Applied Psychology*, *90*(5), 928–944. DOI: 10.1037/0021-9010.90.5.928 PMID: 16162065

Ebrahim, S. S., & Rajab, H. A. (2025). The Future of HR: The Role of AI-Powered Recruitment in Shaping the Modern Workforce. *OAlib*, *12*(1), 1–22. DOI: 10.4236/oalib.1112770

Graham, M. E., Kennavane, E., & Wears, K. H. (2008). Diversity management content in introductory human resource management textbooks. *Academy of Management Learning & Education*, *7*(3), 429–433. DOI: 10.5465/amle.2008.37029277

Johnson, R. D., Lukaszewski, K. M., & Stone, D. L. (2016). The evolution of the field of human resource information systems: Co-evolution of technology and HR processes. *Communications of the Association for Information Systems*, *38*(1), 28. DOI: 10.17705/1CAIS.03828

Macchion, L., Danese, P., & Vinelli, A. (2015). Redefining supply network strategies to face changing environments. A study from the fashion and luxury industry. Operations management research, 8, 15-31.

Nikolaou, I. (2014). Social networking web sites in job search and employee recruitment. *International Journal of Selection and Assessment*, *22*(2), 179–189. DOI: 10.1111/ijsa.12067

Raghavan, M., Barocas, S., Kleinberg, J., & Levy, K. (2020, January). Mitigating bias in algorithmic hiring: Evaluating claims and practices. In *Proceedings of the 2020 conference on fairness, accountability, and transparency* (pp. 469-481). DOI: 10.1145/3351095.3372828

Saad, M. F. M., Nugro, A. W. L., Thinakaran, R., & Baijed, M. (2021, December). A review of artificial intelligence based platform in human resource recruitment process. In 2021 6th IEEE International Conference on Recent Advances and Innovations in Engineering (ICRAIE) (Vol. 6, pp. 1-5). IEEE.

Stone, D. L., Deadrick, D. L., Lukaszewski, K. M., & Johnson, R. (2015). The influence of technology on the future of human resource management. *Human Resource Management Review*, *25*(2), 216–231. DOI: 10.1016/j.hrmr.2015.01.002

Van Hoye, G., & Lievens, F. (2009). Tapping the grapevine: A closer look at word-of-mouth as a recruitment source. *The Journal of Applied Psychology*, *94*(2), 341–352. DOI: 10.1037/a0014066 PMID: 19271794

Voigt, P., & Von dem Bussche, A. (2017). The eu general data protection regulation (gdpr). A practical guide, 1st ed., Cham: Springer International Publishing, 10(3152676), 10-5555.

Zottoli, M. A., & Wanous, J. P. (2000). Recruitment source research: Current status and future directions. *Human Resource Management Review*, *10*(4), 353–382. DOI: 10.1016/S1053-4822(00)00032-2

Chapter 4
The Impact of Artificial Intelligence on Modern Hiring

Wasantha Rajapakshe
https://orcid.org/0000-0002-0757-9030
Sri Lanka Institute of Information Technology, Malabe, Sri Lanka

ABSTRACT

This study explores the transformative impact of AI on talent acquisition, highlighting its evolution within HRM and redefining recruitment in the digital era. It examines AI's integration across key recruitment functions, including resume screening, chatbots, interview scheduling, and predictive analytics for candidate suitability. The research reviews core technologies such as Natural Language Processing (NLP), Machine Learning (ML), Robotic Process Automation (RPA), and facial recognition. While AI enhances efficiency, reduces bias, and supports data-driven decisions, it also introduces ethical and regulatory challenges related to fairness, privacy, and transparency. The study draws upon theoretical models like the Technology Acceptance Model (TAM), Unified Theory of Acceptance and Use of Technology (UTAUT), and Diffusion of Innovation (DOI) to contextualize AI adoption. Finally, it presents a comparative analysis of global trends and Sri Lanka's local context, offering insights into the factors influencing AI adoption in recruitment and the future of digital HR practices.

DOI: 10.4018/979-8-3373-6516-9.ch004

1. INTRODUCTION

1.1 Evolution of AI in Human Resource Management

Artificial Intelligence (AI) has made its mark and transformed the landscape of Human Resource Management (HRM). Its influence has grown significantly, reshaping the traditional role of HR from administrative and operational to strategic and data-driven. This transformation, driven by AI, has automated repetitive tasks, improved decision-making processes, and allowed HR professionals to focus on higher-value functions such as employee engagement, organizational development, and strategic workforce planning.

The integration of AI into HRM can be traced back to the early 2000s when basic applicant tracking systems (ATS) began to digitize the recruitment process (Upadhyay & Khandelwal, 2018). However, these systems offered limited capabilities, mostly serving as digital filing cabinets (Leutner et al., 2022). Over time, advances in machine learning, natural language processing, and data analytics enabled the development of more intelligent and responsive systems. These technologies allowed for the creation of chatbots that could communicate with candidates, algorithms that could analyze resumes at scale, and predictive models that could assess future employee performance or attrition risks (Leutner et al., 2022; Mehta & Mehta, 2020).

Today, AI tools are widely adopted in many areas of HRM, including talent acquisition, learning and development, performance management, and employee well-being. In particular, the COVID-19 pandemic accelerated digital transformation efforts, pushing organizations to adopt remote and AI-assisted technologies faster than ever before. This shift has led to a new era where AI is not just a tool for efficiency but a strategic partner in building agile, resilient, and competitive organizations, inspiring a forward-thinking approach to HRM.

1.2 Defining Talent Acquisition in the Digital Age

Talent acquisition involves identifying, attracting, evaluating, and hiring individuals to meet an organization's workforce needs. Unlike traditional recruitment, which is often reactive and transactional, talent acquisition adopts a holistic approach aligned with long-term business objectives. It encompasses employer branding, workforce planning, candidate relationship management, and the utilization of analytics to optimize hiring decisions (Parasa, 2024).

In the digital era, talent acquisition has undergone significant transformation. Digital platforms such as LinkedIn, online job boards, and company career portals have become essential channels for sourcing candidates. Simultaneously, AI technologies have introduced unprecedented speed, scale, and precision to the hiring process. AI-powered tools can analyze vast datasets to match candidate profiles with job descriptions, identify passive talent, and predict a candidate's potential success within an organization based on behavioral patterns and historical data (Islam et al., 2024).

AI streamlines recruitment operations and enhances the candidate's experience. It offers real-time communication through chatbots, provides personalized job recommendations, and enables virtual interviews with intelligent feedback systems. These innovations make the process more efficient and help organizations stand out in a competitive labor market by delivering more engaging and transparent hiring experiences (Abraham et al., 2025).

As organizations embrace digital transformation, talent acquisition is shifting from a linear, one-size-fits-all process to a dynamic and adaptive strategy. AI plays a central role in this shift, empowering HR professionals with tools and insights to make more informed, data-driven decisions while ensuring fairness, efficiency, and alignment with organizational values (Abdelhay et al., 2025).

2. THE ROLE OF AI IN THE TALENT ACQUISITION PROCESS

Integrating Artificial Intelligence (AI) into talent acquisition processes reshapes the recruitment landscape by enhancing efficiency, improving decision-making, and driving better candidate experiences. The application of AI in recruitment has made the process more streamlined, data-driven, and adaptive to the needs of modern organizations. This section explores key areas where AI plays a critical role, including resume screening and Applicant Tracking Systems (ATS), chatbots for candidate engagement, AI-assisted interview scheduling and communication, and predictive analytics for evaluating candidate suitability.

2.1 Resume Screening and Applicant Tracking Systems (ATS)

One of the most liberating uses of AI in talent acquisition is resume screening and the operation of Applicant Tracking Systems (ATS). Traditionally, HR professionals faced the overwhelming task of manually reviewing thousands of resumes for each job opening. This process was not only time-consuming but also prone to human biases and inconsistencies (Upadhyay & Khandelwal, 2018). However, with the advent of AI-powered resume screening, this process has become far more efficient and objective, freeing up valuable time for more strategic tasks (Bag et al., 2022).

AI in ATS uses machine learning algorithms and natural language processing (NLP) to scan resumes, extracting key information such as skills, qualifications, work experience, and certifications (Van Esch et al., 2019). These systems then match this data to the job description, identifying the most relevant candidates based on predefined criteria. Unlike human recruiters who may overlook certain details or misinterpret information, AI systems can analyze resumes at scale with remarkable accuracy, ensuring that no promising candidates are missed (Black & van Esch, 2020).

Moreover, AI-powered ATS tools are capable of ranking candidates according to their fit for the role, which helps recruiters prioritize top candidates and reduce the time spent on low-quality applications (Sathyaseelan & Siva, 2024). This process not only improves efficiency but also supports diversity and inclusion efforts by removing human biases from the initial screening process (Ajunwa, 2019). However, it is essential to note that the algorithms used in ATS must be continually refined to prevent biases from creeping into the system itself. Additionally, there are potential risks associated with AI in recruitment, such as job displacement and the need for upskilling. HR professionals need to be aware of these risks and plan accordingly (Köchling & Wehner, 2020).

2.2 Chatbots and Automated Candidate Engagement

Chatbots have become indispensable tools in talent acquisition, revolutionizing how candidates interact with employers. These AI-powered virtual assistants engage candidates in real time, providing immediate responses to inquiries, guiding them through the application process, and even conducting preliminary interviews. Chatbots can assist candidates with frequently asked questions (FAQs) related to job openings, company culture, and application status, ensuring that candidates receive timely and accurate information (Badouch et al., 2025).

In addition to providing instant communication, chatbots help HR teams maintain continuous engagement with potential candidates. They can proactively reach out to candidates, follow up on previous interactions, and remind candidates of important deadlines or interviews. This automated engagement enhances the candidate experience by creating a more personalized and responsive communication channel, making candidates feel valued and engaged.

Another key benefit of chatbots in recruitment is their ability to conduct initial screening interviews. Chatbots can gather essential information about candidates' qualifications, work preferences, and availability by asking predetermined questions. They can then assess whether a candidate meets the basic requirements for a job before passing the information to human recruiters. This automation frees up HR professionals to focus on more complex tasks while ensuring that the process is efficient and consistent.

2.3 AI in Interview Scheduling and Communication

AI technologies also play a vital role in optimizing the interview scheduling process, relieving HR professionals from the burden of manual coordination. Traditional interview scheduling can be cumbersome and time-consuming, especially when coordinating between multiple candidates and interviewers with busy schedules. AI-powered scheduling tools can automate this process by analyzing the availability of all parties involved and proposing optimal time slots for interviews. These systems can also send reminders and updates to ensure that candidates and interviewers are prepared, making the process more organized and efficient.

Beyond scheduling, AI can facilitate communication by seamlessly integrating video conferencing platforms. AI tools can facilitate virtual interview scheduling, automatically sending candidates links and instructions. For example, some platforms are equipped with AI-powered systems that analyze a candidate's behavior, speech patterns, and emotional tone during video interviews, providing valuable insights to interviewers about the candidate's communication style, confidence, and engagement levels. These technologies help HR professionals assess the content of an interview and the candidate's non-verbal cues, which are essential in evaluating cultural fit and interpersonal skills.

Moreover, AI-driven systems can transcribe interviews in real time, making it easier for recruiters to review candidate responses later and share feedback with hiring managers. These tools improve the overall efficiency of the interview process and provide valuable data for post-interview analysis, ultimately contributing to better decision-making.

2.4 Predictive Analytics for Candidate Suitability

Predictive analytics is one of the most powerful applications of AI in talent acquisition. By analyzing historical data, AI algorithms can predict the likelihood of a candidate's success within a specific role or organization. This process involves examining factors such as the candidate's experience, educational background, previous job performance, and even personality traits to determine whether they are likely to thrive.

AI-based predictive analytics tools can provide hiring managers objective insights beyond a candidate's resume or interview performance. These tools analyze patterns in data to identify traits and characteristics that correlate with high performance in particular roles. For example, a predictive model may identify that candidates with certain skills or work experience in a fast-paced environment are more likely to succeed in high-pressure positions.

Moreover, AI tools can assess cultural fit by evaluating how candidates align with the organization's values, work styles, and goals. This helps companies avoid costly mismatches, reduce turnover, and enhance employee engagement. The predictive insights provided by AI also contribute to a more data-driven recruitment process, allowing organizations to make better hiring decisions based on measurable evidence rather than gut feelings or subjective judgments.

AI-powered predictive analytics predicts candidate success and assists in workforce planning. By forecasting hiring needs based on market trends, internal employee turnover, and business growth projections, AI helps organizations optimize their talent acquisition strategies. This ensures they hire the right people at the right time, enhancing operational efficiency and reducing recruitment costs.

The role of AI in talent acquisition is rapidly evolving, offering powerful tools that enhance efficiency, improve decision-making, and, importantly, contribute to better candidate experiences. By streamlining processes such as resume screening, candidate engagement, interview scheduling, and predictive analytics, AI enables HR professionals to focus on strategic tasks that require human intuition and creativity. As organizations continue to embrace these advanced technologies, the future of talent acquisition will likely be characterized by even greater automation, personalization, and data-driven insights, all of which aim to enhance the candidate journey.

3. AI TECHNOLOGIES USED IN RECRUITMENT

The recruitment landscape is continuously evolving with the integration of advanced AI technologies. These tools not only automate repetitive tasks but also enhance decision-making by analyzing vast amounts of data and offering insights that would be impossible for humans to derive manually. Key AI technologies such as Natural Language Processing (NLP), Machine Learning Algorithms, Robotic Process Automation (RPA), and Facial Recognition with Emotion Detection play a transformative role in recruitment. This section explores these technologies and their impact on the recruitment process.

3.1 Natural Language Processing (NLP)

Natural Language Processing (NLP) is one of the most powerful AI technologies used in recruitment, particularly in resume screening, candidate matching, and communication. NLP enables machines to understand, interpret, and respond to human language in a meaningful and contextually appropriate way. In the recruitment context, NLP allows AI systems to analyze resumes, cover letters, and job descriptions with high accuracy.

NLP-driven resume screening tools can efficiently scan and extract relevant data from unstructured text, such as job titles, skills, qualifications, and work experience, and compare this information to the requirements of the job opening. This analysis is far more efficient than manual reading and can handle vast volumes of applicants in a fraction of the time. Moreover, NLP-based systems can rank candidates according to their fit for the role, eliminating the need for HR professionals to sift through hundreds or thousands of resumes, thereby enhancing productivity.

In addition to resume screening, NLP is also used in chatbots that engage candidates in real time. These bots use NLP to understand and respond to candidates' inquiries, making communication smoother and more efficient. For example, candidates can ask about the application process, job details, or company culture, and the NLP system will provide instant, accurate responses. This saves time for both candidates and recruiters and improves the candidate's experience by offering personalized and immediate interactions.

3.2 Machine Learning Algorithms

Machine Learning (ML) is another cornerstone of AI in recruitment, empowering HR professionals with their predictive capabilities. ML algorithms analyze historical hiring data to identify patterns and make predictions about future hiring decisions. These algorithms are learnt from previous recruitment cycles, identifying characteristics that are associated with successful hires and using this information to improve decision-making in future recruitment efforts.

For example, ML algorithms can analyze a candidate's past job performance, educational background, skills, and even personality traits to predict their performance in a given role. These algorithms can also assess whether a candidate will be a cultural fit for the organization based on data gathered from employee surveys and job satisfaction metrics.

One of the significant advantages of ML in recruitment is its ability to scale. As the organization gathers more data, the algorithms become more refined and accurate in predicting candidate success. HR teams can continuously improve their hiring strategies by making data-driven decisions rather than relying on intuition or subjective assessments. Furthermore, machine learning models can also be used for candidate sourcing by predicting which passive candidates (those not actively applying for jobs) are most likely to be interested in new opportunities.

Despite its many advantages, machine learning algorithms must be carefully designed to avoid biases in decision-making. These biases can stem from the data fed into the algorithms, which may be biased or incomplete, leading the system to reinforce existing biases. For instance, if historical hiring data is biased towards a certain demographic, the algorithm may inadvertently favor candidates from that demographic, leading to unfair hiring practices. As such, it is essential for HR professionals to continually monitor and evaluate ML systems to ensure they operate ethically and equitably.

3.3 Robotic Process Automation (RPA)

Robotic Process Automation (RPA) refers to the use of software robots (or "bots") to automate routine, rule-based tasks within the recruitment process. RPA is particularly useful for relieving HR professionals of time-consuming and error-prone administrative tasks, such as scheduling interviews, sending email confirmations, and updating candidate records in databases. For example, when a candidate applies for a job, an RPA bot can automatically send an acknowledgment email, input the candidate's information into the ATS, and assign the resume to the appropriate recruiter for review. RPA can also streamline the interview scheduling process, automatically coordinating availability between candidates and interviewers. This reduces the administrative burden on HR staff and ensures that the recruitment process flows smoothly.

RPA is also highly effective in managing large volumes of candidate data. For instance, if an organization conducts a high-volume recruitment campaign, RPA can automatically filter through applications, reject those not meeting the basic criteria, and pass on the relevant candidates for further evaluation. This speeds up the recruitment process and ensures consistency and accuracy in data handling. Additionally, RPA can be used for onboarding, ensuring that all necessary forms, contracts, and documentation are completed before a candidate starts their new role. By automating repetitive administrative tasks, RPA frees HR professionals to focus on more strategic and value-added activities, such as engaging with candidates and making high-level decisions.

3.5 Facial Recognition and Emotion Detection in Video Interviews

Facial recognition and emotion detection technologies are increasingly being integrated into video interviews, providing recruiters with new ways to assess candidates. These technologies analyze a candidate's facial expressions, speech patterns, and body language during a video interview to gauge emotional responses and engagement levels. This can provide a more comprehensive understanding of how a candidate reacts under pressure, their level of confidence, and how well they align with the company's cultural values.

Facial recognition software can detect subtle changes in a candidate's facial expressions, such as smiling, frowning, or raising eyebrows, and assess whether these expressions align with the expressed emotions. Emotion detection algorithms analyze voice intonations, speech patterns, and facial expressions to infer emotions such as happiness, stress, or nervousness. This technology can help recruiters understand the candidate's emotional state, which is important for assessing interpersonal skills, adaptability, and resilience.

While facial recognition and emotion detection technologies provide valuable insights into candidate behavior, they also raise significant ethical and privacy concerns. For example, there are risks of bias in the algorithms used to assess facial expressions, and candidates may feel uncomfortable knowing that their emotions are being analyzed. Moreover, using these technologies raises privacy concerns, as they involve collecting and analyzing personal data. As such, it is essential for organizations to ensure transparency in the use of these technologies, obtain candidate consent before using them in interviews, and adhere to data protection regulations.

Despite the challenges and ethical considerations, when used ethically, facial recognition and emotion detection technologies offer recruiters additional data points that can enhance the recruitment process. These technologies can provide valuable insights into candidate behavior, helping recruiters assess interpersonal skills, adaptability, and resilience. These technologies can contribute to more informed and fair candidate evaluations by offering a more holistic view of candidates.

4. BENEFITS OF AI TALENT ACQUISITION

Integrating AI technologies into talent acquisition offers numerous benefits that improve the hiring process's efficiency, fairness, and overall effectiveness. As organizations increasingly rely on AI-driven solutions, these technologies are reshaping how talent acquisition teams' source, evaluate, and hire candidates. In this section, we will explore the key benefits of AI in talent acquisition, focusing on efficiency and timesaving, bias reduction, enhancing the candidate's experience, and enabling data-driven decision-making.

4.1 Efficiency and Timesaving

One of the most significant advantages of AI in talent acquisition is its ability to increase efficiency and save time. The recruitment process often involves handling large volumes of applications, which can be a time-consuming and resource-intensive task. AI tools, such as Applicant Tracking Systems (ATS), resume screening algorithms, and chatbots, significantly reduce the administrative workload and expedite key stages of the hiring process.

AI-powered resume screening automates the process of shifting through hundreds or thousands of resumes, empowering HR professionals to identify the most suitable candidates based on specific keywords, qualifications, and experience. This automation eliminates the need for manual review, allowing them to focus on the most promising candidates. AI also aids in candidate sourcing by identifying potential talent pools and streamlining job postings across multiple platforms, further reducing the time spent on recruitment marketing.

Moreover, AI-driven chatbots can engage candidates in real time, answering their questions, providing updates on application statuses, and even conducting initial screening interviews. This reduces the need for HR professionals to spend time on routine communications, ensuring that candidates receive timely and consistent interactions. By automating these repetitive tasks, AI frees recruiters to focus on higher-value activities, such as conducting in-depth interviews and making strategic hiring decisions.

4.2 Bias Reduction and Fairness

Another key benefit of AI in talent acquisition is its potential to reduce bias and improve fairness in the hiring process. Traditional recruitment methods, while essential, are often influenced by unconscious biases that can affect hiring decisions. These biases can be based on factors such as a candidate's gender, age, ethnicity, or educational background, which may lead to discriminatory practices and unequal opportunities for certain candidates.

AI technologies, particularly those used for resume screening and candidate evaluation, can help mitigate these biases by focusing purely on objective data, such as skills, experience, and qualifications. For example, AI-powered resume screening algorithms can be trained to disregard demographic information (such as names, photos, and addresses) that might lead to bias, ensuring that candidates are evaluated based solely on their fit for the role.

AI can be used proactively to monitor the recruitment process in real time, identifying potential disparities or biases in the selection process. By analyzing data from previous hiring decisions, AI systems can flag instances where certain groups may be underrepresented, or biases may unintentionally influence decisions. This proactive approach allows HR teams to take corrective action and ensure a more inclusive hiring process, instilling confidence in the fairness of the process.

While AI has the potential to reduce bias, it is important to note that the technology itself can inadvertently perpetuate bias if the data used to train AI models is flawed or biased. Therefore, organizations must take responsibility and continuously review and audit their AI systems to ensure that they are fair, transparent, and free from bias, demonstrating a commitment to fairness.

4.3 Enhancing Candidate Experience

AI has the power to significantly enhance candidate experience, which is a crucial aspect of talent acquisition. In today's competitive job market, candidates have high expectations for a seamless, personalized, and engaging application process. AI technologies can help organizations meet these expectations by providing a more responsive and efficient hiring experience. For example, AI-driven chatbots can engage candidates early in the recruitment process, answering their questions in real time and providing personalized updates. This improves communication between candidates and employers, ensuring candidates feel valued and informed throughout the process. Chatbots can also provide instant feedback to candidates, helping them understand where they stand in the hiring process and reducing the anxiety that often accompanies waiting for updates.

Additionally, AI can help personalize the recruitment experience by matching candidates with roles that best suit their skills and career aspirations. Using data to analyze a candidate's background and preferences, AI systems can recommend jobs that align with their qualifications, experience, and interests. This personalization not only makes the process more relevant to the candidate but also increases the likelihood of a successful hire, as candidates are more likely to stay engaged and committed when the role matches their career goals.

AI also enables organizations to provide a more streamlined application process. Automated resume screening, interview scheduling, and follow-up communications can be managed through AI-powered platforms, ensuring that candidates are not left waiting for responses or overwhelmed by unnecessary administrative steps. As a result, candidates enjoy a more efficient and user-friendly experience, which can improve the employer's brand and attract top talent.

4.4 Data-Driven Decision-Making

AI's most significant contribution to talent acquisition is its capacity to facilitate data-driven decision-making. Unlike traditional methods that rely on subjective assessments or limited data, AI tools empower HR professionals to analyze extensive data from diverse sources like resumes, job descriptions, and candidate performance metrics. This enables them to make more informed and objective decisions, enhancing the quality of their recruitment process.

AI-powered predictive analytics have the potential to significantly improve recruitment outcomes. These tools can assess factors such as past job performance, educational background, and personality traits to predict how well a candidate will perform in the role. By using data to inform hiring decisions, organizations can reduce the risk of hiring mistakes and improve overall recruitment outcomes. This potential for improvement should instill optimism in HR professionals about the future of recruitment with AI.

Moreover, AI can help HR teams optimize their recruitment strategies by identifying patterns in hiring data. For instance, AI algorithms can analyze which sourcing channels produce the best candidates, which interview questions are most predictive of success, and which attributes correlate with long-term employee retention. This data-driven approach allows HR professionals to continually refine their hiring practices, ensuring that they consistently attract and select the best talent. This emphasis on continuous improvement should make HR professionals feel proactive in their approach to recruitment.

Data-driven decision-making also enables HR teams to measure the effectiveness of their recruitment processes over time. AI tools can track key performance metrics, such as time-to-hire, candidate satisfaction, and hiring success rates, providing valuable insights that can be used to optimize future recruitment strategies.

5. CHALLENGES AND ETHICAL CONSIDERATIONS

While AI offers numerous advantages in talent acquisition, its integration into recruitment processes also presents significant challenges and ethical considerations. These challenges often stem from the complexities of machine learning algorithms, data privacy concerns, and the broader implications of AI-driven decision-making. Addressing these challenges is essential to ensure that AI technologies are used responsibly, ethically, and in compliance with relevant laws and regulations.

5.1 Algorithmic Bias and Fairness

One of the most pressing challenges associated with AI in talent acquisition is the issue of algorithmic bias. Algorithms are only as good as the data they are trained on, and if the data used to train these systems is biased, the resulting AI model will also reflect those biases. In the context of recruitment, algorithmic bias can lead to discriminatory hiring practices, where certain groups of candidates—based on gender, age, ethnicity, or other factors—are unfairly disadvantaged.

For example, suppose an AI system is trained on historical hiring data that predominantly reflects the hiring decisions of a particular demographic (such as male candidates for engineering roles). In that case, the system may inadvertently favor candidates who fit that demographic profile. This could lead to biased hiring outcomes, reinforcing existing inequalities in the workplace and undermining diversity and inclusion efforts.

To mitigate algorithmic bias, it is crucial to ensure that AI systems are trained on diverse and representative datasets that reflect a wide range of demographic and experiential backgrounds. Additionally, companies must regularly audit their AI models to identify and address any biases that may emerge over time. By using fairness algorithms, HR professionals can adjust the AI's decision-making criteria to account for demographic and contextual factors, ensuring a more equitable hiring process. While reducing bias in AI systems is possible, it is important to acknowledge that eliminating bias entirely is challenging. As such, organizations must remain vigilant and proactive to ensure fairness in AI-driven recruitment.

5.2 Data Privacy and Security

The use of AI in talent acquisition also raises significant concerns about data privacy and security. Recruitment processes involve the collection and processing of vast amounts of personal and sensitive data, including candidates' resumes, contact information, employment history, and even personal attributes like social media profiles. As AI technologies rely on large data sets to function effectively, safeguarding this information is paramount to ensure candidates' privacy rights are respected.

Data breaches or unauthorized access to candidate data can result in severe consequences, including identity theft, fraud, and reputational damage for the company. Additionally, candidates may feel uncomfortable sharing personal information if they are unsure how their data will be handled or whether it will be securely stored.

To mitigate these risks, organizations must implement robust data protection measures, including encryption, secure storage, and compliance with data protection regulations such as the General Data Protection Regulation (GDPR) in the European Union and the California Consumer Privacy Act (CCPA) in the United States. It is also important to ensure that AI systems are designed with privacy in mind, incorporating features such as data anonymization and minimizing the collection of unnecessary personal information.

Transparency is not just a key element, but a cornerstone in addressing data privacy concerns. Organizations should clearly communicate to candidates how their data will be used, stored, and protected throughout the recruitment process.

Obtaining informed consent from candidates before collecting their data is also a critical step in ensuring compliance with privacy regulations and maintaining trust with job seekers.

5.3 Transparency and Accountability

Transparency and accountability are fundamental ethical considerations when implementing AI in recruitment. The "black-box" nature of many AI algorithms, particularly those based on machine learning, can make it difficult for HR professionals and candidates to understand how decisions are made. This lack of transparency can undermine trust in the system and raise concerns about fairness and discrimination.

For example, if an AI system rejects a candidate's application based on certain factors (such as a particular keyword or qualification), it may not be immediately clear why that decision was made. Without a clear explanation, candidates may feel that they were unfairly evaluated, leading to dissatisfaction and potential legal challenges.

To address this challenge, organizations must prioritize explainability in their AI systems. This means ensuring that AI algorithms are not only effective but also understandable to humans. HR professionals should be able to review and explain the rationale behind AI-driven decisions, especially in cases where candidates are rejected or shortlisted. In addition, AI systems should be designed to allow for human oversight, enabling recruiters to intervene and adjust decisions as needed.

Accountability is not just important, it's crucial. Organizations must take responsibility for the decisions made by their AI systems and be prepared to justify those decisions if challenged. This includes maintaining clear records of how AI models were trained, what data was used, and how the algorithm arrived at its conclusions. By establishing transparent and accountable AI processes, organizations can ensure that their recruitment practices are not just ethical but also aligned with their values.

5.4 Legal and Regulatory Compliance

As AI technologies in recruitment evolve, so too do the legal and regulatory frameworks that govern their use. Organizations must ensure their AI-driven recruitment processes comply with relevant laws and regulations to avoid legal risks and protect candidates and the company. For instance, laws such as the Equal Employment Opportunity (EEO) Act in the United States and the Equality Act in the UK prohibit discrimination based on factors like race, gender, age, and disability. AI systems used in recruitment must be designed and tested to ensure compliance with these anti-discrimination laws. This could involve training the AI system on a diverse set of data to avoid bias and regularly auditing the system's decision-making processes. Failure to do so can result in legal action, fines, and reputational damage.

Additionally, organizations must be mindful of data protection regulations, such as the GDPR in Europe and the CCPA in California, which govern how personal data is collected, processed, and stored. Non-compliance with these regulations can lead to severe financial penalties, such as fines of up to 4% of annual global turnover, and legal consequences, including lawsuits from affected individuals. The reputational damage from such incidents can also be significant.

To navigate these challenges, organizations should work closely with legal and compliance teams to ensure that their AI systems comply with applicable laws. It's important to stress the need for regular audits and assessments of AI models, as they are essential to ensuring ongoing compliance, particularly as regulations related to AI in recruitment continue to evolve.

6. THEORETICAL FRAMEWORKS FOR UNDERSTANDING AI ADOPTION

Adopting new technologies in organizations is a complex process that involves understanding various factors, including perceived benefits, organizational readiness, and user attitudes. In the context of AI adoption in talent acquisition, several theoretical frameworks can help explain why and how organizations and individuals accept and use AI-based systems. This section explores three prominent frameworks: the Technology Acceptance Model (TAM), the Unified Theory of Acceptance and Use of Technology (UTAUT), and the Diffusion of Innovation Theory (DOI). Each framework provides unique insights into the factors influencing AI adoption and its implementation within recruitment processes, offering a glimpse of AI's promising future.

6.1 Technology Acceptance Model (TAM)

The Technology Acceptance Model (TAM), developed by Davis (1989), is one of the most widely used models for understanding how users accept and use new technologies. The model posits that two key factors determine technology acceptance: Perceived Ease of Use (PEOU) and Perceived Usefulness (PU).

- **Perceived Ease of Use (PEOU):** This refers to the degree to which an individual believes that using a particular technology would be free from effort. In the context of AI in talent acquisition, this could refer to how easy AI-driven tools, such as resume screening systems or chatbots, are for HR professionals and candidates to use. The less effort it takes to interact with AI technologies, the more likely users will adopt them.

- **Perceived Usefulness (PU):** This refers to the degree to which an individual believes technology will enhance their job performance. For HR professionals, AI tools that improve the recruitment process's speed, efficiency, and accuracy are likely to be useful. If AI can save time and improve decision-making, it is more likely to be adopted by HR teams.

According to TAM, the more useful and easier to use an AI technology is perceived to be, the more likely it will be accepted and integrated into recruitment processes. This model helps explain why HR professionals may resist adopting AI if they perceive the tools as too complex or not beneficial to their work. Organizations looking to successfully implement AI technologies must focus on improving the usability and demonstrating the clear benefits of the technology.

6.2 Unified Theory of Acceptance and Use of Technology (UTAUT)

The Unified Theory of Acceptance and Use of Technology (UTAUT), developed by Venkatesh et al. (2003), consolidates several technology acceptance theories, including TAM, and introduces additional constructs to explain technology adoption. The UTAUT model posits that the intention to use technology is influenced by Performance Expectancy, Effort Expectancy, Social Influence, and Facilitating Conditions.

- **Performance Expectancy:** This is the degree to which an individual believes that using technology will improve their job performance. In AI adoption for talent acquisition, HR professionals are likely to adopt AI tools if they believe the technology will significantly improve their recruitment outcomes, such as better candidate matching or faster hiring processes. However, it's important to consider the potential impact of AI adoption on job roles and responsibilities. For instance, AI tools may automate certain tasks, freeing up time for HR professionals to focus on more strategic aspects of recruitment.
- **Effort Expectancy:** Similar to TAM's Perceived Ease of Use, this construct refers to the perceived ease of using the technology. If HR professionals find AI-based systems user-friendly and intuitive, they are more likely to embrace them.
- **Social Influence:** This refers to the degree to which an individual perceives those important others (e.g., colleagues, supervisors, industry peers) believe they should use the technology. In a corporate context, the endorsement of

influential figures within the HR department or the wider organization can significantly sway the adoption of AI in recruitment, demonstrating the power of leadership in shaping organizational decisions.

- **Facilitating Conditions:** These are the resources and support available to facilitate technological use. For example, suppose an organization provides adequate training, technical support, and access to resources. In that case, HR professionals can feel reassured and supported in their decision to adopt AI in recruitment. Without these conditions, the adoption rate may decrease, even if technology is useful.

UTAUT highlights the importance of both individual perceptions and organizational support in the adoption process. Therefore, for successful AI adoption in talent acquisition, HR departments should focus on demonstrating the technology's usefulness and ensure that sufficient training and support mechanisms are in place to assist employees in using these tools effectively. This could include providing comprehensive training programs, establishing a dedicated support team, and creating user-friendly manuals and guides.

6.3 Diffusion of Innovation Theory (DOI)

The **Diffusion of Innovation Theory (DOI)**, developed by Rogers in 1962, provides another valuable perspective on technology adoption. This theory focuses on how, why, and at what rate new technologies spread among individuals and organizations. According to the DOI, the adoption of innovation is influenced by several factors, including the Relative Advantage, Compatibility, Complexity, Trialability, and Observability of the innovation (Rogers, 1995).

- **Relative Advantage:** This refers to the perceived benefits of innovation compared to existing technologies or practices. In the context of AI in talent acquisition, if AI systems provide a clear advantage over traditional recruitment methods (such as faster screening, reduced bias, and more accurate candidate matching), they are more likely to be adopted.
- **Compatibility:** This refers to the degree to which an innovation aligns with existing values, practices, and needs. AI systems compatible with current recruitment processes, such as integration with existing Applicant Tracking Systems (ATS), are more likely to be accepted. If AI tools align with HR professionals' existing goals and workflows, they are more likely to adopt them.
- **Complexity:** Similar to **Effort Expectancy** in UTAUT, complexity refers to the perceived difficulty of using the technology. If AI tools are seen as diffi-

cult to implement or operate, adoption rates will be lower. To enhance adoption, AI technologies should be designed to be as user-friendly as possible.

- **Trialability:** This refers to the degree to which an innovation can be experimented with on a limited basis before full-scale adoption. In the context of AI in recruitment, offering HR departments the opportunity to trial AI tools, such as resume screening systems or chatbots, can increase the likelihood of adoption. If organizations can test the technology on a smaller scale and see its effectiveness, they may be more likely to adopt it more broadly.
- **Observability:** This refers to the degree to which the results of the innovation are visible to others. If HR professionals can observe the positive outcomes of AI adoption in other organizations or departments, they may be more inclined to adopt AI technologies themselves.

DOI emphasizes that technology adoption is not immediate but occurs over time, with early adopters paving the way for the majority. For AI in recruitment, early adopters within an organization can serve as champions, demonstrating the benefits of AI and encouraging others to follow suit.

AI is revolutionizing talent acquisition, empowering companies with state-of-the-art tools that significantly enhance operational efficiency, employee engagement, and decision-making. These AI-powered solutions boost operational efficiency, improve hiring outcomes and retention tactics, and streamline the candidate screening process. Understanding how AI will affect HR management is crucial, as this knowledge is key to overcoming the remaining obstacles to widespread AI adoption in talent acquisition.

Many organizations face challenges in identifying the most suitable AI application for the successful implementation of an AI-driven information system. Despite existing research offering various models for technological acceptance, there is a lack of a common framework for comprehending AI adoption in talent acquisition due to varying viewpoints. To bridge this gap, this study identifies determining factors impacting AI adoption in talent recruiting using the Technology Acceptance paradigm (TAM) (Davis, 1989), a popular paradigm that describes how users come to accept and use technology. This study aims to determine how AI can streamline talent acquisition and improve business performance by saving time and cost.

1. How does AI affect workforce engagement, operational effectiveness, and decision-making in talent acquisition?
2. Which important variables, according to the Technology Acceptance Model (TAM), affect the use of AI in hiring?
3. How can businesses use AI to improve hiring and overall business performance through human resource management?

7. CHALLENGES AND ETHICAL CONSIDERATIONS

Embracing Artificial Intelligence (AI) in talent acquisition not only unlocks significant opportunities for efficiency, objectivity, and strategic decision-making but also paves the way for a future of enhanced recruitment processes. However, this journey is not without its challenges and ethical considerations, which we must address with a critical eye to ensure responsible implementation.

- **Bias and Discrimination: One** of the most pressing ethical concerns in AI-driven recruitment is the potential for algorithmic bias. Although AI systems are often promoted as neutral tools, they are trained on historical data that may reflect existing human prejudices or systemic inequalities. If not properly audited and corrected, AI can perpetuate or amplify these biases, leading to discriminatory hiring practices. For example, AI tools may unintentionally favor candidates based on gender, ethnicity, or educational background if these traits correlate with past hiring decisions. Ensuring fairness and equity requires transparent algorithms, regular bias testing, and inclusive data sets.
- **Lack of Transparency and Explainability**

AI models, particularly those based on deep learning, often function as 'black boxes,' making it challenging for HR professionals to comprehend the decision-making process. This lack of transparency presents significant ethical and practical challenges. However, by developing explainable AI (XAI) systems and providing stakeholders with understandable decision-making criteria, we can ensure that the process is transparent, and decisions are made fairly, thereby maintaining accountability.

- **Privacy and Data Security**

AI systems require vast amounts of personal and behavioral data to function effectively. This raises significant concerns regarding data privacy, consent, and security. Candidates may be unaware of how their data is being collected, stored, or analyzed, leading to breaches of trust and potential violations of data protection regulations. Organizations must implement robust data governance frameworks, ensure compliance with local and international laws (such as GDPR or Sri Lanka's Data Protection Act), and maintain informed consent protocols throughout recruitment.

- **Over-reliance on Automation**

The convenience of AI tools can lead to an over-reliance on automation, potentially diminishing the human element of recruitment. Critical soft skills, cultural fitness, and emotional intelligence are difficult to quantify and may be overlooked in highly automated systems. This can result in mechanistic and impersonal recruitment experiences, which may alienate candidates and reduce diversity. A hybrid model—where AI supports rather than replaces human judgment—is essential to maintain the integrity and effectiveness of talent acquisition.

- **Legal and Regulatory Uncertainty**

The regulatory landscape surrounding AI in recruitment is still evolving. Many jurisdictions lack clear guidelines on the ethical use of AI in employment contexts. This creates a gray area for organizations, increasing the risk of non-compliance and legal challenges. Companies operating in multiple regions must navigate varying legal frameworks and be prepared to adapt their practices to meet local standards.

- **Resistance to Change and Technostress**

Internally, HR professionals may resist adopting AI due to fear of job displacement or lack of technological fluency. This "technostress" can hinder effective implementation and reduce user engagement. Addressing these concerns requires comprehensive training, clear communication, and change management strategies emphasizing AI as a tool for augmentation rather than replacement.

The ethical implementation of AI in talent acquisition is not just a technical challenge, but a multidimensional issue that intersects with legal, social, and organizational dynamics. To address these challenges, we must adopt a balanced, human-centric approach that preserves human values while leveraging the strategic advantages of AI. As organizations in Sri Lanka and beyond continue to explore AI-driven recruitment, embedding ethical principles into the design and deployment of these systems will be crucial to fostering responsible innovation and sustainable success.

7. ADOPTION OF AI IN TALENT ACQUISITION: A GLOBAL AND LOCAL PERSPECTIVE

7.1 Trends and Adoption Rates Worldwide

With the development of the internet, especially AI technology, many organizations have transformed traditional talent acquisition to an online basis, facilitating job seekers' easy finding suitable jobs (Jatoba et al., 2023). Job seekers can explore opportunities at their convenience, while employers can efficiently recruit by accessing a pool of qualified candidates through transparent information disclosure. However, with the introduction of AI, many companies have begun integrating it into their recruitment processes, enhancing efficiency and accuracy in candidate selection.

A major change in how businesses handle their workforces is represented by the incorporation of Artificial Intelligence (AI) into Human Resource Management (HRM) (Du, 2024). The need for effective, data-driven HR strategies has never been greater in business contexts that are becoming more complicated and dynamic (Kim & Heo, 2022). AI technologies improve traditional HR functions, including recruitment, employee selection, performance management, and HR planning, and pave the way for a more efficient and effective future. The efficiency and cost savings of AI-based interviews make them a likely choice for future adoption (Kim & Heo, 2022).

By using AI in HRM, managers will behave less unethically and be more accountable and responsible when making AI-driven decisions. AI decision-making aims to advance fairness, openness, and confidence in HR procedures in addition to efficiency and cost savings. Better HRM results are the ultimate result of this (Rodgers et al., 2023; Pereira et al., 2023). It also impacts efficiency, cost savings, and higher-quality hires, enhancing overall HRM effectiveness (Albassam, 2023).

Competency and ease of use are the most influential factors in adopting and using Artificial Intelligence in Talent Acquisition. Talent Management is the strongest predictor of technology adoption, while its practical implementation is primarily driven by technology adoption within Information Technology companies (Vedapradha et al., 2023).

A proactive talent acquisition strategy, incorporating strategic workforce planning, employer branding, continuous talent pipelining, technological integration, skill development, collaboration with educational institutions, data-driven decision-making, and a commitment to diversity and inclusion, is not just a suggestion; it is a roadmap for ensuring long-term, sustainable success (Philip et al., 2024). It puts the power in your hands, allowing you to navigate the AI landscape with confidence and control.

7.2 Exploring AI Adoption in Talent Acquisition in Sri Lanka

7.2.1 Background

As artificial intelligence (AI) continues to redefine operational processes across industries, its application in human resource management, particularly in talent acquisition, has gained significant attention. In Sri Lanka, where technological adoption is steadily increasing, understanding the factors influencing AI integration in recruitment processes is essential. This case study presents findings from an empirical investigation into how HR professionals in Sri Lanka are approaching AI adoption in talent acquisition. The study employed a cross-sectional design using a survey-based data collection method. To ensure relevance and depth of insight, a purposive sampling technique was utilized. Participants were selected based on their active involvement in recruitment and demonstrated knowledge of AI-driven practices within their organizations. This approach ensured that the data collected reflected informed perspectives aligned with the study's objectives.

7.2.3 Theoretical Integration

The findings from this study closely align with and expand upon the Technology Acceptance Model (TAM) introduced by Davis (1989), which posits that *perceived ease of use (PEOU)* and *perceived usefulness (PU)* are primary determinants of technology adoption. This theoretical framework has been widely validated across multiple domains, including digital systems, e-commerce, and e-learning platforms (Alalwan et al., 2017; Vedapradha et al., 2024), and proves equally relevant in the context of AI-driven recruitment in Sri Lanka.

7.2.4 Empirical Insights

As illustrated in **Fig. 1**, the study confirms a strong positive relationship between PEOU and PU, reinforcing the notion that when AI systems are perceived as intuitive and user-friendly, they are more likely to be seen as beneficial by HR professionals. This supports the foundational TAM premise that ease of use significantly enhances perceptions of useful relationship, consistently demonstrated in contemporary technology adoption research.

Figure 1. Factors Affecting AI Adoption in Talent Acquisition in Sri Lanka

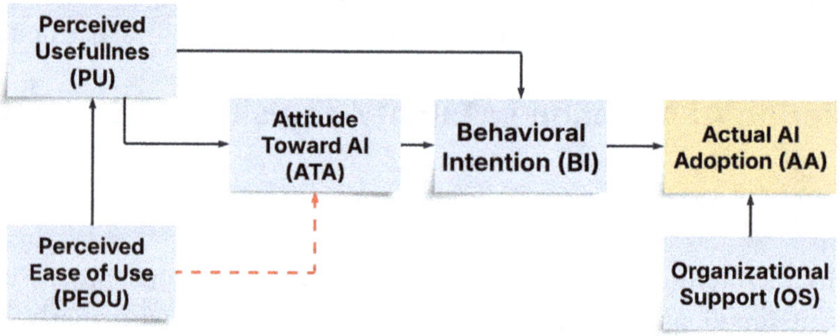

Source: *Author's creation*

Furthermore, the analysis reveals that perceived usefulness (PU) exerts a substantial influence on both attitude toward adoption (ATA) and behavioral intention (BI). This finding underscores the pivotal role of perceived benefits in fostering positive user perceptions and driving commitment to adopt AI in talent acquisition. These results echo the work of Mohan et al. (2024), who highlighted usability as a key predictor of adoption intention and align with findings by Abaddi (2025) in the context of micro, small, and medium enterprises (MSMEs) in Jordan.

More critically, PU emerged as a central determinant of both ATA and BI. The data confirm that individuals who perceive AI as useful are more inclined to develop favorable attitudes and stronger intentions to adopt it. These insights are aligned with Mohan et al. (2024), who identified usability and performance value as key drivers of adoption intent, and with Abaddi (2025), whose research in Jordan's MSMEs also emphasized the centrality of perceived benefit.

In addition, ATA significantly mediates the relationship between PU and BI, affirming TAM's assertion that favorable attitudes translate into greater adoption intent. This mediating role underscores the psychological process through which perceived benefits are internalized and transformed into intention.

7.2.5 Challenging the Model

Interestingly, there is no direct influence of PEOU on ATA. This divergence from traditional TAM findings adds a critical nuance to the model's application in AI contexts. It suggests that ease of use, while influential in shaping perceived usefulness, does not independently shape attitudes toward AI adoption in recruitment. This deviation aligns with recent literature suggesting that users' attitudes toward AI are shaped more by performance outcomes, trustworthiness, and strategic alignment than by ease of interface alone (Dwivedi et al., 2021). In high-capability technologies like AI, users prioritize utility, predictive accuracy, and efficiency over simplicity. As Rai and Selnes (2019) argue, the perceived value of advanced technologies is often assessed through outcome expectancy rather than usability.

This pattern may be explained by the indirect role of PEOU, whereby ease of use enhances PU, which in turn influences ATA. Saif et al. (2024) reported similar findings, suggesting that users need tangible demonstrations of value before usability affects their attitude. Thus, in the AI recruitment context, ease of use acts more as a facilitator than a direct driver of acceptance.

7.2.6 Organizational Influence: Beyond Individual Perceptions

The most notable deviation from classical TAM lies in the determinants of actual adoption (AA). Although BI was found to exert a modest yet significant effect on

AA, the strongest predictor was organizational support (OS). This insight affirms the critical role of organizational infrastructure, leadership advocacy, and strategic alignment in ensuring successful implementation. These findings are consistent with Abaddi (2025) and Black & Ferolie (2018), who emphasized the importance of organizational readiness and contextual enablers in digital transformation efforts. It also aligns with the Unified Theory of Acceptance and Use of Technology (UTAUT) proposed by Venkatesh et al. (2016), which integrates *facilitating conditions* as a key predictor of usage behavior.

8. CONCLUSION AND FUTURE DIRECTIONS

This case study contributes to ongoing efforts to extend the TAM framework to better accommodate the complexities of AI adoption. While PEOU, PU, and ATA remain important, they must be situated within broader organizational and contextual realities. The integration of organizational support into adoption models is no longer optional, it is essential for both theoretical robustness and practical relevance.

Future research should focus on building integrated models that examine the dynamic interplay between individual cognition and organizational factors. This involves going beyond TAM's traditional constructs to include factors such as trust in AI, data governance, change management, and leadership commitment. Such work will offer richer insights into the socio-technical dynamics of AI adoption and inform more effective strategies for technology implementation in human resource management and beyond.

REFERENCES

Abaddi, S. (2025). Factors and moderators influencing artificial intelligence adoption by Jordanian MSMEs. *Management & Sustainability: An Arab Review, 4*(1), 47–73. DOI: 10.1108/MSAR-10-2023-0049

Abdelhay, S., AlTalay, M. S. R., Selim, N., Altamimi, A. A., Hassan, D., Elbannany, M., & Marie, A. (2025). The impact of generative AI (ChatGPT) on recruitment efficiency and candidate quality: The mediating role of process automation level and the moderating role of organizational size. *Frontiers in Human Dynamics, 6*, 1487671. DOI: 10.3389/fhumd.2024.1487671

Abraham, S., Paripoornam, R., & Sharma, G. (2025). The role of artificial intelligence in recruitment and talent acquisition—An empirical study. *Journal of Informatics Education and Research, 5*(1).

Ajunwa, I. (2019). The paradox of automation as anti-bias intervention. *Cardozo Law Review, 41*, 1671.

Alalwan, A. A., Dwivedi, Y. K., Rana, N. P., & Williams, M. D. (2016). Consumer adoption of mobile banking in Jordan: Examining the role of usefulness, ease of use, perceived risk, and self-efficacy. *Journal of Enterprise Information Management, 29*(1), 118–139. DOI: 10.1108/JEIM-04-2015-0035

Albassam, W. A. (2023). The power of artificial intelligence in recruitment: An analytical review of current AI-based recruitment strategies. *International Journal of Professional Business Review, 8*(6), e02089. DOI: 10.26668/businessreview/2023.v8i6.2089

Badouch, M., Boutaounte, M., Zioudi, O., & Mahmoud, H. (2025). The Future of Travel: A Review of Chatbot Recommender Systems in E-Tourism and Smart Tourism. In: Aboudrar, I., Ilahi Bakhsh, F., Nayyar, A., Ouachtouk, I. (eds) *Innovative Technologies on Electrical Power Systems for Smart Cities Infrastructure*. ICESST 2024. Sustainable Civil Infrastructures. Springer, Cham. DOI: 10.1007/978-3-031-86705-7_10

Bag, S., Dhamija, P., Pretorius, J. H. C., Chowdhury, A. H., & Giannakis, M. (2022). Sustainable electronic human resource management systems and firm performance: An empirical study. *International Journal of Manpower, 43*(1), 32–51. DOI: 10.1108/IJM-02-2021-0099

Black, J. S., & van Esch, P. (2020). AI-enabled recruiting: What is it and how should a manager use it? *Business Horizons, 63*(2), 215–226. DOI: 10.1016/j.bushor.2019.12.001

Chapman, D. S., & Gödöllei, A. F. (2017). E-recruiting: Using technology to attract job applicants. In *The Wiley Blackwell Handbook of the Psychology of the Internet at Work* (pp. 211–230). Wiley.

Davis, F. D. (1989). Perceived usefulness, perceived ease of use, and user acceptance of information technology. *Management Information Systems Quarterly, 13*(3), 319–340. DOI: 10.2307/249008

Du, J. (2024). Exploring gender bias and algorithm transparency: Ethical considerations of AI in HRM. *Journal of Theory and Practice of Management Science.*

Dwivedi, Y. K., Hughes, L., Ismagilova, E., Aarts, G., Coombs, C., Crick, T., Duan, Y., ... (2021). Artificial intelligence (AI): Multidisciplinary perspectives on emerging challenges, opportunities, and agenda for research, practice, and policy. *International Journal of Information Management, 57*, 101994. El Khoury (Ed.), *Anticipating future business trends: Navigating artificial intelligence innovations* (Vol. 535, pp. 1–14). Springer, Cham.

Islam, M., Rahman, M. M., Taher, M. A., Quaosar, G. M., & Uddin, M. A. (2024). Using artificial intelligence for hiring talents in a moderated mechanism. *Future Business Journal, 10*(1), 1–16. DOI: 10.1186/s43093-024-00303-x

Jatoba, M. N., Ferreira, J. J., Fernandes, P. O., & Teixeira, J. P. (2023). Intelligent human resources for the adoption of artificial intelligence: A systematic literature review. *Journal of Organizational Change Management, 36*(7), 1099–1124. DOI: 10.1108/JOCM-03-2022-0075

Kim, J.-Y., & Heo, W. (2022). Artificial intelligence video interviewing for employment: Perspectives from applicants, companies, developers, and academicians. *Information Technology & People, 35*(3), 861–878. DOI: 10.1108/ITP-04-2019-0173

Leutner, F., Akhtar, R., & Chamorro-Premuzic, T. (2022). Talent and the Data Science Revolution. In The Future of Recruitment: Using the New Science of Talent Analytics to Get Your Hiring Right (pp. 17-50). Emerald Publishing Limited. DOI: 10.1108/978-1-83867-559-220221002

Parasa, S. K. (2024). Impact of AI in recruitment and talent acquisition. *Human Resource and Leadership Journal, 9*(1), 45–60.

Pereira, V., Hadjielias, E., Christofi, M., & Vrontis, D. (2023). A systematic literature review on the impact of artificial intelligence on workplace outcomes: A multi-process perspective. *Human Resource Management Review, 33*(1), 100857. DOI: 10.1016/j.hrmr.2021.100857

Philip, B., Mathew, G. A., Sebastian, R. T., Eshwari, B., Roopa, M. B., & Mathews, S. B. (2024). Strategizing talent acquisition for fostering future workforce success: Addressing millennial turnover and hiring challenges in a rapidly evolving business landscape. In R.

Rai, R. S., & Selnes, F. (2019). Conceptualizing task-technology fit and the effect on adoption–A case study of a digital textbook service. *Information & Management, 56*(8), 103161. DOI: 10.1016/j.im.2019.04.004

Rodgers, W., Murray, J. M., Stefanidis, A., Degbey, W. Y., & Tarba, S. Y. (2023). An artificial intelligence algorithmic approach to ethical decision-making in human resource management processes. *Human Resource Management Review, 33*(1), 100925. DOI: 10.1016/j.hrmr.2022.100925

Rogers, E. M. (1995). Diffusion of Innovations: Modifications of a Model for Telecommunications. In Stoetzer, M. W., & Mahler, A. (Eds.), *Die Diffusion von Innovationen in der Telekommunikation. Schriftenreihe des Wissenschaftlichen Instituts für Kommunikationsdienste* (Vol. 17). Springer. DOI: 10.1007/978-3-642-79868-9_2

Saif, N., Khan, S. U., Shaheen, I., ALotaibi, F. A., Alnfiai, M. M., & Arif, M. (2024). Chat-GPT; validating technology acceptance model (TAM) in education sector via ubiquitous learning mechanism. *Computers in Human Behavior, 154*, 108097. DOI: 10.1016/j.chb.2023.108097

Sathyaseelan, D. D., & Siva, D. S. (2024). Role of Artificial Intelligence in Reshaping the Human Resource Practices. *Educational Administration: Theory And Practice, 30*(4), 354–359.

Upadhyay, A. K., & Khandelwal, K. (2018). Applying artificial intelligence: Implications for recruitment. *Strategic HR Review, 17*(5), 255–258. DOI: 10.1108/SHR-07-2018-0051

Van Esch, P., Black, J. S., & Ferolie, J. (2019). Marketing AI recruitment: The next phase in job application and selection. *Computers in Human Behavior, 90*, 215–222. DOI: 10.1016/j.chb.2018.09.009

Vedapradha, R., Hariharan, R., Praveenraj, D. D., Sudha, E., & Ashok, J. (2023). Talent acquisition—Artificial intelligence to manage recruitment. *E3S Web of Conferences, 376*, 05001.

Venkatesh, V., Morris, M. G., Davis, G. B., & Davis, F. D. (2003). User acceptance of information technology: Toward a unified view. *Management Information Systems Quarterly, 27*(3), 425–478. DOI: 10.2307/30036540

Chapter 5
Teaching Methods for AI-Driven HR Practices

P. Venkadesh
https://orcid.org/0000-0001-6582-3153
V.S.B College of Engineering Technical Campus, Coimbatore, India

R. Mathusoothana S. Kumar
Noorul Islam Centre for Higher Education, Kumaracoil, India

L. Shalini
Bharath Institute of Higher Education and Research, Chennai, India

S.V. Divya
https://orcid.org/0009-0004-4321-8066
V.S.B College of Engineering Technical Campus, Coimbatore, India

R. Sukesh
V.S.B College of Engineering Technical Campus, Coimbatore, India

ABSTRACT

Using Artificial Intelligence (AI) in Human Resources (HR) has completely changed HR work. Now, decisions about managing workers are smarter and based on data. AI uses tools like machine learning, predictive analysis, and natural language processing, and these are key for recruitment, keeping employees satisfied, managing talent, and organizational planning. So, how we teach HR professionals also needs to change. This chapter talks about new teaching methods focused on AI in HR. It highlights learning from different areas, hands-on learning, and thinking about ethics. It offers a detailed plan for what should go into teaching materials, the key skills needed, and includes practical tools, real-world examples, and ways to test

DOI: 10.4018/979-8-3373-6516-9.ch005

understanding. The goal is to help teachers and students create and run programs that fit the changing HR field. By doing this, future HR leaders will be well-prepared for a workplace driven by data and digital technology.

1. INTRODUCTION

In today's fast-evolving digital landscape, Artificial Intelligence (AI) is transforming how organizations identify, evaluate, and hire talent. Among all Human Resource (HR) functions, recruitment and talent acquisition have experienced the most rapid and impactful integration of AI technologies. From automated resume screening and candidate scoring to AI-driven interviews and predictive hiring analytics, modern recruitment processes are becoming faster, data-informed, and increasingly complex. As these changes unfold, there is a growing demand for HR professionals who are not only fluent in people management but also adept at navigating intelligent recruitment systems. The traditional approach to teaching HR must be reimagined to reflect these industry realities. Educational institutions and training providers now face the critical responsibility of equipping learners with both the technical skills and ethical judgment required to work with AI in recruitment.

This chapter specifically explores effective teaching methods for preparing students, educators, and professionals to engage with AI-based recruitment tools and platforms. It emphasizes the design of interdisciplinary curricula that integrate recruitment-specific AI applications such as Natural Language Processing (NLP) for resume parsing, machine learning algorithms for candidate ranking, and AI-powered video interview assessments.

In addition to the technical dimensions, the chapter highlights the importance of ethical practices in recruitment technology. Topics such as algorithmic bias, fairness audits, and data privacy are discussed as essential learning objectives within an AI-enhanced recruitment curriculum. To bridge theory and practice, the chapter outlines pedagogical strategies such as case-based learning, real-world simulations, and project-based assignments focused on AI in hiring. It also provides practical examples of how to structure training programs and integrate industry tools like HireVue, Pymetrics, and Eightfold AI.

By the end of this chapter, educators will be equipped with a comprehensive teaching framework designed to prepare the next generation of HR professionals for the challenges and opportunities of AI-powered recruitment. This future-ready approach ensures that learners are not just tech-savvy but also ethically grounded, strategically aware, and human-centered in their application of AI within the hiring lifecycle.

Research Gap and Original Contribution

Despite the growing use of AI in hiring, there is limited research on how to teach AI-based recruitment tools and techniques in structured learning environments. While prior studies have explored the application of AI in Recruitment functions and the evolving role of HR professionals, few have systematically addressed how to teach these emerging competencies within structured academic and corporate learning environments. Most existing literature focuses either on AI technology or Recruitment practice in isolation. This chapter fills a critical gap by presenting an integrated framework that combines pedagogy, curriculum design, technology tools, and ethical governance specifically for AI-driven HR education. It also introduces original pedagogical strategies and interdisciplinary curriculum models that can be directly implemented by educators, making it both practically relevant and academically significant.

2. LITERATURE SURVEY

Human Resource Management (HRM) is undergoing rapid transformation through the integration of Artificial Intelligence (AI). Traditionally rooted in personal judgment and manual processes, HR has now become increasingly driven by intelligent systems and data-centric decision-making. Early uses of AI focused on administrative tasks such as resume screening, applicant tracking, and interview scheduling, significantly improving efficiency and freeing HR professionals to focus on strategic initiatives (Tambe, Cappelli, & Yakubovich, 2019; Bessen, 2018).

Today, the capabilities of AI have evolved. Modern tools now support advanced functions like employee attrition prediction, performance forecasting, leadership assessment, and succession planning (Daugherty & Wilson, 2018; Eubanks, 2018). In recruitment specifically, platforms such as HireVue, Eightfold AI, and Pymetrics are being used to evaluate resumes, assess candidate fit, and conduct AI-analyzed interviews (Chamorro-Premuzic, Winsborough, Sherman, & Hogan, 2016; Raghavan, Barocas, Kleinberg, & Levy, 2020). These tools not only improve process speed but also enable data-driven decisions and pattern recognition that humans might overlook.

Despite these advancements, the adoption of AI in HR has faced cultural and ethical barriers. Concerns about fairness, loss of empathy, transparency, and algorithmic bias have made many HR professionals hesitant to rely on AI (Yanamala, K. K. R., 2023; Robert et al., 2020). However, the perception is gradually changing. AI is increasingly seen as an augmenting partner—enhancing human judgment rather than replacing it (Eubanks, 2018; Bessen, 2018).

Academic interest in AI for HR has grown significantly. Research is increasingly grounded in behavioral science and ethics. Theories such as bounded rationality and expectancy theory are used to assess how AI alters decision-making and employee experience (Pratama, M. P et al, 2023; Ghosh & Scott, 2023). Simultaneously, AI demands new professional competencies—ranging from data literacy and digital fluency to ethical reasoning and algorithmic auditing (Gelinas, Sadreddin, & Vahidov, 2022; Ng, 2019).

In response to these evolving demands, educational institutions are revising HR curricula to include training in AI technologies, recruitment analytics, and responsible data practices (UNESCO, 2022; Gonzalez-Gonzalez & Jiménez-Zarco, 2023). Pedagogical strategies such as project-based learning and AI tool simulations are now being used to train students for AI-integrated HR roles (Pisica et al., 2023; Bates et al., 2020). Some studies stress the importance of incorporating generative AI in hiring and instructional design (Choi, Kim, Lee, & Moon, 2024), while others highlight the need for digital equity and fairness audits in candidate evaluation (Delcker et al., 2024).

Still, challenges persist. Issues like algorithmic bias, lack of explainability, privacy concerns, and a significant digital skills gap among HR professionals continue to limit AI's full integration (Raghavan et al., 2020; Qiu & Zhao, 2019). Recent studies point out that many HR professionals feel underprepared to use AI tools effectively (Ng, 2019; Chiu et al., 2023), and call for structured training programs that blend ethical awareness with hands-on technical practice.

Ultimately, AI is redefining what it means to work in HR. It's no longer just a tool for automation—it is a strategic asset that informs hiring, enhances decision-making, and shapes the future of work. The next generation of HR professionals must be capable of blending human insight with machine intelligence—thoughtfully, responsibly, and inclusively (Crompton & Burke, 2024).

3. UNDERSTANDING AI IN HUMAN RESOURCES

Artificial Intelligence (AI) in Human Resource (HR) management is no longer a futuristic concept but a present reality transforming how organizations attract, manage, retain, and engage talent. For educators aiming to equip learners with relevant and impactful HR knowledge, understanding AI's scope and application is vital. AI technologies are increasingly being leveraged to automate repetitive administrative tasks, analyse large volumes of data for strategic decision-making, and enhance the overall employee experience. A foundational understanding of key AI types—such as Machine Learning (ML), Natural Language Processing (NLP), Robotic Process Automation (RPA), and Predictive Analytics—is essential. ML is used to learn from historical data and predict outcomes such as employee attrition or engagement. NLP interprets and analyses text from resumes, chatbot interactions, and feedback forms, while RPA streamlines rule-based processes like payroll and onboarding. Predictive analytics aids in forecasting hiring needs, performance trajectories, and potential turnover.

The practical applications of AI span multiple HR functions. In recruitment and selection, AI systems can efficiently scan thousands of resumes based on predefined metrics, and platforms like HireVue and Pymetrics utilize ML and NLP to assess candidate suitability through voice tone, facial expressions, and responses. During onboarding, AI-driven chatbots assist new employees by answering FAQs and streamlining documentation, thus improving the onboarding experience. AI also plays a crucial role in gauging employee engagement by analysing sentiment from emails, surveys, and internal communications. In performance management, smart dashboards consolidate real-time data to personalize development plans. For learning and development, AI curates customized training paths based on identified skill gaps. Furthermore, workforce planning is enhanced through predictive modelling, enabling accurate forecasting of headcount requirements and succession plans. The benefits of AI integration in HR are multifaceted. It significantly boosts efficiency by automating screening, onboarding, and routine data entry tasks.

It fosters personalization in development programs and internal communication. Data-driven insights improve decision accuracy and reduce bias, while automation drives cost savings by reducing manual workload. Moreover, AI enhances employee retention by identifying early warning signs and recommending timely interventions. However, these advantages come with ethical and legal challenges. Algorithms trained on biased datasets may inadvertently reinforce existing inequalities, and black-box models may lack transparency in decision-making. Additionally, managing sensitive employee data necessitates strict compliance with regulations such as the General Data Protection Regulation (GDPR). Educators must therefore not only teach how to use AI tools but also emphasize critical evaluation to ensure ethical usage and regulatory adherence.

Diagram: AI Applications in HR Life Cycle

The Artificial Intelligence Applications in Human Resource Life as shown in Figure 1

Figure 1. AI Applications in HR Life Cycle

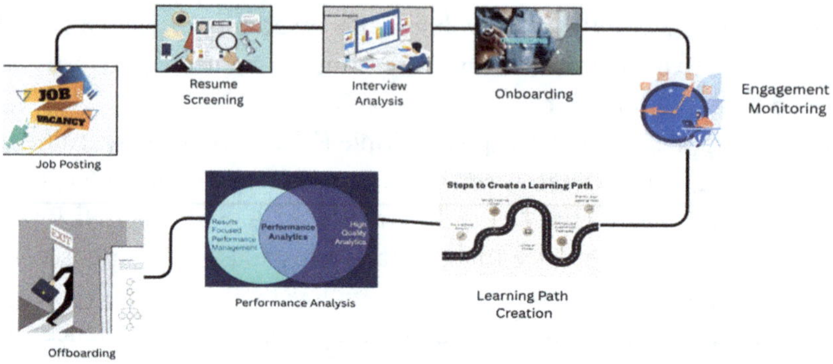

4. CORE COMPETENCIES FOR AI-DRIVEN HR PRACTICES

The integration of Artificial Intelligence (AI) into recruitment is not just changing how candidates are sourced and selected—it is redefining what it means to be an effective HR professional in the digital age. As AI systems become central to resume screening, candidate assessment, and interview analytics, HR practitioners must develop a distinct set of competencies that blend technical fluency with human-centric judgment.

To prepare students and professionals for AI-enhanced talent acquisition roles, educational programs must prioritize the following four core competency domains:

A. Technical Proficiency in AI-Based Hiring Tools

Professionals must gain hands-on experience with AI recruitment platforms such as HireVue, Pymetrics, Eightfold AI, and X0PA AI. Understanding how these tools use Natural Language Processing (NLP), video analytics, and machine learning to score candidates is crucial. Students should be able to:

- Analyze and interpret AI-generated hiring recommendations.
- Configure and test resume screening models.
- Work with datasets to build simple predictive hiring algorithms.

Educators can support this through lab-based activities, sandbox tools, and mock recruitment campaigns.

B. Ethical and Legal Literacy in Algorithmic Hiring

With AI influencing who gets shortlisted or rejected, it is essential that future HR professionals understand the ethical implications of automated decision-making. Competencies in this area include:

- Identifying algorithmic bias in candidate scoring systems.
- Understanding legal frameworks such as EEOC guidelines and GDPR as they relate to hiring data.
- Conducting fairness audits on hiring algorithms. Simulation-based learning, legal case reviews, and role-playing scenarios can help students build responsible hiring mindsets.

C. Data Literacy for Recruitment Analytics

AI in recruitment depends heavily on structured and unstructured data—from resumes and social media to interview transcripts and assessment scores. Learners should develop:

- Skills to clean, structure, and analyze candidate data.
- Proficiency in tools like Excel, Power BI, or Python for recruitment analytics.
- An understanding of key metrics like time-to-hire, candidate quality index, and conversion rates. Capstone projects using anonymized applicant datasets can foster applied learning in this area.

D. Human-Centered Design and Candidate Experience

Despite automation, recruitment remains a deeply human process. AI should be used to enhance not replace human interaction. Key competencies here include:

- Designing recruitment workflows that blend AI tools with personal touchpoints.
- Ensuring inclusive, empathetic candidate experiences in digital environments.
- Advocating for transparency and fairness in every stage of AI-assisted hiring.

Teaching methods such as empathy mapping, diversity-centered recruitment simulations, and feedback loop analysis help develop this mindset.

These four domains form a competency matrix that can guide curriculum developers, instructors, and learners in building meaningful, career-ready skill sets for the AI-driven recruitment era. By ensuring that technical training is balanced with ethical awareness and people-first thinking, we can prepare future professionals to shape recruitment systems that are intelligent, inclusive, and impact-driven.

Diagram: Core Competencies Matrix

The Competencies of AI-Driven in Human Resources as shown in Figure 2.

Figure 2. Core Competencies Matrix

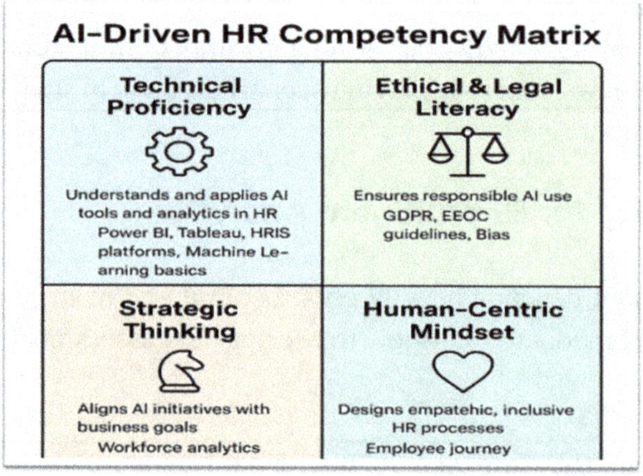

5. CURRICULUM DESIGN FOR AI-DRIVEN RECRUITMENT EDUCATION

As recruitment becomes more data-centric and technology-driven, academic institutions and corporate training programs must reconfigure their curricula to meet the demands of AI-powered talent acquisition. Traditional HR syllabi are no longer sufficient to prepare professionals for systems that analyze resumes using Natural Language Processing (NLP), conduct AI-enabled video interviews, or recommend candidates using machine learning models.

This section outlines a strategic, layered curriculum design tailored to developing competencies specifically for AI-integrated recruitment.

A. Curriculum Objectives

An AI-driven recruitment curriculum should be anchored in the following objectives:

1. Build foundational understanding of AI technologies used in hiring.
2. Train learners in hands-on application of recruitment-specific AI tools.
3. Foster ethical awareness in automated candidate selection processes.
4. Prepare students to lead AI-based hiring initiatives in real-world organizations.

B. Core Modules and Course Topics

The proposed curriculum may span a 12–16-week course and include the following core modules:

- **Week 1–2: Introduction to AI in Recruitment**

Topics: AI trends in HR, automation in hiring, overview of modern recruitment platforms.

- **Week 3–4: Tools and Technologies for AI Hiring**

Tools: HireVue, Pymetrics, LinkedIn Recruiter Insights, Eightfold AI.
Activities: Tool demos, platform walkthroughs, sandbox exercises.

- **Week 5–6: Data-Driven Recruitment and Predictive Hiring**

Topics: Resume parsing, candidate scoring models, prediction of job-fit and attrition risk.
Tools: Python, Google Colab, Kaggle datasets.
Projects: Build and test a simple candidate ranking model.

- **Week 7–8: Ethics and Bias in AI Recruitment**

Topics: Algorithmic fairness, transparency, legal compliance (EEOC, GDPR).
Activities: Case discussions, fairness audits, AI black-box deconstruction.

- **Week 9–10: Designing AI-Enabled Recruitment Pipelines**

Topics: Blending automation with human judgment, candidate experience, diversity analytics.
Capstone: Redesign a recruitment process using AI tools.

- **Week 11–12: Industry Exposure and Tool Integration**

Activities: Guest lectures, live recruitment challenges, mock AI interviews.

- **Week 13–14: Final Capstone Project**

Deliverable: End-to-end AI recruitment plan—tool integration, data pipeline, ethical review.

C. Teaching and Learning Formats

- **Blended Learning:** Mix of video lectures, interactive labs, and live tool demonstrations.
- **Project-Based Assignments:** Students design AI hiring workflows and defend their ethical reasoning.
- **Simulation Labs:** Practice candidate screening, interview evaluation, and resume parsing using real AI platforms.
- **Peer Review and Reflection:** Encourage collaborative learning and ethical self-assessment.

D. Assessment Criteria

Student performance should be evaluated on:

- Technical accuracy in using AI recruitment tools.
- Analytical reasoning in interpreting candidate data.
- Ethical rigor in decision-making.
- Communication of AI outcomes to non-technical stakeholders.

Competency-based rubrics aligned with industry expectations will ensure that learners are assessed for job readiness, not just academic understanding.

E. Curriculum Adaptability and Scalability

Given the pace of technological change, the curriculum should be reviewed and updated annually. New topics such as:

- **Generative AI in job description design**
- **Voice and facial expression analysis in interviews**
- **AI-supported DEI hiring initiatives** can be introduced through modular formats, micro-credentials, or short bootcamps.

By embedding recruitment-specific content, tools, and ethics throughout the curriculum, institutions can ensure their learners are not only AI-literate, but truly recruitment-ready.

A visual framework aligning curriculum levels with AI-Recruitment Education competencies is shown in Figure 3.

Figure 3. AI-HR Curriculum Framework showing layered progression of AI competencies from foundational knowledge to advanced strategic applications in HR education.

Educators are encouraged to incorporate project-based learning, guest speakers from industry, and co-designed learning modules to ensure relevance and applicability. Regular content updates and alignment with industry standards help maintain course integrity and long-term impact. A curriculum built on these principles can produce HR professionals who are not only technologically competent but also ethically grounded and strategically prepared for the evolving demands of AI-enhanced workplaces.

This aligns with recent research that highlights the critical role of interdisciplinary frameworks in AI-focused higher education to enhance scalability and global relevance (Gonzalez-Gonzalez & Jiménez-Zarco, 2023).

Teaching Methods and Pedagogical Approaches for AI-Enabled Recruitment Training

Delivering education in AI-driven recruitment demands more than lectures on algorithms—it requires immersive, experiential strategies that bridge theory and industry practice. As organizations increasingly adopt tools like HireVue, Pymetrics, and Eightfold AI for hiring, educators must integrate these technologies into instructional design to prepare learners for real-world talent acquisition environments.

The following pedagogical approaches are designed to cultivate both the technical and ethical competencies essential in AI-powered recruitment.

Project-Based Learning (PBL)

Project-Based Learning engages students in solving real-world recruitment problems using AI tools. Sample projects may include:

- Designing an AI-enabled resume screening system using open-source datasets.
- Creating bias mitigation strategies for candidate scoring algorithms.
- Prototyping a chatbot that handles initial candidate queries and pre-screening.

These projects promote critical thinking, collaboration, and tool fluency.

Case-Based and Scenario Learning

Students analyze real-world case studies from companies like:

- Unilever, which uses Pymetrics and HireVue for gamified AI interviews.
- Accenture, which built internal AI tools for workforce planning and internal hiring.

Using structured frameworks, learners evaluate recruitment outcomes, identify ethical risks, and propose improvements. Cases may also include failed or controversial deployments, prompting students to critique AI implementation from technical, legal, and human-centric perspectives.

Simulation and Role-Playing Exercises

Simulations offer learners hands-on experiences with recruitment workflows. For example:

- Mock hiring scenarios where students act as HR professionals using AI platforms to screen applicants.
- Role-plays between candidates and AI-driven chatbots (e.g., Tobi by Vodafone) to assess usability, inclusivity, and transparency.

These exercises help students connect technology with empathy and decision-making.

Flipped Classroom Model

Instructors deliver pre-class content—such as videos on AI tools, ethics primers, or company demos—through LMS platforms. Classroom time is then dedicated to:

- Live tool explorations (e.g., running a resume parser in real time).
- Ethical debates on algorithmic fairness.
- Group presentations on AI hiring strategies.

This approach increases student engagement and promotes active learning.

AI Hackathons and Design Sprints

Short, intensive events allow students to build rapid solutions for recruitment challenges, such as:

- Automating candidate pre-screening using sentiment analysis.
- Designing a dashboard to predict employee fit based on historical hiring data.

Mentored by faculty and industry professionals, these events simulate the fast-paced innovation environments of real HR tech teams.

Reflective and Ethical Learning Activities

To ensure learners do not become "tech-only" thinkers, reflective tasks are essential. These may include:

- Weekly learning journals analyzing AI recruitment tools from the perspective of fairness and privacy.
- Critical essays comparing traditional hiring with AI-powered methods.
- Ethical audits of mock recruitment pipelines.

This cultivates a deeper awareness of the impact of AI on candidate experience and workforce diversity.

Collaborative Industry Engagement

Invite guest speakers from HR tech companies and organize live sessions where students:

- Interact with recruiters using AI systems in real roles.
- Test enterprise recruitment tools in sandbox environments.
- Participate in feedback sessions from professionals on their capstone hiring projects.

This closes the gap between academia and the fast-changing AI recruitment industry.

By combining technology-enabled, reflective, and industry-informed pedagogical practices, this approach ensures that learners are not only proficient in AI tools but also equipped to lead recruitment processes with ethical integrity and human-centered insight.

These relationships are illustrated in the integrated pedagogical strategy model shown in Figure 4.

Figure 4. Integrated Pedagogical Strategy Model connecting instructional methods—flipped classroom, project-based learning, simulations, reflective journals, and industry mentoring—to competency development in AI-HR education.

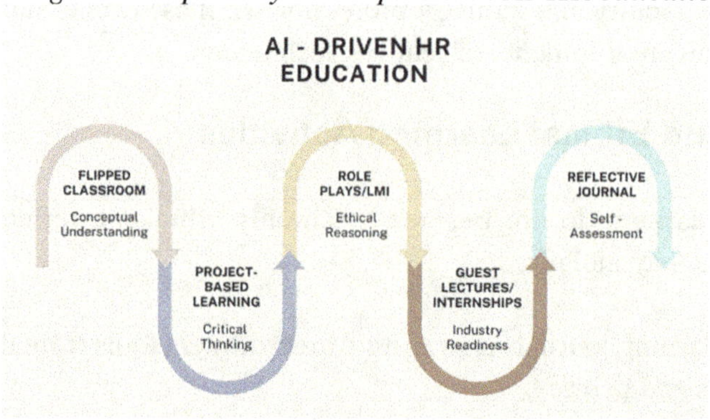

6. PRACTICAL IMPLEMENTATION OF AI-ENABLED RECRUITMENT EDUCATION IN CLASSROOM AND TRAINING PROGRAMS

To effectively prepare learners for AI-enhanced hiring, classroom instruction must move beyond theory and offer structured, technology-integrated, hands-on training. Practical implementation bridges the gap between academic learning and real-world recruitment needs, equipping students to use AI tools responsibly and effectively throughout the hiring lifecycle.

Technology-Enabled Learning Environments

Bridging the gap between academic knowledge and workplace readiness in AI-driven HR education requires a strategic and well-resourced approach. A key component is creating a technology-ready classroom environment. Smart classrooms equipped with high-speed internet, cloud-based AI tools, and HR-specific software such as IBM Watson and SAP SuccessFactors foster interactive and immersive learning experiences. These tools allow students to directly engage with the technologies they will use in the workplace, building both confidence and competence. Flexible course delivery models, including blended learning, further enhance this strategy. By combining online theory modules with in-person, practical workshops, students benefit from the flexibility of asynchronous learning while applying concepts in hands-on settings. Modular formats and micro-credentials offer tailored learning paths that align with individual interests and career goals, while bootcamps and intensive workshops provide fast-paced upskilling opportunities for working professionals.

Experiential and Applied Learning

At the heart of impactful AI-HR education are hands-on exercises and project-based learning. Students engage with real-world tools like LinkedIn Recruiter Insights and Eightfold AI through interactive labs and assignments. Using anonymized datasets, they develop essential skills in ethical data analysis and AI application within HR contexts. Simulated environments replicate actual HR decision-making processes, offering learners practical exposure to strategic dilemmas and ethical challenges. Building on these experiences, capstone projects serve as a comprehensive application of acquired knowledge. Students design and prototype AI-driven HR solutions, integrating technical, ethical, and strategic competencies. These projects are evaluated by both academic faculty and industry professionals, ensuring alignment with real-world expectations and giving students critical feedback from experienced practitioners.

Industry Integration and Professional Exposure

Industry engagement plays a pivotal role in preparing students for the dynamic AI-HR landscape. Guest lectures, live project collaborations, and field visits offer firsthand insights into the practical applications and challenges of AI in modern HR settings. These experiences help bridge the gap between classroom learning and industry practice, exposing students to emerging trends and professional workflows. To support continuous relevance in a rapidly evolving field, ongoing skill development is crucial. Students are encouraged to pursue Massive Open Online Courses (MOOCs), online certifications, and participate in professional networks such as SHRM and AIHR. These opportunities not only help learners stay current but also enhance their employability and professional credibility.

Evaluation, Feedback, and Future Readiness

To ensure the success and sustainability of AI-HR educational programs, institutions must implement robust evaluation and feedback mechanisms. Regular feedback from students enables adaptive improvements to course design, content delivery, and teaching methodologies. Competency-based assessments, focused on real-world problem-solving, validate students' readiness to lead AI-driven initiatives within HR departments. These assessments emphasize the practical application of knowledge, ensuring graduates are not only technically proficient but also capable of ethical reasoning and strategic decision-making. By aligning curriculum design, innovative pedagogy, and practical implementation, institutions can cultivate a new generation of HR leaders—professionals who are technologically fluent, ethically aware, and equipped to navigate and drive AI-powered transformation in the human resources domain.

The AI-Driven Workflow for Classroom and Training Program Enhancement as shown in Figure 5

Figure 5. AI-Driven Workflow for Classroom and Training Program Enhancement

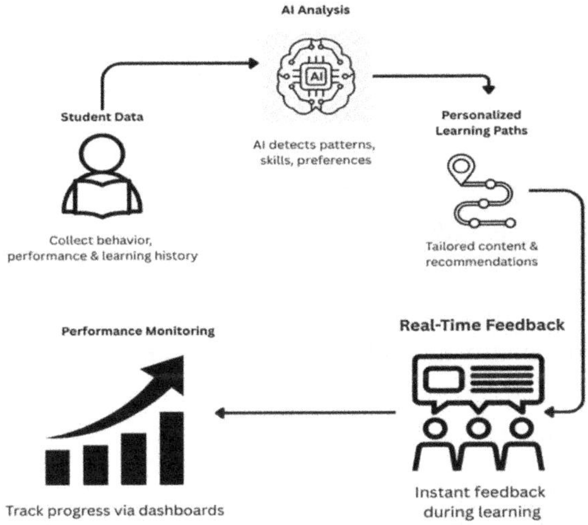

7. CASE STUDIES AND REAL-WORLD APPLICATIONS IN AI-ENABLED RECRUITMENT

Case-based learning offers powerful insights into how organizations across industries are leveraging Artificial Intelligence (AI) to revolutionize recruitment. By analyzing real implementations, successes, and challenges, learners can connect classroom concepts to industry realities and develop critical thinking around ethical deployment, candidate experience, and long-term strategic value.

This section presents selected case studies from global corporations and public institutions that exemplify the integration of AI into recruitment workflows.

A. Unilever: Gamified AI Recruitment at Scale

Unilever reimagined its graduate hiring process by integrating Pymetrics (for neuroscience-based assessments) and HireVue (for AI-analyzed video interviews). Candidates completed game-based tasks to evaluate cognitive traits, followed by asynchronous video interviews scored by machine learning algorithms.

Impact:

- Time-to-hire reduced by 75%.
- Candidate satisfaction increased due to greater flexibility and transparency.

- Bias audits were built into the algorithm to ensure fairness.

Learning Application: Students can reverse-engineer the process, assess the ethical considerations, and replicate part of the workflow using open-source datasets and simulation tools.

B. Accenture: Internal Mobility with Talent Intelligence Platforms

Accenture deployed an internal AI Talent Intelligence Platform that mapped employee skills and recommended lateral moves, internal job matches, and reskilling pathways.

Impact on Recruitment:

- Reduced external hiring by 15%.
- Improved internal mobility and retention.
- Machine learning matched roles with current employees more accurately than traditional recruiters.

Learning Application:

This case introduces learners to predictive hiring, internal sourcing strategies, and algorithm-driven workforce planning.

C. Vodafone: AI Chatbot 'Tobi' for Candidate Experience

Vodafone implemented Tobi, an AI-driven chatbot, to manage job seeker interactions, guide applicants through the recruitment process, and answer FAQs during onboarding.

Impact:

- 24/7 support enhanced candidate experience.
- Reduced recruiter workload on administrative tasks.
- Highlighted the limitations of AI in handling sensitive or complex candidate queries.

Learning Application:

Students can design their own recruitment chatbots using Dialogflow or IBM Watson, followed by role-plays testing conversational design, empathy, and accessibility.

D. LinkedIn: AI for Inclusive Recruitment

LinkedIn used AI models to analyze job descriptions, flag biased language, and recommend neutral alternatives. Its algorithms also monitored hiring trends to identify underrepresented groups.

Impact:

- Improved gender and ethnic diversity across roles.
- Boosted engagement with job posts.
- Demonstrated the value of explainable AI in building trust.

Learning Application:

This case allows learners to discuss ethics, audit AI outputs, and explore how algorithm design affects diversity, equity, and inclusion in recruitment.

E. Government of India and Microsoft: AI-Powered Reskilling and Job Matching

The National Skill Development Corporation (NSDC), in collaboration with Microsoft, launched a platform using AI to assess skill gaps, personalize learning, and connect candidates with job openings across sectors.

Impact:

- 10,000+ mid-career professionals upskilled.
- 28% increase in placement rates.
- Raised concerns around data sharing between government and corporate partners.

Learning Application:

Students can evaluate the balance between data-driven recruitment and privacy policies, as well as policy implications of AI use in public-sector hiring.

F. TALENTiQ at a European University: Academic Hiring Reinvented

A large European university deployed TALENTiQ, an AI platform that analyzed academic CVs, filtered compliance issues, and ranked candidates based on institutional priorities such as diversity, research alignment, and experience.

Impact:

- 45% reduction in time-to-hire.
- Improved match quality per post-hire evaluation.
- Periodic audits ensured transparency and reduced bias in shortlisting.

Learning Application:

This case helps students understand how AI can support niche hiring and institutional goals beyond just speed and efficiency.

By examining these diverse examples, students can develop a nuanced understanding of how AI is shaping recruitment across sectors. These case studies also expose learners to ethical trade-offs, technology limitations, and the importance of human oversight in candidate selection processes.

8. TOOLS AND TECHNOLOGIES FOR TEACHING AI IN RECRUITMENT

Effective instruction in AI-based recruitment demands more than theoretical exposure—it requires learners to work with the very tools reshaping modern hiring. Integrating real-world technologies into the curriculum equips students with the practical skills needed to navigate AI-powered hiring workflows and critically assess their outcomes.

This section outlines essential platforms and tools that educators can incorporate into classroom and training environments to teach AI in recruitment meaningfully and interactively.

A. AI Recruitment Platforms and Sandboxes

Hands-on engagement with recruitment platforms allows students to simulate candidate selection and decision-making.

- **HireVue:** Enables learners to explore AI-analyzed video interviews, facial expression scoring, and voice tone analysis.
- **Pymetrics:** Offers insight into gamified candidate assessments based on cognitive and emotional profiling.
- **Eightfold AI / X0PA AI:** Allow students to experiment with resume parsing, skill matching, and predictive fit scoring.
- **LinkedIn Talent Insights:** Useful for exploring talent mapping, job market analytics, and recruitment funnel data.

Educators may use demo accounts or simulated datasets to walk students through mock hiring campaigns.

B. Natural Language Processing (NLP) and Resume Parsing Tools

AI-driven resume parsing is at the heart of automated candidate screening. Students should be able to:

- Use **spaCy**, **NLTK**, or **HuggingFace** models in platforms like Google Colab to extract entities from resumes.
- Build keyword-matching systems for role-fit analysis.
- Analyze structured vs. unstructured resume formats for parsing accuracy.

Instructors can use anonymized or sample CV datasets from Kaggle or institutional repositories.

C. Machine Learning and Predictive Hiring Tools

To understand how candidate scoring and hiring predictions work, students can use:

- **Google Colab + Python (scikit-learn, pandas):** To build and train hiring prediction models.
- **Tableau or Power BI:** For visualizing applicant scores, diversity metrics, or shortlisting funnels.
- **AutoML Tools (e.g., H2O.ai or Microsoft Azure AutoML):** For building no-code recruitment prediction systems.

Sample exercises include predicting applicant success rates based on past hiring data or simulating AI bias detection using explainability libraries like **SHAP** or **LIME**.

D. Chatbot Design Tools for Candidate Engagement

Recruitment chatbots play a growing role in pre-screening and FAQs. Students can build and test their own using:

- **Dialogflow (Google)**
- **IBM Watson Assistant**
- **Microsoft Bot Framework**

Projects can include designing candidate-friendly workflows, ensuring inclusive language, and evaluating chatbot responsiveness.

E. Simulation and Role-Play Platforms

AI simulations help replicate real hiring interactions. Tools include:

- **HR Avatar** and **Mursion:** Virtual interviews, conflict resolution, and performance evaluations with AI avatars.
- **CapsimInbox:** Allows scenario-based role-play in hiring decisions, ethical dilemmas, and leadership hiring strategies.

These platforms foster empathy, ethical awareness, and contextual understanding of AI use in high-stakes hiring.

F. Collaborative Learning and Industry Workflow Tools

To reflect workplace dynamics, teaching should include collaboration tools used in HR teams:

- Slack / Microsoft Teams: For mock recruiter-candidate conversations.
- Trello / Miro / Notion: For visualizing hiring pipelines, tracking candidate journey, and brainstorming AI tool integrations.

These tools help students simulate a real HR tech team environment while completing group projects or hackathons.

G. Learning Management Systems with AI Capabilities

Instructors can host modules, assessments, and sandbox exercises using:

- Canvas, Moodle, or Blackboard (with AI plug-ins for adaptive feedback)
- Coursera for Campus, edX, and LinkedIn Learning for certified, self-paced AI-in-HR courses
- Panopto for analyzing learner engagement in recruitment simulation videos

The Practice has shown in Figure 6.

Figure 6. Predictive Features for Employee Attrition Using Machine Learning in Google Colab

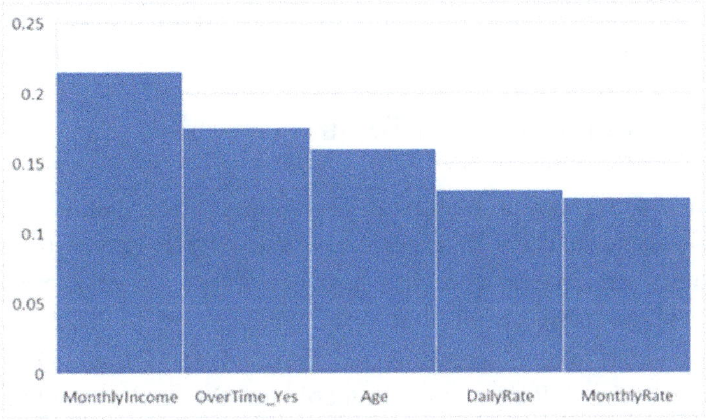

HR Technology Suites with AI Capabilities

Modern enterprise HR platforms now feature integrated AI functionalities. Tools such as SAP SuccessFactors, Workday, Oracle HCM Cloud, and Zoho People allow learners to simulate processes including resume parsing, candidate scoring, employee sentiment analysis, and talent mobility forecasting. These platforms replicate full-cycle HR workflows, providing hands-on experience in decision support and workforce planning. Academic trial versions or sandbox environments are often available, facilitating safe exploration within educational settings.

Chatbots and Virtual Assistants

Natural Language Processing (NLP) is a core component of AI in HR. Educators can instruct students to design HR-specific chatbots using tools such as Dialogflow, IBM Watson Assistant, or Microsoft Bot Framework. By building conversational agents to answer FAQs or guide onboarding workflows, students gain practical exposure to NLP, dialogue design, and user experience principles.

Learning Management Systems and AI-Personalized Platforms

Learning Management Systems (LMS) such as Moodle, Canvas, and Blackboard are increasingly enhanced with AI features, enabling personalized learning paths and adaptive feedback mechanisms. These systems support real-time progress tracking and intelligent content recommendation. Platforms like Coursera for Campus, edX, and LinkedIn Learning can be embedded into course design to supplement core instruction with flexible, self-paced modules. Additionally, AI-enhanced video analytics tools such as Panopto offer insights into learner engagement through heatmaps and retention metrics.

Simulation and Visualization Tools

Simulation-based training platforms—including HR Avatar, Mursion, and CapsimInbox—allow learners to experience realistic HR scenarios powered by AI. These systems simulate tasks such as hiring interviews, conflict resolution, and performance reviews using virtual avatars, enhancing critical thinking and ethical reasoning. Visualization tools like Tableau, Power BI, and Google Data Studio are essential for converting HR data into actionable insights and strategic dashboards.

Collaboration and Project Management Tools

HR education increasingly emphasizes collaboration across functions. Tools like Slack, Trello, Miro, and Microsoft Teams can be used to organize team-based projects that integrate HR, business, and data science components. These platforms mirror contemporary workplace environments and support the development of soft skills such as communication, coordination, and decision-making under time constraints.

By combining industry-grade tools with structured pedagogical design, instructors can empower students to engage with recruitment technologies not as passive users but as informed, ethical decision-makers. These tools allow learners to prototype, test, critique, and innovate AI-driven hiring processes within a safe, educational context.

9. CHALLENGES, FUTURE DIRECTIONS, AND POLICY IMPLICATIONS IN AI-DRIVEN HR EDUCATION

As Artificial Intelligence (AI) becomes central to modern hiring, the need to educate future professionals on its applications in recruitment is both urgent and complex. However, embedding AI recruitment training into academic and professional settings presents significant challenges. Simultaneously, the future holds promise—driven by innovation, evolving learner needs, and shifting industry expectations.

This section outlines the critical challenges in implementation, explores emerging trends, and offers strategic policy recommendations to align AI-recruitment education with ethical, technological, and labor market imperatives.

A. Challenges in Implementing AI-Based Recruitment Education

1) Institutional Gaps in Curriculum Development

Many HR programs still treat recruitment as a theoretical or administrative task, lacking modules on AI resume screening, predictive hiring, or algorithmic fairness. Curriculum approval cycles are slow, and faculty often lack cross-disciplinary exposure to both HR and AI.

2) Shortage of Faculty Expertise

Instructors may lack familiarity with platforms like HireVue or Pymetrics, or with teaching data analytics and ethical audits in hiring. Without targeted upskilling or industry mentorships, instructors are unable to deliver AI recruitment instruction at scale.

3) Limited Access to Recruitment Tech Infrastructure

AI hiring tools are often proprietary, expensive, or restricted to enterprise use. Many institutions—especially in low-resource regions—lack access to sandboxes or datasets needed for hands-on recruitment training.

4) Ethical Complexity and Regulatory Uncertainty

Recruitment AI poses sensitive issues around bias, discrimination, and transparency. Educators must teach not just tool usage but also how to audit candidate scoring models, respect candidate privacy, and comply with global hiring laws like the GDPR and EEOC standards.

5) Disconnection from Industry Practice

Without real-world case integration or industry partnerships, AI education risks becoming theoretical. Students need exposure to actual workflows, recruitment metrics, and post-deployment evaluation practices to become employable and adaptable.

B. Future Directions in AI Recruitment Education

1) Integration of Generative AI into Candidate Evaluation

Tools like ChatGPT and Gemini are entering recruiting workflows—from drafting job descriptions to evaluating candidate writing. Educators must now include instruction on generative AI ethics, bias, and real-time content analysis in recruitment contexts.

2) Micro-Credentials in AI Talent Acquisition

Stackable certifications focused on "AI in hiring," "bias audits in recruitment," or "chatbot-led candidate engagement" are gaining popularity. Institutions can offer these through modular learning platforms to support agile, just-in-time learning.

3) Simulated and Immersive Hiring Environments

Virtual Reality (VR) and Augmented Reality (AR) are being piloted to simulate AI interviews and recruiter decision-making. These technologies help learners explore emotional cues, candidate experience, and AI limitations in an interactive manner.

4) Predictive Career Guidance through AI Analytics

AI platforms are increasingly used to guide students not just into jobs—but into the right jobs. Recruitment education will soon need to teach how to interpret candidate-job fit predictions, manage algorithmic suggestions, and address systemic hiring bias.

5) Employer Co-Developed Curricula

Leading HR tech companies are beginning to co-author course content and sponsor tool licenses. This trend will expand, offering learners early exposure to industry-grade systems while keeping educational content updated.

C. Policy Implications and Strategic Recommendations

1) Mandating AI-Recruitment Literacy

National education frameworks must recognize AI-driven recruitment as a core skill within HR and business education. Accreditation bodies should require instruction in hiring automation, candidate data ethics, and algorithmic fairness.

2) Public Funding for Educational AI Tool Access

Governments should subsidize access to AI hiring sandboxes and datasets—especially in underserved institutions—to promote equity in technology adoption and professional mobility.

3) Faculty Development and Certification

Dedicated programs must be launched to certify faculty in teaching AI-based hiring. These should blend pedagogy, ethics, and tool usage, ideally co-designed with AI companies.

4) Data Governance and Consent Frameworks in Education

As AI tools are embedded into LMS and training programs, policies must define how learner data is used, how performance is evaluated algorithmically, and how student privacy is preserved—mirroring practices in recruitment environments.

5) Inclusive Curriculum Design

Special efforts must be made to ensure that AI hiring education includes content on diversity, accessibility, and anti-discrimination practices, with built-in tools for students to audit their own projects.

By addressing these strategic pillars—curriculum, ethics, accessibility, and collaboration—AI-driven recruitment education can evolve from niche pilot efforts to globally recognized academic and training standards. Educators, industry leaders, and policymakers must co-create this future to ensure recruitment remains fair, efficient, and profoundly human—even in an algorithmic age.

The Ecosystem of AI-Driven HR Education: Challenges, Innovations, Policies, and Strategies as shown in Figure 7.

Figure 7. The Ecosystem of AI-Driven HR Education: Challenges, Innovations, Policies, and Strategies

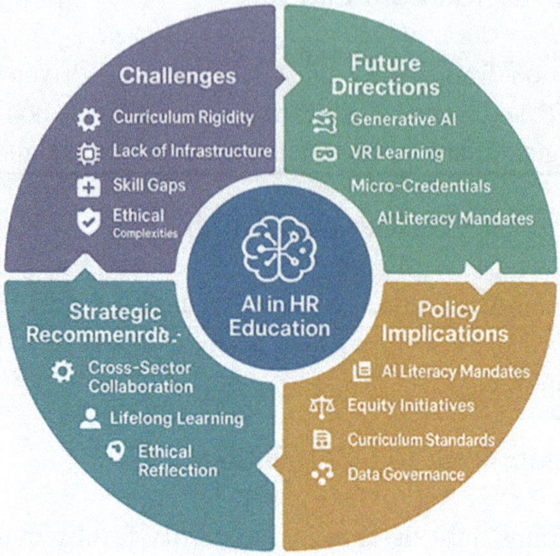

10. CONCLUSION AND RECOMMENDATION

The transformative impact of Artificial Intelligence (AI) and big data on Human Resource Management (HRM) signifies a paradigm shift in both industry practice and educational frameworks. Once perceived primarily as an administrative function, HR now plays a strategic role in driving organizational performance—and AI stands at the center of this evolution.

This chapter has outlined the conceptual foundations of AI in HR, highlighted the pedagogical shift required to meet emerging workforce demands, and proposed curriculum design strategies tailored for AI-enhanced HR education. It has also introduced interdisciplinary teaching methods, practical tools, and real-world case studies, offering a comprehensive model for preparing future HR professionals.

Challenges related to ethical governance, institutional inertia, and technological access were critically examined, along with forward-looking trends such as generative AI, virtual reality-based instruction, and micro-credentialing. These developments suggest that HR education must move beyond content delivery to cultivate adaptability, ethical thinking, and innovation.

To fully realize the potential of AI in HR education, coordinated action is required across stakeholders:

- **Educators** must continuously update their skills and integrate interdisciplinary content, ensuring learners are both technically fluent and ethically informed.
- **Institutions** should invest in infrastructure and faculty development, while fostering industry partnerships to enhance curriculum relevance.
- **HR professionals** are encouraged to embrace a culture of lifelong learning, upskilling through short courses and certifications, and critically evaluating AI tools for fairness and impact.
- **Policy makers** must support inclusive and scalable models for AI education through funding, accreditation standards, and data governance frameworks.

A forward-thinking approach to curriculum design should prioritize not only technical competence but also human values—fairness, inclusion, and accountability. AI-informed HR strategies hold the potential to make workplaces more efficient, equitable, and responsive to employee needs. However, achieving this requires education systems that prepare learners to implement these tools strategically and responsibly.

Limitations of the Study

While this chapter offers a comprehensive overview of AI-driven HR education, it is important to acknowledge its limitations. First, the analysis is largely conceptual and literature-based, with limited empirical validation of outcomes from implemented curricula. Second, the chapter primarily focuses on higher education and corporate training environments, which may not fully reflect the unique challenges faced in low-resource or vocational settings. Third, given the fast-paced evolution of AI tools, some platform-specific recommendations may become outdated quickly. Future research should aim to include longitudinal studies, diverse educational contexts, and comparative analyses of pedagogical effectiveness across geographies and learning models.

Key Takeaways

AI is no longer a nicety in HR education but an essential skill for future HR professionals. Pedagogical innovation is needed: teaching AI for HR cannot be based on passive or lecture-based learning. Curriculum design needs to be interdisciplinary, pulling together aspects of computer science, business, psychology, ethics, and data analytics. Ethics needs to be integrated into every phase of learning, not delivered as a separate module. Faculty development and investment in infrastructure are preconditions for effective implementation. Industry partnerships are necessary to ensure curricula remain relevant and practice-based. Policy support is required to standardize, scale, and democratize access to AI-based HR education.

Actionable Recommendations

- **For Academic Institutions**: Modernize HR curricula to include AI technologies like natural language processing, machine learning, and workforce analytics. Offer faculty development programs and establish partnerships with HR tech firms for internships, guest lectures, and co-developed coursework.
- **For HR Practitioners**: Promote lifelong learning through micro-credentials and short AI-focused courses. Foster AI literacy within HR teams, and apply AI tools ethically to improve talent acquisition, engagement, and evaluation.
- **For Policy Makers**: Enforce AI competency requirements in HR education standards. Support institutions through targeted funding and ensure digital equity in access to AI learning platforms. Develop accreditation guidelines and privacy regulations aligned with the use of AI in education and workforce development.

Directions for the Future

As AI becomes increasingly embedded in work and learning environments, the future of HR education will depend on flexibility, personalization, and ethical alignment. Areas for continued exploration include:

- **AI-Co-Created Curriculum**: Leveraging generative AI to design customized learning materials and content.
- **Global Credential Portability**: Establishing international standards for AI-HR competencies to enable recognition across borders.
- **Predictive Career Guidance**: Using AI analytics to support career path planning based on individual strengths and market trends.
- **Decentralized Learning Ecosystems**: Applying blockchain and Web3 technologies for learner-owned credentials and secure data exchange.
- **Outcome-Based Research**: Conducting longitudinal studies on the impact of AI in HR education on employability, critical thinking, and ethical awareness.

Final Reflection

Integrating AI into HR education is not merely a matter of adopting new tools—it is about empowering a generation of professionals to lead with insight, integrity, and inclusivity. As educators, researchers, and practitioners, we are collectively responsible for shaping a future in which technology amplifies human values rather than replacing them.

By preparing students to engage critically with AI in HR, we are not only teaching systems—we are educating tomorrow's leaders to build equitable, data-informed, and humane organizations.

11. APPENDIX AND SUPPLEMENTARY MATERIALS

To support educators, curriculum designers, and HR professionals in the effective implementation of AI-driven human resource education, this appendix provides a comprehensive collection of tools, resources, templates, and references. These materials are intended to be directly applied or adapted to various educational contexts, including classroom instruction, professional training, and academic research, thereby facilitating a deeper understanding and practical application of AI technologies in HR.

A sample instructional module has been developed to span a three-week period within a broader curriculum focused on AI-driven HR practices. This module emphasizes both the practical and ethical dimensions of applying artificial intelligence in recruitment and talent acquisition processes. Its primary objective is to equip students and professionals with a nuanced understanding of the capabilities, as well as the limitations, of AI tools used to enhance talent acquisition strategies. Specifically, the module aims to develop learners' ability to comprehend how AI algorithms analyse structured and unstructured data—such as resumes, social media profiles, and skill assessments—to match candidate profiles with job descriptions effectively. This fosters critical thinking about the benefits and challenges of integrating AI within recruitment workflows. The appendix further highlights several prominent AI tools and platforms widely used in HR education. IBM Watson provides sophisticated AI-driven analytics and chatbot frameworks that support HR data analysis and generate predictive insights for workforce planning. LinkedIn Talent Insights offers a workforce intelligence platform that aids in talent mapping and skill gap analysis, enabling HR professionals to make informed strategic decisions. Pymetrics leverages AI to conduct behavioural and cognitive assessments, promoting fair and objective talent evaluation and matching processes. Complementing these specialized tools, online learning platforms such as Coursera and edX deliver comprehensive courses on AI, HR technologies, and associated ethical considerations, providing learners with a well-rounded theoretical foundation alongside practical skill.

To assist curriculum developers, a detailed five-week template is proposed for structuring AI in HR courses. The initial week introduces fundamental concepts of AI in HR through interactive lectures and case study discussions, assessed via quizzes and reflective exercises to reinforce understanding. The second week focuses on HR data analytics, featuring demonstrations of relevant tools and hands-on dataset exploration, with group data reports as a form of assessment to encourage collaboration and applied learning. Ethical implications are addressed in the third week through debates and ethical dilemma simulations, culminating in policy proposal drafts that challenge learners to engage thoughtfully with the societal impact of AI. The fourth week involves role-playing exercises where participants simulate recruitment scenarios using AI tools, assessed through video presentations that demonstrate their applied knowledge. The course concludes with a capstone project in the fifth week, requiring learners to design and present an AI-enhanced HR process, synthesizing their accumulated knowledge into a practical, real-world application.

In summary, this appendix offers actionable and adaptable materials designed to serve as immediate references for those launching or upgrading AI-augmented HR education programs. Educators and practitioners are encouraged to contextualize the content to their unique environments, experiment with various instructional formats, and actively share innovations within their professional networks. Such collaborative efforts will contribute to the ongoing refinement and advancement of AI-driven HR education, ensuring it remains relevant and impactful in an ever-evolving technological landscape.

REFERENCES

Bates, T., Cobo, C., Mariño, O., & Wheeler, S. (2020). Can artificial intelligence transform higher education? *International Journal of Educational Technology in Higher Education, 17*(1), 42. Advance online publication. DOI: 10.1186/s41239-020-00218-x

Bessen, J. E. (2018). AI and jobs: The role of demand. In Agrawal, A., Gans, J., & Goldfarb, A. (Eds.), *The economics of artificial intelligence: An agenda* (pp. 291–307). National Bureau of Economic Research., DOI: 10.2139/ssrn.3078715

Chamorro-Premuzic, T., Winsborough, D., Sherman, R. A., & Hogan, R. (2016). New talent signals: Shiny new objects or a brave new world? *Industrial and Organizational Psychology: Perspectives on Science and Practice, 9*(3), 621–640. DOI: 10.1017/iop.2016.6

Chiu, T. K. F., Xia, Q., Zhou, X., Chai, C. S., & Cheng, M. (2023). Systematic literature review on opportunities, challenges, and future research recommendations of artificial intelligence in education. *Computers and Education: Artificial Intelligence, 4*, 100118. DOI: 10.1016/j.caeai.2022.100118

Choi, G. W., Kim, S. H., Lee, D., & Moon, J. (2024). Utilizing generative AI for instructional design: Exploring strengths, weaknesses, opportunities, and threats. *TechTrends, 68*(4), 832–844. DOI: 10.1007/s11528-024-00967-w

Crompton, H., & Burke, D. (2023). Artificial intelligence in higher education: The state of the field. *International Journal of Educational Technology in Higher Education, 20*(1), 22. DOI: 10.1186/s41239-023-00392-8

Crompton, H., & Burke, D. (2024). The educational affordances and challenges of ChatGPT: State of the field. *TechTrends, 68*(2), 380–392. DOI: 10.1007/s11528-024-00939-0

Daugherty, P. R., & Wilson, H. J. (2018). *Human + machine: Reimagining work in the age of AI*. Harvard Business Review Press. https://dl.acm.org/doi/10.5555/3235249

Delcker, J., Heil, J., Ifenthaler, D., Seufert, S., & Spirgi, L. (2024). First-year students' AI competence as a predictor for intended and de facto use of AI tools for supporting learning processes in higher education. *International Journal of Educational Technology in Higher Education, 21*(1), 13. DOI: 10.1186/s41239-024-00452-7

Gelinas, D., Sadreddin, A., & Vahidov, R. (2022). Artificial intelligence in human resources management: A review and research agenda. *Pacific Asia Journal of the Association for Information Systems, 14*(6), 1–42. DOI: 10.17705/1pais.14601

Ghosh, R., & Scott, J. E. (2023). The adoption of artificial intelligence in human resources management: A systematic literature review. *Journal of Business Research, 150*, 1–15. DOI: 10.1016/j.jjimei.2023.100208

Gonzalez-Gonzalez, C. S., & Jiménez-Zarco, A. I. (2023). Artificial intelligence in higher education: The state of the field. *International Journal of Educational Technology in Higher Education, 20*(1), 7. Advance online publication. DOI: 10.1186/s41239-023-00392-8

Pisica, A. I., Edu, T., Zaharia, R. M., & Zaharia, R. (2023). Implementing artificial intelligence in higher education: Pros and cons from the perspectives of academics. *Societies (Basel, Switzerland), 13*(5), 118. DOI: 10.3390/soc13050118

Pratama, M. P., Sampelolo, R., & Lura, H. (2023). Revolutionizing education: harnessing the power of artificial intelligence for personalized learning. *Klasikal: Journal of education, language teaching and science, 5*(2), 350-357. DOI: 10.52208/klasikal.v5i2.877

Qiu, L., & Zhao, L. (2019). Opportunities and challenges of artificial intelligence to human resource management. *Academic Journal of Humanities & Social Sciences, 2*, 144–153. https://francis-press.com/papers/349

Raghavan, M., Barocas, S., Kleinberg, J., & Levy, K. (2020). Mitigating bias in algorithmic hiring: Evaluating the impact of fairness interventions. In *Proceedings of the 2020 Conference on Fairness, Accountability, and Transparency (FAT)** (pp. 469–481). DOI: 10.1145/3351095.3372828

Robert, L. P., Pierce, C., Morris, L., Kim, S., & Alahmad, R. (2020). Designing fair AI for managing employees in organizations: A review, critique, and design agenda. *arXiv preprint arXiv:2002.09054*. https://arxiv.org/abs/2002.09054

Tambe, P., Cappelli, P., & Yakubovich, V. (2019). Artificial intelligence in human resources management: Challenges and a path forward. *California Management Review, 61*(4), 15–42. DOI: 10.1177/0008125619867910

UNESCO. (2022). *AI and education: Guidance for policymakers*. United Nations Educational, Scientific and Cultural Organization. https://unesdoc.unesco.org/ark:/48223/pf0000376709

Yanamala, K. K. R. (2023). Transparency, privacy, and accountability in AI-enhanced HR processes. *Journal of Advanced Computing Systems, 3*(3), 10–18. DOI: 10.69987/JACS.2023.30302

Chapter 6
Sentiment and Emotion Analysis in Video Interviews Using Deep Learning Techniques

Rituraj Jain
https://orcid.org/0000-0002-5532-1245
Marwadi Uinversity, Rajkot, India

ABSTRACT

The chapter discusses techniques for integrating sentiment and emotion analysis in video interviews using state-of-the-art deep learning approaches. Integrating multiple forms of data, including facial expressions, speech and text, automates and improves the evaluation of job candidates during the recruitment process. Deep learning models including CNNs, RNNs and transformers allow for precise analysis of emotions and provide a better understanding of the context in video interviews. Medium provides information on renowned datasets, key preprocessing steps, powerful deep learning models, real-world examples and significant ethical challenges. The chapter highlights emerging advancements in federated learning, explainable AI and multimodal fusion as important areas for future research, emphasizing the importance of responsible application in AI-involved recruitment.

1. INTRODUCTION

Artificial intelligence is transforming how companies discover, evaluate and recruit the best talent available. With tougher competition in the global job market and remote work on the rise, video interviews have now become essential for or-

DOI: 10.4018/979-8-3373-6516-9.ch006

ganizations to quickly assess candidates remotely. Deep learning-based sentiment and emotion analysis has become increasingly important in improving the accuracy and fairness of video interview evaluations.

Sentiment analysis searches for feelings, attitudes and emotional reactions expressed in written content. Video interviews allow recruiters to employ sentiment analysis on transcripts or answers to assess candidates' feelings, views and emotional expressions. Emotion analysis analyzes human emotions by examining facial expressions, voice tone and other cues from the candidate's body language. Integrating sentiment analysis and emotion analysis offers recruiters detailed information about candidates' personality, interaction approaches and how they may fit into the company environment.

Deep learning has shown exceptional ability to handle and interpret rich, multivariate information found in videos and speech. Deep learning algorithms learn complex hierarchies of data representations themselves, resulting in more precise and in-depth interpretations of how people think and feel. This method allows for the identification of subtle behaviors and patterns hidden from human evaluation and is scalable enough to analyze numerous video interviews consistently.

Emotion analysis in video interviews is beneficial in many human resources and recruitment scenarios. Such methods allow major organizations quickly to assess a large number of applicants and select candidates who are likely to display superior soft skills and adaptability. It can considerably shorten the time and effort needed to evaluate potential hires at the beginning of the hiring process. Employing AI analysis reduces the risk of bias in the recruitment process, allowing for a more diverse and inclusive workforce. These issues have made this topic more crucial in the current hiring process. Because of remote work and distributed teams, video interviews are widely used during the hiring process in most companies. Due to the rise of remote interviews, there is a need for new ways to assess whether an applicant is skilled for the job vacancy. They are now working to hone their skills in picking up soft skills and emotional intelligence beyond just reviewing resumes and conducting traditional job interviews.

Employing AI emotion and sentiment analysis is one way HR teams try to make the recruitment process fairer and more efficient. Such approaches give insight using data, which can make the selection process more reliable and efficient. We should also make sure to review how these tools handle ethics, their limitations, and how their decisions are made clear to people.

In Figure 1, the process is shown from the start of collecting data, processing it to extract needed features, using deep learning models to analyze, and making a conclusion.

Figure 1. End-to-End Emotion and Sentiment Classification Flow for Video Interview Analytics.

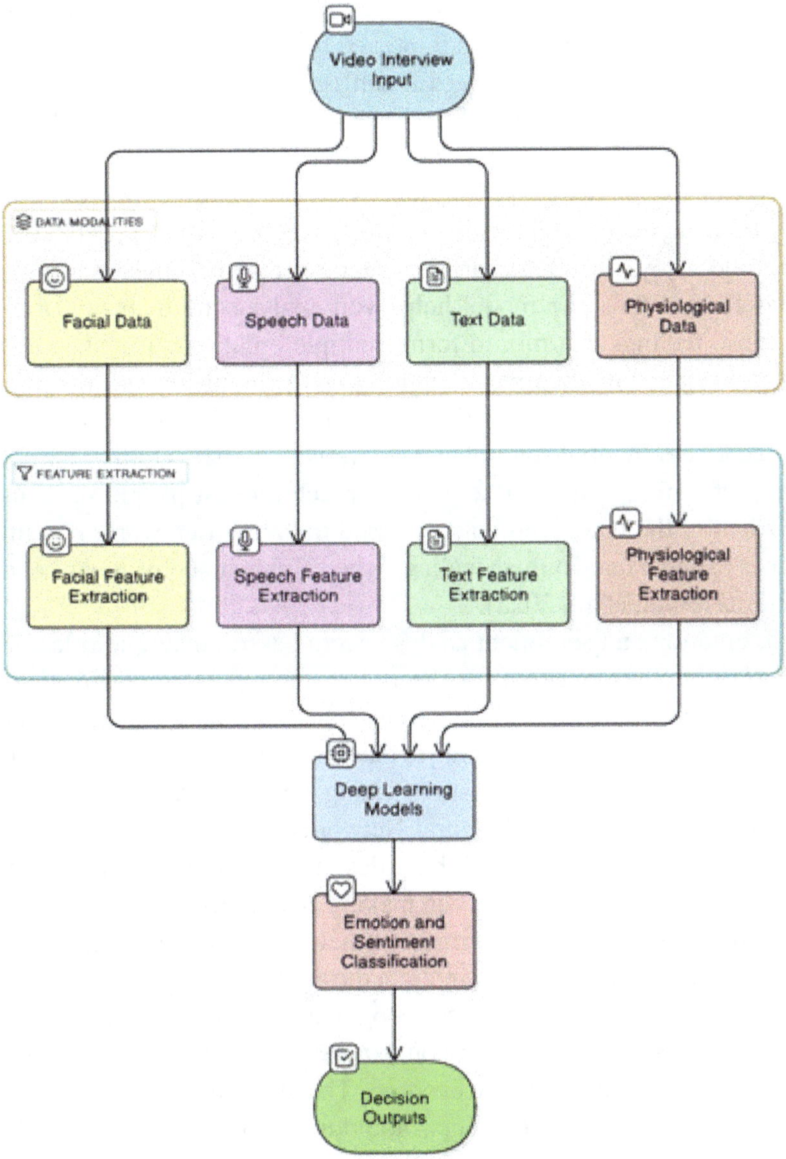

2. FOUNDATIONS OF EMOTION AND SENTIMENT ANALYSIS

Emotion and sentiment analysis is based on pre-defined emotion taxonomies. Emotion and sentiment analysis was improved by Ekman's six basic emotions and Plutchik's wheel of emotions. As per Ekman's model, there are six key emotions. There are six emotions we commonly experience in life: happiness, sadness, anger, fear, disgust, and surprise. It is commonly utilized in emotion recognition because it is easy to use and shares the same patterns everywhere. The wheel of emotions created by Plutchik covers eight main emotions. According to Li et al. (2023) using Plutchik's model, joy, trust, fear, surprise, sadness, disgust, anger, and anticipation are the basic emotions. The model helps you analyze the intensity of emotions and how those feelings can mix to form multiple emotions. It makes it easier to identify new methods in affective computing by distinguishing sentiment analysis from emotion analysis. Sentiment analysis involves finding out if a text shows a positive, negative or neutral sentiment. Generally, the goal is to measure how well a brand is performing in the market or how much interest people show in it. The idea is to identify the main emotion expressed in the written work. It is important for machines to understand human feelings when aiming to help humans or discover social patterns (Hung et al., 2023).

At first, emotion and sentiment analysis were based on simple rules, and now, advanced AI technology takes over. In the past, systems used simple rules and pattern matching to animate sentences with emotions. Since text data became more abundant and complex, researchers began turning to machine learning to improve their models and their ability to process information. Using Support Vector Machines, Naive Bayes classifiers, Convolutional Neural Networks and Bidirectional Long Short-Term Memory networks, researchers have designed a variety of models. Including theory from psychology is critical when making an emotion recognition model that is accurate and trustworthy. Furthermore, it helps to supplement emotion-related lexicons and include how emotions interact during training (Li et al., 2023). There is currently more emphasis on how to recognize emotions in conversations. This task requires understanding the chat context, feelings of the people involved, and how they change all along the conversation. The study of emotion recognition in dialogue demonstrates that researchers should use knowledge from both language and psychology fields. As emotion and sentiment analysis advances, scientists are trying new ways to join various inputs like text, audio, and images to improve their detection. Various studies make use of audio and text to enhance emotion recognition (Makhmudov et al., 2024). Multimodal approaches have shown that they can compensate when a single mode is inadequate for describing emotions.

The comparison between Ekman's basic emotion categories and Plutchik's wheel of emotions is illustrated in Figure 2. It points out that some emotion classification models are simpler than others, while some are more detailed.

Figure 2. Comparison of Ekman's Basic Emotions and Plutchik's Wheel of Emotions

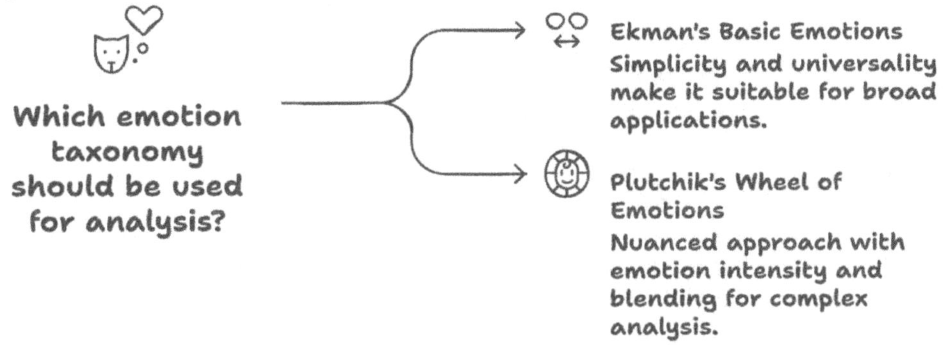

3. VIDEO INTERVIEW ANALYTICS

3.1 Structure of video interviews

Audio and video recordings are used to capture a conversation between an interviewer and the person being interviewed in a video interview. We can analyze these interviews to learn more about the interaction participants had. Among the primary data modalities from video interviews are:

1. This includes how people look, interact through their faces and eyes, move their heads, and present their body movements. To give an example, being professionally dressed is strongly related to good performance in interviews ($\rho = .62$), which is closely followed by eye contact ($\rho = .45$) and head movements ($\rho = .43$) (Martín-Raugh et al., 2022).
2. This data discusses various qualities of voice, pitch, speed, and other vocal features. It is possible to tell what a person thinks or feels by listening to their tone of voice (Changjiang et al., 2024).
3. By turning the responses into transcriptions, their language usage and meanings can be studied (Wang et al., 2022).
4. Studies have shown that measuring heart rate is a way to assess mental health status (Jiang et al., 2024).

One can explore both types of data separately or merge them for complete comprehension of how interviews work. They have accessed information from the text, audio, and video clips to develop their understanding of the subject. It may be possible for the method to tell the difference between words and gestures, as well as show us more about the emotions and experiences of people from marginalized groups. AI and machine learning make it possible for systems to draw useful findings from information in different formats. Changes in facial features, tone of voice, language, and actions can be used to find psychiatric disorders or determine someone's mental condition (Jiang et al., 2024; Zhang et al., 2024).

3.2 Available data types

With more video interviews being evaluated with multiple data modalities to extract insights about the candidate's emotions, behavior and response. Facial expression, speech and text are such rich data for evaluators. Analysis of facial expression is very important for emotion identification during interview. Gunawan et al. (2020) mention that a deep learning model such as CNN, is efficient in emotion recognition of human by using the facial cues. Results indicate that contextual datasets containing information such as the driver emotion facial expression dataset, are very powerful and can significantly boost the performance of emotion recognition. For instance, (Kanjanawattana et al., 2023) the tools for facial analysis can recognize emotions like anger, sadness, happiness or neutral. They are useful for HR professionals to evaluate candidates.

The recognition is further improved using speech based emotion analysis. While Bharti et al. (2022) developed methods for handling audio signals using CNN and Bi-GRU, no speech based methods were explored for processing pesticide alarm and warning signals. Emotion detection works for speech with this certainty, as adding other modalities introduces bias (Zhang et al., 2020). Transcribed responses in Bharti et al. (2022) shed light on candidates' mood and sentiment and in this paper NLP is used for sentiment analysis in language. Speaking patterns and facial expressions alongside automated text analysis ultimately reveal more accurate emotional insights, said Chaudhari et al. (2023).

In recent research work of Wang et al. (2022), multimodal models such as M2 Lens, are proposed together that characterize and integrate various types of data to better interpret the emotions. However, when audio and video along with text were combined as modalities, accuracy was improved to 68.38% (Zhang et al., 2020) and 86.40% (Chaudhari et al., 2023) utilizing transformers with attention mechanisms. Patterns of brain activity for facial perception were found by Volynets et al. (2020). In addition, Gkintoni et al. (2025) and similar research claim that emotion prediction is possible up to 90% with physiological and neural signals.

Whilst these advances have taken place, challenges persist in processing real time data, standardizing protocols and in tackling ethical problems such as privacy, bias and confidentiality (Gkintoni et al., 2025; Saumard, 2023; Zhang & Tan, 2023).

Table 1 presents the important data modalities for video interview analysis, along with their main features, analysis practices, and insights. When facial expressions, speech, text, and emerging body signals are combined, emotion detection in interviews is more accurate and provides richer information.

Table 1. Summary of Data Modalities, Analytical Techniques, and Performance Outcomes in Video Interview Emotion Recognition

Data Type	Key Features/Signals	Techniques Used	Insights and Observations
Facial Expressions	Emotions like anger, sadness, happiness, neutral	CNNs, DEFE dataset, Mini-Xception	Helps assess demeanor and reactions; neural mirroring supports deeper recognition accuracy
Speech (Audio)	Tone, pitch, prosody, vocal confidence	CNN, Bi-GRU, MFCCs, RNNs	Indicates confidence and emotional state; context influences recognition performance
Text (Transcription)	Word choice, sentiment, emotional tone	NLP, sentiment classifiers, transformers	Reveals communication style and intent; enhanced when fused with visual/audio data
Multimodal Integration	Facial + Speech + Text + EEG/Physiology	Transformer-based fusion, attention mechanisms	Improves accuracy significantly (e.g., up to 86.4%); enables nuanced and real-time analysis

3.3 Challenges in automated assessment

Researchers are exploring the usage of AI to analyze video interviews, but also face some issues. Organizations are beginning to turn to people analytics to assist in human resources decisions by analyzing interview responses. But the accuracy depends on the exact qualities that are being detected. It has been found that machine learning can provide a more accurate assessment of interviewers' judgment on personality traits than self-reported traits in mock video interviews. Predicting interviewer ratings resulted in higher cross-validated accuracy than self-report predictions (Hickman et al., 2021). This points to AI being more capable of noticing how candidates are perceived by others than how they see themselves.

Various issues need to be considered in implementing video interviews that are automated. Risks related to these concerns are issues with protecting information, runaway biases, and making the AI decision process clear (Bulut & Beiting-Parrish, 2024). Some people are concerned about using AI to make serious choices about who to employ. It is also important to note that problems with data quality, processing rate, and the variety of applicant profiles may appear when integrating AI systems (Al-Quraishi et al., 2024; Badouch & Boutaounte, 2024).

4. DEEP LEARNING TECHNIQUES IN EMOTION RECOGNITION

4.1 CNNs for facial expression detection

Facial expression detection and emotion recognition have benefited a lot from techniques such as Convolutional Neural Networks. Conventional methods are not as effective as CNNs in analyzing facial images for finding emotions (Depuru et al., 2022). They can automatically uncover the relevant aspects of facial expressions from information provided in real-time, without explicit instructions. To recognize emotions from faces, scientists usually follow three important steps: first, locate the face, then extract its features, and finally assign emotions to the face (Jaiswal et al., 2020). It makes it possible for the network to directly correlate images to emotions without having to build special features first. It has been established that CNNs accurately detect the seven basic emotions: happiness, sadness, anger, fear, disgust, surprise, and neutral (Dada et al., 2023) .

According to several studies, CNN-based systems have achieved excellent results. In particular, the same researchers obtained accuracies of 70.14% and 98.65% on the FERC-2013 and JAFFE datasets using their CNN framework (Jaiswal et al., 2020). Reportedly (Depuru et al., 2022), the FER challenge dataset showed an average accuracy of 84.50% in another study. The CNN-10 model achieved the best results on the CK+ dataset, getting 99.9% accuracy, along with 84.3% on FER-2013 and 95.4% on JAFFE. Many scientists have tried various solutions to improve the work of CNNs. For instance, GCN models developed with faces' landmark graphs helped solve issues related to extra data and imbalanced training.

It is also effective to use two CNNs, one for emotion and the other for identity, to learn features that are later merged into a Tandem Facial Expression Feature. The method reported an accuracy of 99.31% on the CK+ dataset and 84.29% on the FER+ dataset, according to a 2021 study (Li et al., 2021). Transfer learning has also been used to recognize emotions. According to the study by Chowdary et al. in 2021, fine-tuning four deep learning models so they can be fine-tuned enhanced the accuracy to about 96% for emotion recognition on the CK+ dataset. The outcomes suggest that CNNs can be used to effectively detect facial expressions.

One case study explores the utilization of convolutional neural networks (CNNs) for emotion recognition from video. Researchers applied it on fer2013 dataset and get the 97% accuracy on training set and 57.4% accuracy on testing set on depression detection (Gunawan et al., 2020). In this example, we show that deep learning can be used to identify emotional states from video data and how this could be useful for video interview scenarios.

Interestingly some of the studies report that when multiple data sources are used (multimodal approaches) emotional recognition accuracy can be improved. For instance, coupling EEG data with physiological signals resulted in improving classification accuracy, in some cases (Gkintoni et al. 2025; Badouch, Boutaounte, et al., 2025a), up to 90\% and beyond. Although we should not apply this approach to the standard video interviews, this can be useful in the presence of other data that can assist emotion detection in interview settings.

4.2 RNNs/LSTMs for speech-based emotion analysis

RNNs and LSTM networks are used in this task because they handle time series data and maintain long connections. A study found that models like this can recognize emotions from speech better than classic machine learning approaches (Abbaschian et al., 2021). Among all models, LSTM networks have made a significant difference in emotion recognition. They keep track of a person's emotions within a defined time period (Li et al., 2021). Chowdary et al. (2022) indicate that LSTM could recognize emotions in EEG signals with an average accuracy of 97% or higher. Zhang et al. (2020) state that LSTM networks commonly find the emotions in speech, achieving 94.58% and 72.50% correct rates on different datasets. There are some weaknesses that cannot be avoided with these networks. They are not always easy to train and might produce errors known as gradient explosion or gradient disappearance (Li et al., 2021). According to some experts, there are suggested approaches that use adaptations and combinations of methods. A recent study built the CRNN-MAs model, combining a CNN for time-frequency recognition and an LSTM for sequence learning (Jiang et al., 2022). On the other hand, ABMD includes residual dilated causal convolution blocks plus dilated convolution and multi-head attention. According to a 2022 paper by Kakuba et al., the model performs with RNN-style models and focuses on how parts of speech relate to one another. When running on SAVEE, RAVDESS, and EMODB, the model achieved accuracy scores of 93.75%, 85.89%, and 95.93%, respectively.

4.3 Transformers for multimodal fusion

The use of deep learning has vastly enhanced how we recognize emotions in multiple forms, and transformers have proved indispensable for processing various inputs. Transformers make it easier to join different types of knowledge and skills to find the best outcome. Transformers are used to combine data from audio and text for speech emotion recognition. The model to achieve this was a cross-modal transformer that learned the connections between audio and text. The model then has a self-attention network to identify the most significant emotional details in the fused multimodal inputs (Maji et al., 2023). Based on the IEMOCAP dataset, the approach was more proficient for the emotions of happiness, neutral, sadness, and anger. There are cases where transformers are implemented in the field of video emotion recognition. A new MERDCCA model was proposed in 2021, which extracts unimodal features with gated recurrent units and cross-modal correlations with an encoder-decoder network based on deep canonical correlation analysis (Zhang et al., 2021; Badouch, Boutaounte, et al., 2025b). This method outperformed traditional methods when tested on public datasets.

Researchers have introduced a hypercomplex multimodal network with a new fusion module using hypercomplex multiplications (Lopez et al., 2023). This method, employed in areas where things are very complex, models the hidden connections among different EEG and peripheral features to improve their fusion. The reason transformers are helpful is that they aim to connect different colors based on how they overlap. Because of attention in transformers, the model is able to focus on important features from different modalities, which led to better results in emotion recognition. Transformers have shown to perform well in merging data types for emotion recognition, but other approaches including CNNs and RNNs are equally if not more important and are often combined with transformers. The way information is fused in multimodal emotion recognition systems affects its performance (Lian et al., 2023).

4.4 Recent frameworks

Recently developed frameworks based on deep learning have greatly improved the way emotions are recognized. EmoNet is a system for recognizing emotion in speech that is based on EmoSet, a large corpus of emotional utterances. This model depends on ResNet combined with residual adapters, and these are adapted from general visual recognition systems to the task of emotion recognition in speech. Using EmoNet, researchers were able to efficiently train a multi-domain SER model on 26 sets of data, leading to better results for 21 of them (Gerczuk et al., 2023). Users can gain access to the framework for free and use its command line to interact with various applications in transfer learning across several corpora.

Xception-based mini-Xception, similar to CNNs, is effective in detecting facial emotions. This technology allows it to identify someone based on expressions and their facial features. The authors identified a very high accuracy of nearly 95.60% when they utilized the mini-Xception technique and FER-2013 dataset for their research. A new model called DSP-EmotionNet has been presented to recognize emotions in EEG by using topological and spatial information. It improves the accuracy of detecting emotions in EEG recordings by using the SATFEM module to study activity characteristics. The model performed better than any previous studies on both the SEED and SEED-IV datasets, achieving 82.5% and 65.9% accuracy (Lu et al., 2024).

DeepVANet is known for being a practical method for finding out the valence and arousal of emotions. First, it uses ConvLSTM to obtain faces, then uses Conv1D for bio-sensing data, and lastly puts these features together. Researchers have found that DeepVANet is much more accurate than others, achieving around 99.22% correctness on DEAP and MAHNOB-HCI datasets (Zhang et al., 2021). Speech emotion recognition has improved with the introduction of the Deep Stride Convolutional Neural Network (DSCNN). Reducing the number of convolutional layers leads to an increase in speed, without reducing the level of accuracy. It was shown by Wani et al. (2020) that DSCNN performed better on SAVEE speech data when spectrogram representations were used.

Table 2. Overview of Deep Learning Models, Modalities, Techniques, and Performance in Emotion Recognition Systems

Technique/Model	Modality	Methodology/Architecture	Dataset(s) Used	Reported Accuracy or Outcome	References
CNN	Facial Expression	Hierarchical feature learning, end-to-end classification	FER-2013, JAFFE, CK+	70.14% (FER), 98.65% (JAFFE), 99.9% (CK+)	Jaiswal et al., 2020; Dada et al., 2023
Tandem CNN (TFE)	Facial Expression	Joint emotion-identity learning with CNNs	FER+, CK+	84.29%–99.31%	Li et al., 2021
Transfer Learning CNNs	Facial Expression	ResNet50, VGG19, Inception V3, MobileNet (fine-tuned)	CK+	~96%	Chowdary et al., 2021
LSTM/RNN	Speech/EEG	Sequential modeling of speech/ emotional time-series	EMO-DB, CASIA, EEG	72.50%–97%	Zhang et al., 2020; Chowdary et al., 2022
CRNN-MAs	Speech	CNN + LSTM with multiple attention modules	Not specified	High, task-dependent	Jiang et al., 2022
ABMD	Speech	RDCC + multi-head attention	RAVDESS, EMODB, SAVEE	85.89%–95.93%	Kakuba et al., 2022
Transformers	Multimodal	Cross-modal & self-attention fusion	IEMOCAP, MERDCCA	Improved over baselines	Maji et al., 2023; Zhang et al., 2021
EmoNet	Speech	Multi-corpus SER with ResNet and residual adapters	EmoSet (26 corpora)	Improved in 21 of 26 corpora	Gerczuk et al., 2023
mini-Xception	Facial Expression	Lightweight CNN for joint face and emotion classification	FER-2013	~95.60%	B et al., 2024
DSP-EmotionNet	EEG	SATFEM with domain adaptation	SEED, SEED-IV	65.9%–82.5%	Lu et al., 2024

continued on following page

Table 2. Continued

Technique/Model	Modality	Methodology/Architecture	Dataset(s) Used	Reported Accuracy or Outcome	References
DeepVANet	Multimodal	ConvLSTM + Conv1D for valence-arousal recognition	DEAP, MAHNOB-HCI	Up to 99.22%	Zhang et al., 2021
DSCNN	Speech	Lightweight CNN with spectrogram inputs	SAVEE	87.8%	Wani et al., 2020

5. DATASETS AND TOOLS

5.1 Common datasets (e.g., RAVDESS, IEMOCAP, EmotiW, SEMAINE)

Many researches in this field refer to RAVDESS, IEMOCAP, and EmoDB datasets in SER, since these are widely used. The RAVDESS dataset is often used because it is regarded highly by specialists in the field. Ong et al. (2023) and Dolka et al. (2021) has applied this database, where eight different emotions are documented. Furthermore, there are recommendations to use the IEMOCAP dataset because it has a variety of samples of emotional speech (as discussed by Kumar et al., 2021; Pastor et al., 2023). It has been observed that EmoDB is widely used in SER studies, with the studies relying on it reporting reliable accuracy (Bhangale & Kothandaraman, 2023). The references explain using the SAVEE dataset (Pastor et al., 2023) and the TESS dataset (Dolka et al., 2021). The results in research papers can be vastly different when researchers use the same datasets. The research conducted by Ong et al. (2023) led to 67.72%, Dolka et al. (2021) reached 88.72%, and Kumar et al. (2021) obtained 91.67% accuracy (Dolka et al., 2021; Ong et al., 2023; Kumar et al., 2021). There are chances that these variations come from how each study applied its method, extracted its features, or used its model architecture. SER research uses several tools and techniques. Typically, MFCC and LPCC are applied as methods for extracting important features (Bhangale & Kothandaraman, 2023). In recent time, classification is accomplished with algorithms like Support Vector Machines, Random Forests, and k-Nearest Neighbors (Farooq et al., 2020). Researchers in the field of SER more frequently use deep learning models, such as CNNs and RNNs (Ullah et al., 2023; Bhangale & Kothandaraman, 2023). Some research also relies on pre-trained models such as wav2vec 2.0 for extracting features (Pastor et al., 2023; Pepino et al., 2021).

5.2 Preprocessing strategies

The method used to prepare data plays a key part in improving the effectiveness of machine learning algorithms. Different methods are applied to tackle different types of data quality and representation issues. Standardizing or normalizing data is generally used to prepare data for learning models, and is specifically useful for small, large, or medium-sized datasets (Mahmud Sujon et al., 2024). Reduced dataset features can be made richer by using the feature extraction techniques PCA and CAE. Some of the most common methods for handling class imbalance involve sampling, such as RUS, SMOTE, and SMOTE Tomek (Salekshahrezaee et al., 2023). When preprocessing texts, it is necessary to do tokenization, remove stop words, and stem words, but there are problems such as constructing stop words for a specific field and over/under stemming (Kathuria et al., 2020). The methods used to preprocess data can affect the results of the classification algorithm differently (Alshdaifat et al., 2021). For example, using combination strategies and AdaBN in brain-computer interfaces improves the performance of deep learning models used to transfer data between different datasets (Xu et al., 2021). Effective preprocessing in Arabic text classification mainly depends on processes such as stemming, selecting the right features, and the type of data (Muaad et al., 2022).

5.3 Annotation tools and benchmarks

Annotation tools are necessary for putting together large amounts of properly labeled data for machine learning. The SUSTech POINTS system was created to simplify annotation of 3D point clouds in datasets for self-driving cars and includes user-friendly features (Li et al., 2020). It has modules for pictures and 3D points that focus on finding errors and let users label images and clouds. A number of tools can be utilized by natural language processing systems for annotating radiology reports. Research involving CheXpert, RadReportAnnotator, GPT-4, and cTAKES tools on chest radiograph data found high accuracy for most findings, though revealed biases when analyzing elderly patients (Santomartino et al., 2024). Researchers found that automated tools were not always as accurate as human judgment for assessing different linguistic features (Picoral et al., 2021). PMLB, which stands for Penn Machine Learning Benchmarks, gives access to a wide variety of machine learning benchmarks, making them available with standard APIs or the web interface (Romano et al., 2021). A toolkit that offers multiple annotation formats and 15 performance metrics for object detection was developed to help evaluate different algorithms through various datasets (Padilla et al., 2021). Some solutions to this issue include actively cleaning labels in a dataset. Methodological improvements in labeling focus on choosing samples that are easiest to annotate, decreasing time and improving the quality of the data (Bernhardt et al., 2022).

The main parts of sentiment and emotion recognition, such as the datasets and methods, are summarized in Table 3. The system provides training data, estimates model accuracy, and includes specialized annotations for evaluating emotions displayed in video interviews.

Table 3. Key Datasets, Preprocessing Methods, and Annotation Tools Used in Sentiment and Emotion Recognition for Video Interviews

Category	Name / Type	Purpose or Characteristics	Performance / Notes	References
Emotion Datasets	RAVDESS	Audio-visual, 8 emotions, widely used in SER	Accuracy ranges from 67.72% to 91.67%	Ong et al., 2023; Dolka et al., 2021; Kumar et al., 2021
	IEMOCAP	Dyadic motion capture dataset for speech emotion	High diversity; widely benchmarked	Pastor et al., 2023; Kumar et al., 2021
	EmoDB	German speech dataset with 7 emotions	High performance in SER tasks	Bhangale & Kothandaraman, 2023
	SAVEE	English male actors expressing basic emotions	Used for video/ audio-based classification	Pastor et al., 2023
	TESS	Emotional speech by two age groups of women	Focused on emotion-age analysis	Dolka et al., 2021
Preprocessing	MFCC, LPCC	Feature extraction for audio signals	Commonly used in SER pipelines	Bhangale & Kothandaraman, 2023
	Standardization / Normalization	Scaling numeric data	Enhances model performance depending on dataset size	Mahmud Sujon et al., 2024
	SMOTE, RUS, SMOTE-Tomek	Handles class imbalance	Improves recall/ sensitivity in minority classes	Salekshahrezaee et al., 2023
	Text: Tokenization, Stemming, Stop Words	Text cleanup for NLP tasks	Requires domain-specific tuning	Kathuria et al., 2020; Alshdaifat et al., 2021
	AdaBN + Alignment	Normalization across domains (e.g., EEG)	Boosts transfer learning performance	Xu et al., 2021

continued on following page

Table 3. Continued

Category	Name / Type	Purpose or Characteristics	Performance / Notes	References
Annotation Tools	SUSTech POINTS	3D point cloud annotation for visual datasets	Efficient GUI and error correction tools	Li et al., 2020
	CheXpert, RadReport, GPT-4, cTAKES	NLP-based medical text annotation	Accuracy with age-related bias noted	Santomartino et al., 2024
	Penn ML Benchmarks (PMLB)	Benchmark suite for ML evaluation	Standardized datasets with easy access	Romano et al., 2021
	Object Detection Toolkit	Multi-format support with 15+ metrics	Enhances comparative evaluation of detectors	Padilla et al., 2021
	Active Label Cleaning	Prioritizes re-labeling using label correctness/ difficulty heuristics	More efficient than random re-annotation	Bernhardt et al., 2022

6. CASE STUDIES IN RECRUITMENT CONTEXTS

6.1 Use cases in real hiring platforms

AI and machine learning are being used in recruitment at many organizations and are mentioned in numerous reports. In 2016, Unilever chose HireVue and Pymetrics to help develop an AI-supported system for recruiting, selecting, and onboarding (Hu, 2023). Natural language processing, gamification, and verbal computer-mediated communication were used to automate and help with various steps in hiring, including finding, qualifying, and interviewing job applicants. Unilever saved both time and costs and effectively increased the performance of its HRM division by using this AI solution. AI is now being used by online recruitment platforms to make sure job seekers get the most suitable job. Researchers suggested a technique that finds patterns in interviews and compares them, predicting whether the match will prosper or not, using both positive and negative cases (Yang et al., 2022). The main goal was to allow both parties to make their own choices, which helps match them well.

Jiang et al. (2020) studied how blending different features could lead to better algorithms for pairing employees and jobs. They trained deep learning models on resumes and job descriptions, taking into account previous applications and using entity recognition to determine what the two sides are looking for. It was found to be the most successful after testing it with real data for 10 months. You can find

AI when using common freelancing websites to apply for jobs. Research reviewing TaskRabbit found that fair assessment algorithms play a key role in the hiring process. It was discovered that fair ranking usually improved the hiring of minority candidates, though it depended greatly on the specific role and the candidates themselves. LinkedIn is among the other big players in online recruitment that use AI to match job seekers to employers (Sühr et al., 2021). Still, the investigation pointed out that both the environment of trying to get hired and the possible prejudices of employers should be considered to ensure a fair hiring process.

6.2 AI-based hiring tools

Highly regarded AI-based tools, including HireVue and MyInterview, have improved the way many organizations recruit by reducing the effort required. They use AI to judge candidates by means of video chats, online gaming, and by examining their CVs (Kazim et al., 2021). For example, HireVue determines the personalities of candidates by using game-based assessments and video interviews, while MyInterview depends mainly on video interviews (Kazim et al., 2021). The 2016 agreement between Unilever and HireVue along with Pymetrics was well-known in the use of AI in recruitment. The goal was to make a system that uses AI for covering recruitment, selection, and onboarding steps. Unilever gained important cost and time savings while their HRM performance improved thanks to the implementation. But, it's necessary to consider that they may introduce fresh concerns about bias and data security (Hu, 2023).

It turns out that candidates tend to think positively about using AI in recruitment, although there are still some risks to consider. They find it easy and helpful, and the reduced response time is seen as the main plus point. On the other hand, users pointed out that the system lacks fine details, might make mistakes sometimes, and is not fully developed (Horodyski, 2023). There has been a lot of debate about the use of AI in hiring. A major example involved a 100-million-dollar lawsuit filed by Context Systems against African American, Latina American, Arab American, and other job applicants and employees. It is claimed that errors within the AI hiring system led to results that were unfair to some groups (Omar & Burrell, 2023). It emphasizes why we need to ensure that AI-driven tools for recruitment are built with care for ethics and accurate results.

6.3 Performance evaluation and recruiter feedback

Today, the use of real-time feedback applications has become valuable for both evaluating performance and offering feedback during recruitment. Such systems make it possible for managers and employees to give, request, and receive competency-based feedback using various devices and no longer require traditional formal performance reviews. By performing reviews like these, the company can help employees learn and enhance innovation swiftly. An examination of real-time feedback usage in performance appraisals uncovered some notable outcomes. Feedback is more critical when it comes from managers rather than colleagues or those reporting to you. It was also found that men give women higher marks than they give men, while women see the gender gap as equal for both sexes. Research shows that positive real-time feedback matters more for future performance ratings than negative feedback (Rivera et al., 2021).

This partnership shows that Unilever is using artificial intelligence to help with hiring and selection. Using this system that includes social networking, video games, and computer-based communication has greatly improved the speed, affordability, and overall performance of HRM (Hu, 2023). Yet, there are also concerns about discrimination and privacy with the use of AI in recruitment. Researchers found that in a Swedish food retail company, algorithmic recruitment actually led to a decrease in diversity. The main factor was not bias in the algorithm, but a complicated interaction between humans and algorithms, which Bursell & Roumbanis (2024) highlighted in AI recruitment processes. New predictive models have been developed with the help of AI in recruitment. One such model draws on AI to extract soft skills mentioned in job applications and testing, which are then used to recommend appropriate candidates. The goal is to lessen hiring errors, control expenses related to hiring, and lower the risk of losing workers (Lamjid et al., 2024).

7. EVOLVING ROLE OF INTERVIEWERS IN AI-ASSISTED VIDEO INTERVIEWS

Interviewers in AI assisted video interviews are becoming more important in their role, as they need to analyse sentiment and emotion in the input video during the interview process. As a front door to the organization, Asynchronous Video Interviews (AVIs) with AI assistance have been widely adopted in the pre employment screening process, bringing new challenges and opportunities for both the applicant and the interviewer (Suen and Hung 2023). Human emotions detection in video content during user interaction has been proved by deep learning techniques (Ballesteros et al., 2024; Jaiswal et al., 2020), particularly convolutional neural network techniques. AI powered systems can detect facial expressions to identify the emotions which might increase interviewer's capability to evaluate campaigners' reactions and sentiments during the interview process (Gunawan et al., 2020). Nonetheless such systems may not be sufficiently accurate, especially in situations dominated by various images and similar emotional patterns (Ballesteros et al., 2024). What is interesting from the study in (Suen & Hung, 2023) is the human interviewers didn't perform any better at detecting deceptive impression management behaviors in any interview mode, except in AVIs with extensive faking. This indicates that design components of AI–assisted assessment can add to human judgment in the discovery of specific behaviors that require a lot of effort for interviewers to discover. Attention based methods, when integrated into deep neural networks, have proved effective in sentiment analysis tasks that can be generalised to improve emotion recognition in video interviews (Kardakis et al., 2021). To wrap things up, the future of interviewers in AI assisted video interviews is algorithmic based on human expertise and used to analyse sentiment and emotion of the candidate. Although AI systems are able to give important information about emotional state of candidates as well as their possible deceptive intent, human interviewers continue to be of great relevance in candidate assessment. In the near future, for the expected benefits in accuracy and reliability of the emotion detection in video interviews, new advances in deep learning techniques (such as the hybrid model one proposed in (Bharti et al., 2022) will help make this system even more efficient in the human hiring process.

8. CHALLENGES AND ETHICAL CONSIDERATIONS

8.1 Bias and fairness in emotion analysis

Researchers in the field face many challenges related to bias and fairness in emotions studied by AI. The way human raters tag emotions can introduce a bias in SER (Chien & Lee, 2023). As a result, people are treated unfairly and biases in gender-based feelings are reinforced. Because AI is being used so quickly in health and banking, many are concerned about its effect on bias and fairness (Palakurti, 2025) . There are several potential sources for bias in emotion analysis, which come from information collected, how it is processed, and from human evaluation (Shuford, 2024). They might result in prejudiced outcomes, which support harmful stereotypes and add to current differences in society. To deal with these issues, many researchers have suggested several strategies. For example, a new framework was introduced in Chien and Lee (2023) where debiasing is accomplished using a fairness constraint and gender-wise learning. Bias can be controlled further by performing data preparation, changing machine learning models, and embedding explanatory features in systems (Gupta, 2023). Furthermore, using fairness metrics, ensuring diverse training data, and continuously monitoring the system play key roles in making AI algorithms fairer (Akinrinola et al., 2024).

8.2 Privacy concerns with facial and speech data

Using FRT and speech data in the healthcare, government, and consumer sectors can create important safety concerns about privacy. They might endanger our privacy, since they gather and process biometric details without always letting us decide. Because of the use of AI and EHRs in healthcare, patient information and IT safety are more important than ever. According to research, 58.9% of pharmacists in MENA feel concerned about data privacy risks when introducing AI (Hasan et al., 2024). In the same way, the pandemic has made it harder for healthcare entities to defend sensitive patient data from cyber threats (Burrell et al., 2023). The concerns about privacy in augmented reality can indirectly influence what users intend to do. Developing clear privacy disclosures can lead to people being less inclined to use a product and less likely to recommend it, due to its perceived usefulness and how much it engages users (Cowan et al., 2021). This points out the connection between what users feel about privacy and how they behave with facial data technology. Gathering and examining biometric information such as a person's face or voice often leads to increased digital surveillance and can make our privacy much riskier. Because of AI and Big Data, it is increasingly important to have well-constructed regulations and systems that guard privacy rights while allowing us to benefit from these technologies (Idoko et al., 2024).

Figure 3 points out what AI recruitment can do and what it might lack in this field. Though improvements in efficiency and bias reduction are important, concerns about ethics and job context must also be looked at thoroughly.

Figure 3. Key Pros and Cons of Using AI in Video Interview-Based Recruitment, Highlighting Efficiency Gains and Fairness Potential Against Risks of Bias, Context Dependence, and Ethical Challenges.

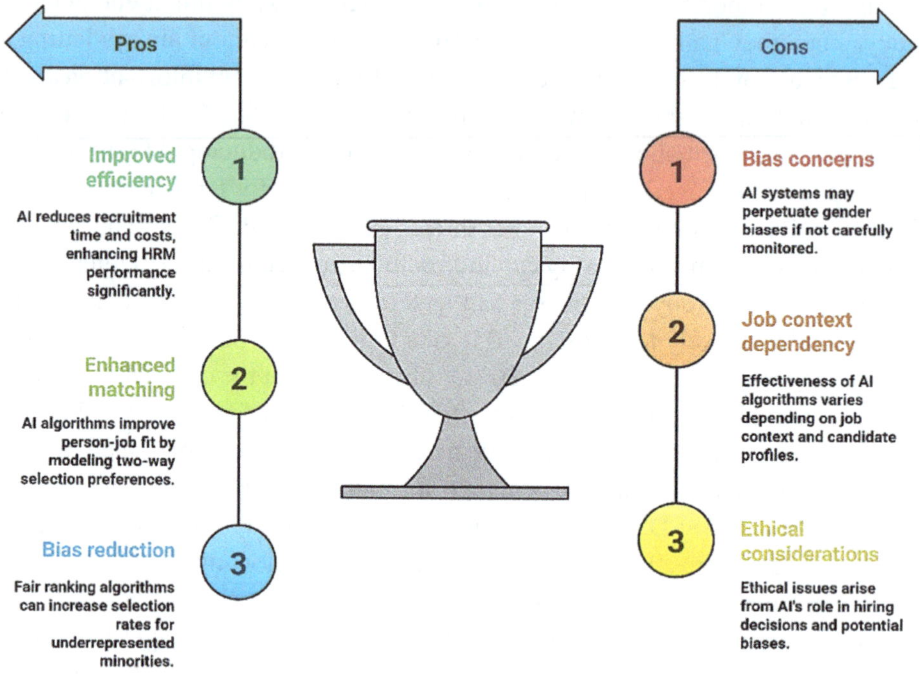

Video interviewing and sentiment analysis which are AI based recruitment strategies, also have a huge potential for benefits for organizations, it is for example helping in boosting efficiency, reducing cost as well as for better quality hire (Albassam, 2023). The use of AI in recruitment however bring with it ethical and legal concern. For example, algorithmic bias and discrimination (Albassam, 2023). Facial expression based sentiment analysis and emotion detection, both applicable to video interviews, are areas of popular research with many applications including marketing, public safety and human resources (Chutia & Baruah, 2024). Motion obtained from images is used for emotion detection. Deep learning techniques, specifically Convolutional Neural Networks (CNNs) have achieved results with accuracies 70.14% (FERC-2013) and 98.65% (JAFFE) (Jaiswal et al., 2020). However, sentiment analysis of social media has shortcomings including overlooking long distanced semantic links of emotional features and over reliance on manual annotation (Li & Li, 2023). The same problems may also occur for video interview analysis. With AI powered recruitment tools comes a number of advantages that can be derived but their implementation requires careful thought so that they don't fall on the wrong side of ethical and legal issues. AI may further be integrated in recruitment processes where it detects bias; specifically in video interviews and emotion analysis one should build the balance between utilizing the technology advancement and remedying the technology bias. In the future, research should concentrate on devising impartial algorithms, setting moral principles and investigating cutting edge techniques to reinforce framework trustworthiness and suitability in enlistment et cetera (Albassam, 2023; Halkiopoulos et al., 2025).

9. FUTURE DIRECTIONS

Examining emotions and feelings in video interviews with deep learning must account for ethical questions. With federated learning, models can be trained unitedly by experts using different owners' data without sharing their data directly. Implementing multi-party computation increases the precision and makes the tool suitable for several personality prediction models. Teamwork between AI and humans is needed to guarantee their models do not discriminate. Creating a system that uses human feedback mixed with computers while putting privacy and fairness first is part of it. This learning method makes it possible to construct models across several groups with privacy being upheld. Creating a strong AI system needs solutions for handling manipulation, escaping stealth problems, and making systems perform well as a group. This makes the thinking behind the system easier for people to understand.

Dealing with AI in the selection of employees requires creating an ethical framework at this time. The focus is also on ensuring the privacy of facial and speech information and making sure such tools are transparent. This means that appropriately merging facial expressions, audio, text, and physiological details will help greatly in emotion recognition. For practical applications, these approaches must handle real-time processing. We are also seeing a growing focus on personalization and adjusting to different emotions in context, such as what culture or position a person has and at which stage of the interview. Over time, studying the patterns of emotions during many interviews can indicate future job and cultural fit.

Altogether, the area offers plenty of promise, but progress should be balanced with efforts to deal with ethical, technical, and practical matters. Reaching the height of these technologies' achievements will need the cooperation of different fields and being responsible along the way.

10. CONCLUSION

With artificial intelligence and deep learning increasingly defining the future of recruitment, video interviews are becoming a disruptive medium for assessing people beyond asking standard questions. In this chapter an integration of emotion and sentiment analysis within video interviews is explored and the potential of deep learning approaches (such as CNNs, LSTMs and transformers) towards extracting facial and linguistic cues to predict how the candidate behaves, is engaged and what internal psychological states they display is investigated. We looked at how various datasets and preprocessing strategies lie betwixt the accuracy of such systems and the metrics of evaluation used to validate their performance. As well as the technical depth of these systems, this chapter also explored how these systems are implemented and integrated with Applicant Tracking Systems, how vendors are selected, what data security measures are taken and how the transition is made within the HR team. Additionally, ethical and legal implications were critically examined concerning such problems as algorithmic bias, candidate privacy, transparency and psychological impact of being assessed by AI systems.

Importantly, the chapter rectified this imbalance by noting recruiters are now tasked with making sense of AI outputs, while keeping human judgement in hiring decisions. In addition, we presented the candidate's point of view, highlighting the requirement of trustworthy, explainable and fair AI applications. Finally, the chapter presents a forward looking look on future trends, e.g., multimodal data integration, federated learning for privacy preserving analytics and adaptive, culturally sensitive AI models. In the end, the use case of AI in recruitment is huge; however, despite its advantages, it can only be successful if maintained human centric, based on ethics and consistent with organizational values.

REFERENCES

Abbaschian, B. J., Elmaghraby, A., & Sierra-Sosa, D. (2021). Deep Learning Techniques for Speech Emotion Recognition, from Databases to Models. *Sensors (Basel), 21*(4), 1249. DOI: 10.3390/s21041249 PMID: 33578714

Akinrinola, O., Ugochukwu, C., Ofodile, O., & Okoye, C. (2024). Navigating and reviewing ethical dilemmas in AI development: Strategies for transparency, fairness, and accountability. GSC Advanced Research and Reviews, 18(3), 050–058.

Al-Quraishi, T., Al-Quraishi, N., Alnabulsi, H., Al-Qarishey, H., & Ali, A. H. (2024). Big Data Predictive Analytics for Personalized Medicine: Perspectives and Challenges. *Applied Data Science and Analysis, 2024*, 32–38. DOI: 10.58496/ADSA/2024/004

Alshdaifat, E., Hussein, F., Alshdaifat, D., El-Salhi, S. M. F. S., & Alsarhan, A. (2021). The Effect of Preprocessing Techniques, Applied to Numeric Features, on Classification Algorithms' Performance. *Data, 6*(2), 11. DOI: 10.3390/data6020011

B, S., Meeradevi, M., S, S., Alex, S. A., Kanavalli, A., S, R., & G, S. (2024). Machine learning model for emotion detection and recognition using an enhanced Convolutional Neural Network. Journal of Integrated Science and Technology, 12(4).

Badouch, M., Boulmane, Es., Mahmoud, H., Zioudi, O., & Boutaounte, M. (2025b). Smart Tourism: How AI is Reimagining the Travel Experience. In Aboudrar, I., Ilahi Bakhsh, F., Nayyar, A., & Ouachtouk, I. (Eds.), *Innovative Technologies on Electrical Power Systems for Smart Cities Infrastructure. ICESST 2024. Sustainable Civil Infrastructures*. Springer. DOI: 10.1007/978-3-031-86705-7_18

Badouch, M., & Boutaounte, M. (2024). Design and implementation of a hotel recommendation system using deep learning. In Advances in marketing, customer relationship management, and e-services book series (pp. 388–408). DOI: 10.4018/979-8-3693-3172-9.ch019

Badouch, M., Boutaounte, M., Mahmoud, H., & Elmobark, N. (2025a). AI-Powered Smart Tourism Reimagining Travel. In Advances in computational intelligence and robotics book series (pp. 431–464).

Ballesteros, J. A., Ramírez, V. G. M., Moreira, F., Pelaez, C. A., & Solano, A. (2024). Facial emotion recognition through artificial intelligence. *Frontiers of Computer Science*, 6.

Bernhardt, M., Lungren, M. P., Glocker, B., Alvarez-Valle, J., Bannur, S., Tanno, R., Tezcan, K. C., Castro, D. C., Monteiro, M., Oktay, O., Schwaighofer, A., & Nori, A. (2022). Active label cleaning for improved dataset quality under resource constraints. *Nature Communications*, *13*(1), 1161. DOI: 10.1038/s41467-022-28818-3 PMID: 35246539

Bhangale, K., & Kothandaraman, M. (2023). Speech Emotion Recognition Based on Multiple Acoustic Features and Deep Convolutional Neural Network. *Electronics (Basel)*, *12*(4), 839. DOI: 10.3390/electronics12040839

Bharti, S. K., Shukla, P. K., Mahmoud, A., Varadhaganapathy, S., Bouye, M., Gupta, R. K., & Hingaa, S. K. (2022). Text-Based Emotion Recognition Using Deep Learning Approach. Computational Intelligence and Neuroscience, 2022(45–60), 1–8.

Bulut, O., & Beiting-Parrish, M. (2024). The Rise of Artificial Intelligence in Educational Measurement: Opportunities and Ethical Challenges. *Chinese/English Journal of Educational Measurement and Evaluation*, *5*(3). DOI: 10.59863/MIQL7785

Burrell, D. N., Springs, D., Jones, A. J., Muller, S. R., Wright, J. B., Richardson, K., Burton, S. L., Huff, A. J., Brown-Jackson, K. L., & Nobles, C. (2023). The Managerial Ethical and Operational Challenges of Hospital Cybersecurity (pp. 444–458). igi global.

Bursell, M., & Roumbanis, L. (2024). After the algorithms: A study of meta-algorithmic judgments and diversity in the hiring process at a large multisite company. *Big Data & Society*, *11*(1), 20539517231221758. DOI: 10.1177/20539517231221758

Chaudhari, A., Krishna, A., Travieso-González, C. M., & Bhatt, C. (2023). Facial Emotion Recognition with Inter-Modality-Attention-Transformer-Based Self-Supervised Learning. *Electronics (Basel)*, *12*(2), 288. DOI: 10.3390/electronics12020288

Chien, W.-S., & Lee, C.-C. (2023). Achieving Fair Speech Emotion Recognition via Perceptual Fairness. 17, 1–5.

Chowdary, M. K., Hemanth, D. J., & Anitha, J. (2022). Emotion Recognition from EEG Signals Using Recurrent Neural Networks. *Electronics (Basel)*, *11*(15), 2387. DOI: 10.3390/electronics11152387

Chowdary, M. K., Nguyen, T. N., & Hemanth, D. J. (2021). Deep learning-based facial emotion recognition for human–computer interaction applications. *Neural Computing & Applications*, *35*(32), 23311–23328. DOI: 10.1007/s00521-021-06012-8

Cowan, K., Javornik, A., & Jiang, P. (2021). Privacy concerns when using augmented reality face filters? Explaining why and when use avoidance occurs. *Psychology and Marketing*, *38*(10), 1799–1813. DOI: 10.1002/mar.21576

Craig, S. L., Goulden, A., Eaton, A. D., & Mcinroy, L. B. (2021). Engaging the Senses in Qualitative Research via Multimodal Coding: Triangulating Transcript, Audio, and Video Data in a Study With Sexual and Gender Minority Youth. *International Journal of Qualitative Methods, 20*, 160940692110136. DOI: 10.1177/16094069211013659

Dada, E. G., Joseph, S. B., Oluwagbemi, O. O., Emebo, O., & Oyewola, D. O. (2023). Facial Emotion Recognition and Classification Using the Convolutional Neural Network-10 (CNN-10). *Applied Computational Intelligence and Soft Computing, 2023*, 1–19. DOI: 10.1155/2023/2457898

Depuru, S., Nandam, A., Sivanantham, S., Amala, K., Akshaya, V., & Saktivel, M. (2022). Convolutional Neural Network based Human Emotion Recognition System: A Deep Learning Approach. 1–4.

Dolka, H. (2021). *M, A. X. V., & Juliet, S.* Speech Emotion Recognition Using ANN on MFCC Features.

Farooq, M., Raja, F. R., Baloch, N. K., Zikria, Y. B., Hussain, F., & Yu, H. (2020). Impact of Feature Selection Algorithm on Speech Emotion Recognition Using Deep Convolutional Neural Network. *Sensors (Basel), 20*(21), 6008. DOI: 10.3390/s20216008 PMID: 33113907

Gerczuk, M., Ottl, S., Amiriparian, S., & Schuller, B. W. (2023). EmoNet: A Transfer Learning Framework for Multi-Corpus Speech Emotion Recognition. *IEEE Transactions on Affective Computing, 14*(2), 1472–1487. DOI: 10.1109/TAFFC.2021.3135152

Gkintoni, E., Aroutzidis, A., Antonopoulou, H., & Halkiopoulos, C. (2025). From Neural Networks to Emotional Networks: A Systematic Review of EEG-Based Emotion Recognition in Cognitive Neuroscience and Real-World Applications. *Brain Sciences, 15*(3), 220. DOI: 10.3390/brainsci15030220 PMID: 40149742

Gunawan, T. S., Rosnelly, R., Kartiwi, M., Riza, B. S., Haryanto, E. V., Ashraf, A., & Janin, Z. (2020). Development of video-based emotion recognition using deep learning with Google Colab. *Telkomnika, 18*(5), 2463. DOI: 10.12928/telkomnika.v18i5.16717

Gupta, N. (2023). Artificial Intelligence Ethics and Fairness: A study to address bias and fairness issues in AI systems, and the ethical implications of AI applications. *Revista Review Index Journal of Multidisciplinary, 3*(2), 24–35. DOI: 10.31305/rrijm2023.v03.n02.004

Hasan, H. E., Jaber, D., Khabour, O. F., & Alzoubi, K. H. (2024). Ethical considerations and concerns in the implementation of AI in pharmacy practice: A cross-sectional study. *BMC Medical Ethics*, *25*(1), 55. DOI: 10.1186/s12910-024-01062-8 PMID: 38750441

Hickman, L., Ng, V., Saef, R., Woo, S. E., Bosch, N., & Tay, L. (2021). Developing and evaluating language-based machine learning algorithms for inferring applicant personality in video interviews. *Human Resource Management Journal*, *34*(2), 255–274. DOI: 10.1111/1748-8583.12356

Horodyski, P. (2023). Applicants' perception of artificial intelligence in the recruitment process. *Computers in Human Behavior Reports*, *11*, 100303. DOI: 10.1016/j.chbr.2023.100303

Hu, Q. (2023). Unilever's Practice on AI-based Recruitment. Highlights in Business. *Economics and Management*, *16*, 256–263.

Hung, L. P., & Alias, S. (2023). Beyond Sentiment Analysis: A Review of Recent Trends in Text Based Sentiment Analysis and Emotion Detection. *Journal of Advanced Computational Intelligence and Intelligent Informatics*, *27*(1), 84–95. DOI: 10.20965/jaciii.2023.p0084

Idoko, I., Manuel, H., Igbede, M., Ukaegbu, C., Akpa, F., & Adeoye, T. (2024). Big data and AI in employment: The dual challenge of workforce replacement and protecting customer privacy in biometric data usage. Global Journal of Engineering and Technology Advances, 19(2), 089–106.

Jaiswal, A., Deb, S., & Krishnama Raju, A. (2020, Jun 1). Facial Emotion Detection Using Deep Learning.

Jiang, J., Ye, S., Wang, W., Xu, J., & Luo, X. (2020). Learning Effective Representations for Person-Job Fit by Feature Fusion. 2549–2556.

Jiang, P., Zhao, L., Xu, X., Tao, H., & Zou, C. (2022). Convolutional-Recurrent Neural Networks With Multiple Attention Mechanisms for Speech Emotion Recognition. *IEEE Transactions on Cognitive and Developmental Systems*, *14*(4), 1564–1573. DOI: 10.1109/TCDS.2021.3123979

Jiang, Z., Seyedi, S., Griner, E., Abbasi, A., Rad, A. B., Kwon, H., Cotes, R. O., & Clifford, G. D. (2024). Multimodal Mental Health Digital Biomarker Analysis From Remote Interviews Using Facial, Vocal, Linguistic, and Cardiovascular Patterns. *IEEE Journal of Biomedical and Health Informatics*, *28*(3), 1680–1691. DOI: 10.1109/JBHI.2024.3352075 PMID: 38198249

Kakuba, S., Han, D. S., & Poulose, A. (2022). Attention-Based Multi-Learning Approach for Speech Emotion Recognition With Dilated Convolution. *IEEE Access : Practical Innovations, Open Solutions*, *10*, 122302–122313. DOI: 10.1109/ACCESS.2022.3223705

Kanjanawattana, S., Kittichaiwatthana, P., Praneetpholkrang, P., & Srivisut, K. (2023). Deep Learning-Based Emotion Recognition through Facial Expressions. Journal of Image and Graphics, 140–145.

Kardakis, S., Perikos, I., Hatzilygeroudis, I., & Grivokostopoulou, F. (2021). Examining Attention Mechanisms in Deep Learning Models for Sentiment Analysis. *Applied Sciences (Basel, Switzerland)*, *11*(9), 3883. DOI: 10.3390/app11093883

Kathuria, A., Singla, R. K., & Gupta, A. (2020). A Review of Tools and Techniques for Preprocessing of Textual Data (pp. 407–422). springer singapore.

Kazim, E., Koshiyama, A. S., Hilliard, A., & Polle, R. (2021). Systematizing Audit in Algorithmic Recruitment. *Journal of Intelligence*, *9*(3), 46. DOI: 10.3390/jintelligence9030046 PMID: 34564294

Kumar, P., Iwamura, M., Roy, P. P., Jain, S., & Raman, B. (2021). End-to-end Triplet Loss based Emotion Embedding System for Speech Emotion Recognition. 13, 8766–8773.

Lamjid, A., Ennejjai, I., Anass, A., Soumia, Z., & Mabrouki, J. (2024). Enhancing the hiring process: A predictive system for soft skills assessment. Data and Metadata, 3.

Li, C., Chen, B., Cummins, N., Schuller, B. W., & Zhao, Z. (2021). Hierarchical Attention-Based Temporal Convolutional Networks for Eeg-Based Emotion Recognition. 1240–1244.

Li, E., Li, D., Li, C., Wang, S., Hao, Q., & Wu, X. (2020). SUSTech POINTS: A Portable 3D Point Cloud Interactive Annotation Platform System. abs 1903 11027, 1108–1115.

Li, M., Liu, X., Li, X., Huang, X., Xu, H., & Song, Z. (2021). Facial Expression Recognition with Identity and Emotion Joint Learning. *IEEE Transactions on Affective Computing*, *12*(2), 544–550. DOI: 10.1109/TAFFC.2018.2880201

Li, W., Zeng, G., Chen, X., Cui, Y., Guo, G., Cao, D., Ma, Y., & Li, G. (2023). A Spontaneous Driver Emotion Facial Expression (DEFE) Dataset for Intelligent Vehicles: Emotions Triggered by Video-Audio Clips in Driving Scenarios. *IEEE Transactions on Affective Computing*, *14*(1), 747–760. DOI: 10.1109/TAFFC.2021.3063387

Li, Y., Chan, J., Peko, G., & Sundaram, D. (2023). Mixed emotion extraction analysis and visualisation of social media text. *Data & Knowledge Engineering*, *148*, 102220. DOI: 10.1016/j.datak.2023.102220

Lian, H., Zong, Y., Zhao, Y., Li, S., Lu, C., & Tang, C. (2023). A Survey of Deep Learning-Based Multimodal Emotion Recognition: Speech, Text, and Face. *Entropy (Basel, Switzerland)*, *25*(10), 1440. DOI: 10.3390/e25101440 PMID: 37895561

Lopez, E., Grassucci, E., Comminiello, D., & Chiarantano, E. (2023, Jun 4). Hypercomplex Multimodal Emotion Recognition from EEG and Peripheral Physiological Signals.

Lu, W., Zhang, X., Xia, L., Ma, H., & Tan, T.-P. (2024). Domain adaptation spatial feature perception neural network for cross-subject EEG emotion recognition. *Frontiers in Human Neuroscience*, *18*, 18. DOI: 10.3389/fnhum.2024.1471634 PMID: 39741785

Mahmud Sujon, K., Binti Hassan, R., Choi, K., Abdus Samad, M., Tusnia Towshi, Z., & Othman, M. A. (2024). When to Use Standardization and Normalization: Empirical Evidence From Machine Learning Models and XAI. *IEEE Access : Practical Innovations, Open Solutions*, *12*, 135300–135314. DOI: 10.1109/ACCESS.2024.3462434

Maji, B., Swain, M., Guha, R., & Routray, A. (2023). Multimodal Emotion Recognition Based on Deep Temporal Features Using Cross-Modal Transformer and Self-Attention. 1–5.

Makhmudov, F., Kultimuratov, A., & Cho, Y.-I. (2024). Enhancing Multimodal Emotion Recognition through Attention Mechanisms in BERT and CNN Architectures. mdpi ag.

Martín-Raugh, M. P., Randall, J. G., Kell, H. J., Banfi, J. T., & Anguiano-Carrasco, C. (2022). Speaking without words: A meta-analysis of over 70 years of research on the power of nonverbal cues in job interviews. *Journal of Organizational Behavior*, *44*(1), 132–156. DOI: 10.1002/job.2670

Muaad, A. Y., Chola, C., Benifa, J. V. B., Guru, D. S., Gumaei, A. H., Davanagere, H. J., Al-Antari, M. A., & Alsalman, H. (2022). Arabic Document Classification: Performance Investigation of Preprocessing and Representation Techniques. *Mathematical Problems in Engineering*, *2022*, 1–16. DOI: 10.1155/2022/3720358

Omar, M., & Burrell, D. N. (2023). Organizational Dynamics and Bias in Artificial Intelligence (AI) Recruitment Algorithms (pp. 269–290). igi global.

Ong, K. L., Lim, H. S., Lim, K. M., & Lee, C. P. (2023). Speech emotion recognition with light gradient boosting decision trees machine. [IJECE]. *International Journal of Electrical and Computer Engineering*, *13*(4), 4020. DOI: 10.11591/ijece.v13i4.pp4020-4028

Padilla, R., Dias, T. L. B., Passos, W. L., Netto, S. L., & Da Silva, E. A. B. (2021). A Comparative Analysis of Object Detection Metrics with a Companion Open-Source Toolkit. *Electronics (Basel)*, *10*(3), 279. DOI: 10.3390/electronics10030279

Palakurti, N. R. (2025). Ethical Considerations of AI and ML in Insurance Risk Management: Addressing Bias and Ensuring Fairness. International Journal of Multidisciplinary Research in Science, Engineering and Technology, 08(01).

Pastor, M. A., Lleida, E., Miguel, A., Ribas, D., & Ortega, A. (2023). Cross-Corpus Training Strategy for Speech Emotion Recognition Using Self-Supervised Representations. *Applied Sciences (Basel, Switzerland)*, *13*(16), 9062. DOI: 10.3390/app13169062

Pepino, L., Ferrer, L., & Riera, P. (2021, Aug 30). Emotion Recognition from Speech Using wav2vec 2.0 Embeddings.

Picoral, A., Reppen, R., & Staples, S. (2021). Automated annotation of learner English. *International Journal of Learner Corpus Research*, *7*(1), 17–52. DOI: 10.1075/ijlcr.20003.pic

Rivera, M., Kumar, S., Qiu, L., & Petrucci, T. (2021). Are Traditional Performance Reviews Outdated? An Empirical Analysis on Continuous, Real-Time Feedback in the Workplace. *Information Systems Research*, *32*(2), 517–540. DOI: 10.1287/isre.2020.0979

Romano, J. D., Moore, J. H., Goldberg, D. J., Chakraborty, P., Le, T. T., Ray, N. L., Himmelstein, D., La Cava, W., Fu, W., & Gregg, J. T. (2021). PMLB v1.0: An open-source dataset collection for benchmarking machine learning methods. *Bioinformatics (Oxford, England)*, *38*(3), 878–880. DOI: 10.1093/bioinformatics/btab727 PMID: 34677586

Salekshahrezaee, Z., Leevy, J. L., & Khoshgoftaar, T. M. (2023). The effect of feature extraction and data sampling on credit card fraud detection. *Journal of Big Data*, *10*(1), 6. DOI: 10.1186/s40537-023-00684-w

Santomartino, S. M., Zech, J. R., Hall, K., Jeudy, J., Parekh, V., & Yi, P. H. (2024). Evaluating the Performance and Bias of Natural Language Processing Tools in Labeling Chest Radiograph Reports. *Radiology*, *313*(1), e232746. DOI: 10.1148/radiol.232746 PMID: 39436298

Saumard, M. (2023). Enhancing Speech Emotions Recognition Using Multivariate Functional Data Analysis. *Big Data and Cognitive Computing*, *7*(3), 146. DOI: 10.3390/bdcc7030146

Shuford, J. (2024). Exploring Ethical Dimensions in AI: Navigating Bias and Fairness in the Field. Journal of Artificial Intelligence General Science (JAIGS) ISSN:3006-4023, 103–124.

Suen, H.-Y., & Hung, K.-E. (2023). Comparing job applicant deception in asynchronous vs synchronous video interviews, with and without AI-assisted assessments. *Information Technology & People*, *38*(2), 963–983. DOI: 10.1108/ITP-02-2023-0189

Sühr, T., Hilgard, S., & Lakkaraju, H. (2021). Does Fair Ranking Improve Minority Outcomes? Understanding the Interplay of Human and Algorithmic Biases in Online Hiring. 989–999.

Ullah, R., Ullah, I., Khurshaid, T., Shah, W. A., Alibakhshikenari, M., Anjam, F., Asif, M., Ali, S. M., Shah, S., & Wuttisittikulkij, L. (2023). Speech Emotion Recognition Using Convolution Neural Networks and Multi-Head Convolutional Transformer. *Sensors (Basel)*, *23*(13), 6212. DOI: 10.3390/s23136212 PMID: 37448062

Volynets, S., Saarimäki, H., Nummenmaa, L., & Smirnov, D. (2020). Statistical pattern recognition reveals shared neural signatures for displaying and recognizing specific facial expressions. *Social Cognitive and Affective Neuroscience*, *15*(8), 803–813. DOI: 10.1093/scan/nsaa110 PMID: 33007782

Wang, X., Qu, H., Wang, Y., Yang, M., Jin, Z., & He, J. (2022). M2Lens: Visualizing and Explaining Multimodal Models for Sentiment Analysis. *IEEE Transactions on Visualization and Computer Graphics*, *28*(1), 802–812. DOI: 10.1109/TVCG.2021.3114794 PMID: 34587037

Wani, T. M., Mansor, H., Kartiwi, M., Gunawan, T. S., Qadri, S. A. A., & Ismail, N. (2020). Speech Emotion Recognition using Convolution Neural Networks and Deep Stride Convolutional Neural Networks. 1–6.

Xu, L., Wang, K., Jung, T.-P., Xu, M., Ma, Z., & Ming, D. (2021). Enhancing transfer performance across datasets for brain-computer interfaces using a combination of alignment strategies and adaptive batch normalization. Journal of Neural Engineering, 18(4), 0460e5.

Yang, C., Zhao, W. X., Zhang, T., Hou, Y., Song, Y., & Wen, J.-R. (2022). Modeling Two-Way Selection Preference for Person-Job Fit.

Zhang, H., Han, H., & Huang, H. (2020). Attention-Based Convolution Skip Bidirectional Long Short-Term Memory Network for Speech Emotion Recognition. *IEEE Access : Practical Innovations, Open Solutions*, *9*, 5332–5342. DOI: 10.1109/ACCESS.2020.3047395

Zhang, K., Li, Y., Wang, Z., Wang, J., & Li, X. (2021). Feature Fusion for Multimodal Emotion Recognition Based on Deep Canonical Correlation Analysis. *IEEE Signal Processing Letters*, *28*, 1898–1902. DOI: 10.1109/LSP.2021.3112314

Zhang, T., & Tan, Z. (2023). Deep Emotion Recognition using Facial, Speech and Textual Cues: A Survey. institute of electrical electronics engineers.

Zhang, X., Wang, M.-J., & Guo, X.-D. (2020). Multi-modal Emotion Recognition Based on Deep Learning in Speech. *Video and Text.*, *30*, 328–333.

Zhang, Y., Rahman, S., & Hossain, M. Z. (2021). DeepVANet: A Deep End-to-End Network for Multi-modal Emotion Recognition (pp. 227–237). springer.

Zhang, Z., Zhang, S., Ni, D., Wei, Z., Yang, K., Jin, S., Huang, G., Liang, Z., Zhang, L., Li, L., Ding, H., Zhang, Z., & Wang, J. (2024). Multimodal Sensing for Depression Risk Detection: Integrating Audio, Video, and Text Data. *Sensors (Basel)*, *24*(12), 3714. DOI: 10.3390/s24123714 PMID: 38931497

Chapter 7
Virtual Reality for Interview Simulations

P. Venkadesh
https://orcid.org/0000-0001-6582-3153
V.S.B College of Engineering Technical Campus, Coimbatore, India

S. Ninisha Nels
Noorul Islam Centre for Higher Education, Kumaracoil, India

S.V. Divya
https://orcid.org/0009-0004-4321-8066
V.S.B College of Engineering Technical Campus, Coimbatore, India

K.V. Shiny
https://orcid.org/0000-0002-6603-4268
Bharath Institute of Higher Education and Research, Chennai, India

M. Sudhan
V.S.B College of Engineering Technical Campus, Coimbatore, India

ABSTRACT

Virtual Reality (VR) is transforming recruitment by offering immersive, interactive simulations that replicate real job scenarios. Unlike traditional interviews, VR enables recruiters to assess behavioral traits, decision-making, communication, and cultural fit with greater precision. Powered by Artificial Intelligence (AI) and Big Data, VR systems analyze verbal and non-verbal cues to predict job performance, reduce bias, and improve hiring outcomes. Industries such as emergency medicine, software engineering, and retail have successfully adopted VR, resulting in better employee retention and reduced training costs. Gamified and AI-driven environments enhance candidate engagement through avatar-based interactions, real-time feed-

DOI: 10.4018/979-8-3373-6516-9.ch007

back, and collaborative problem-solving. VR can simulate high-pressure scenarios to evaluate emotional intelligence, adaptability, and leadership—traits often overlooked in conventional interviews. This Chapter deals with how Virtual Reality helps for Interview simulations in conduction a smooth and efficient interview virtually.

1. INTRODUCTION

The hiring process significantly influences an organization's success. Conventionally, recruitment relies on structured interviews, resume reviews, and aptitude tests. Although these methods establish a foundation for evaluating candidates, they often fail to capture real-world behaviors, problem-solving skills, and cultural alignment. Moreover, traditional interviews can be time-intensive, susceptible to bias, and challenging to standardize across large or global hiring efforts.

With digital technology's rapid evolution, organizations are adopting innovative tools to streamline and enhance recruitment. Technologies like Artificial Intelligence (AI), Machine Learning (ML), and data analytics have transformed hiring by automating resume filtering, predicting job performance, and refining candidate matching. Virtual Reality (VR) emerges as a transformative tool, providing immersive, interactive environments that replicate real-world work scenarios.

VR allows recruiters to evaluate candidates beyond traditional question-answer interviews. Through VR headsets and motion-tracking systems, candidates engage in simulated job settings tailored to specific roles, such as leading teams, handling customer issues, or debugging code. These simulations enable recruiters to assess soft skills like communication, leadership, and adaptability, alongside technical expertise, in realistic settings. Unlike conventional interviews, which can be hypothetical and subjective, VR assessments deliver practical, data-driven insights.

As companies complete for top-tier talent in an increasingly digital and remote-first world, the demand for innovative and equitable hiring practices is at an all-time high. VR is not just a futuristic concept it is already being adopted by global organizations across the industries including technology, healthcare, finance and retail. Whether used for organizations identify and evaluate the best candidates.

Despite growing interest in Virtual Reality (VR) for recruitment, most existing studies focus narrowly on specific user groups (e.g., clinical populations) or technical feasibility without addressing the broader organizational, ethical, and cultural contexts. There is limited guidance on how companies can practically implement VR interview systems at scale, and few works explore the balance between candidate experience, technical performance, and fairness. In particular, there is a lack of integrated discussion that connects AI-driven analytics, system design, soft-skill evaluation, and legal compliance in a single framework. Moreover, little attention has been given to global accessibility, localization strategies, and support for underrepresented or differently abled candidate groups. This chapter addresses these critical gaps by offering a comprehensive, interdisciplinary overview that merges theoretical foundations, technical architectures, real-world case studies, and ethical considerations. In doing so, it contributes a novel, end-to-end perspective on immersive hiring practices using VR.

The global shift to remote work, the rise of digital hiring, and the growing demand for fair, efficient, and immersive recruitment solutions make VR-based interviews more relevant than ever. Traditional hiring methods are struggling to capture nuanced behavioral traits and create consistent experiences across locations. With increasing concerns around bias, inclusivity, and candidate engagement, organizations are now looking for tools that blend innovation with ethical design. Virtual Reality offers a unique convergence of simulation, AI, and user experience, making it a promising frontier in recruitment. This chapter is positioned to fill a critical gap by offering not just theoretical insights but also practical frameworks for implementation, accessibility, and ethical alignment.

This chapter aims to provide a comprehensive exploration of VR for interview simulations, It delves into the core components of VR technology in recruitment, including system design, AI integration, behavioural analytics and predictive hiring. The chapter also examines the advantages and challenges of VR-based interviews, ethical considerations such as GDPR/CCPA compliance and real-world case studies of successful implementation. Finally, it discusses future trends and innovations that are expected to shape the next generation of virtual hiring tools.

2. LITERATURE REVIEW

Over the past decade virtual reality (VR) has shifted from a futuristic curiosity to a credible instrument for identifying, preparing, and selecting talent. Pioneering work by Luo et al. (2024) shows that seemingly subtle design choices—such as the realism of a simulated office or the balance between personal and technical questions—materially change how anxious and forthcoming candidates become, underscoring the importance of thoughtful scenario engineering. The most mature application of this idea is VR Job Interview Training (VR-JIT). A series of linked studies by Smith et al. (2016) with job-seekers who have substance-use disorders, by Smith et al. (2015) with people living with schizophrenia, and by Smith, Parham & Mitchell (2023) with prison-based populations all report the same headline finding: a short course of VR-JIT measurably improves interview skill and at six-month follow-up translates into higher odds of competitive employment. Complementing these clinical investigations, a Frontiers in Virtual Reality study on interview "perspective" (2024) demonstrates that simply viewing a simulation from a first-person rather than third-person camera can strengthen self-efficacy—another reminder that micro-level design details matter.

Outside the laboratory, organisations are using VR to keep hiring agile and engaging. During the pandemic documented how Indian technology firms pivoted to fully virtual recruitment drives, reporting better candidate throughput and stronger employer branding. In school-based transition services found that VR-JIT could be rolled out at scale with high user satisfaction, while a budget-impact analysis by Danielson et al. (2024) showed that once headsets and licences are pooled across programmes, VR interviewing is no more expensive than conventional assessment centres. Determining exactly how much "dose" is needed, Parham & Ryzin (2024) concluded that even three to five guided sessions yield significant skill gains for youth with disabilities, and a quasi-experimental study by Smith et al. (2022) confirmed that those gains hold when training is delivered across multiple campuses.

Commercial case studies echo the research describes how Walmart used VR to rehearse Black-Friday scenarios and then adapted the same platform for candidate screening, noting sharper retention of new hires but warning that glossy simulations can inflate expectations if job realities are not equally compelling. A separate WIRED report on Lloyds Banking Group's graduate assessment found that candidates praised the fairness of a shared 360-degree puzzle room, while recruiters valued the automated behavioural analytics generated in real time. Those analytics draw heavily on techniques first proven in healthcare. A meta-analysis by Kyaw et al. (2019) shows that VR consistently boosts skill transfer and decision-making in medical education, and observational work by Moro et al. (2017) links the technology to higher engagement during complex procedural training. The learning sciences offer parallel evidence: Izard et al. (2017) found that VR outperforms desktop interfaces in sustaining attention, whereas Zeng et al. (2024) demonstrated that immersive symptom-management coaching reduces distress for cancer patients—findings that collectively support the claim that VR can evoke realistic stressors without compromising psychological safety.

VR also proves valuable where safety is paramount. In mining, Moro et al. (2019) showed that simulated emergencies improve response accuracy and recall, a principle transferable to leadership assessments that require calm under pressure. Likewise, education research by Parong & Mayer (2018) confirms that immersive 3-D environments deepen conceptual understanding, suggesting that VR hiring tasks can validly probe higher-order reasoning rather than rote recall. The field is now being extended by augmented and mixed reality; a meta-analysis by Kriklenko et al. (2022) concludes that blending physical and virtual cues enables adaptive feedback that feels personalised, opening the door to interview systems that adjust difficulty on the fly.

Notwithstanding these gains, two concerns recur. First, upfront costs remain non-trivial, although amortisation models proposed by Danielson et al. (2024) and cloud-streaming solutions are reducing the barrier to entry. Second, privacy and fairness demand vigilance. An early position paper by Smith et al. (2014) warned that rich behavioural telemetry must be handled under strict governance to prevent new forms of bias; today, GDPR-compliant data vaults and algorithmic audits are becoming standard practice. Taken together, the literature paints a consistent picture: when grounded in sound instructional design and ethical data use, VR gives recruiters a richer, more equitable view of human potential than traditional interviews can offer, and it does so in a format that candidates increasingly recognise as both modern and engaging.

3. UNDERSTANDING VIRTUAL REALITY IN HR

Virtual Reality (VR) refers to a computer-generated mimic of a three-dimensional world where the user can experience surroundings in an extremely immersive and realistic way. Through the utilization of equipment like headsets with high-definition screens and motion tracking sensors, as well as haptic gloves or controllers, VR positions the user within a virtual environment where they are not observers but active agents. In contrast to conventional digital interfaces that display information on two-dimensional screens, VR offers an intense feeling of presence by stimulating the user's visual, auditory, and tactile senses. This level of immersion allows VR to be very effective at simulating real-world situations, which is why it has been used across various fields like education, entertainment, military training, and most recently, human resources (HR) and talent acquisition.

In order to learn what can change HR practices with VR, it is necessary to look at the technology's fundamental building blocks. VR equipment consists of head-mounted devices such as Oculus Quest, HTC Vive, or Meta Quest, which cast 3D worlds into the subject's point of view. Motion controllers allow the manipulation of virtual items by moving one's hands with gestures such as grabbing, pointing, or navigating. Body movements and orientation are tracked by sensors and tracking systems in order to align the user's physical actions in the real world with the virtual world. Haptic devices provide realism by giving users feedback physically, so they can “feel” resistance or textures in the virtual world. From the software side, simulation platforms serve to plan and manage the simulated environments, typically combined with AI and analytics tools to monitor user performance, gesture, voice commands, and engagement measurements. Cloud-based architecture provides scalability, remote access, and multi-user collaboration, particularly useful for decentralized workforces. User Interface (UI) and User Experience (UX) design is essential to making these systems easy to use, responsive, and accurate in mirroring real-life workflows.

VR deployment in HR has been picking up pace as companies try to improve recruitment, training, and employee engagement to be more effective, inclusive, and scalable. One of the most influential applications is Virtual Job Simulations, in which candidates are virtually put into actual job environments to carry out role-specific tasks. This approach enables managers to evaluate technical and problem-solving skills within context. For example, customer service candidates can engage with virtual customers to showcase their conflict resolution skills, and engineers can diagnose mock equipment malfunctions. Also, Behavioural and Soft Skill Evaluations can be done via VR by seeing how interviewees interact in team challenges or leadership scenarios, giving insights into traits such as communication, empathy, and teamwork—abilities hard to gauge using resumes or traditional interviewing.

With the increase in remote labor and outsourcing of talent globally, VR is emerging as a revolutionary technology in remote and international hiring. It helps organizations carry out thorough tests and interviews without having to make the candidates travel, saving time and money while maintaining consistency in assessment. As the technology becomes more mature, we should expect to witness increasingly sophisticated capabilities such as real-time language interpretation, AI-powered feedback, and adaptive learning tracks, which will make VR not just an instrument of simulation but a platform for smart workforce building.

4. CONCEPTS OF INTERVIEW SIMULATIONS IN VIRTUAL RECRUITMENT

Interview simulations are a modern hiring method that simulates real-life job situations in a controlled and systematic setting. While conventional interviews only analyze applicants on the basis of verbal answers to predetermined questions, simulation-based interviews are meant to analyze how people truly react and decide when they are presented with job-related challenges. Such simulations are especially useful when assessing not only soft skills like communication, flexibility, and emotional intelligence but also technical or occupation-specific competencies, with a holistic understanding of a candidate's fit for a job. By placing the candidates in realistic situations, simulations enable the recruiters to see the actions instead of hearing theoretical responses, leading to better and unbiased judgments. For job applicants, the simulation is frequently more interactive and participative and offers a substantive chance to showcase their capabilities in action.

The integration of Virtual Reality (VR) into interview simulations has elevated their effectiveness by significantly enhancing realism and immersion. In a VR setting, simulations can become fully interactive, three-dimensional experiences that deeply engage the candidate's senses. To take one example, a task simulation in VR could put an application software developer into a simulated virtual tech lab where they engage with code and virtual tools in the moment, or a customer service applicant can work through AI-driven avatars simulating actual customers. The interactive quality of VR enables simulations to mimic real-world job settings, so they are not merely tests but experiential introductions to the job. This realism is necessary for two important reasons. First, it creates genuine responses from applicants since they are likely to act naturally when they perceive the setting to be closely like actual work conditions. This allows recruiters to gain clearer visions of a candidate's functional skills and emotional reactions. Second, VR simulations provide accurate job previews to applicants, which creates realistic expectations and enhances job satisfaction after hiring. By getting candidates used to the pressure and subtlety of the job beforehand, it is less likely that they will be caught off guard by the realities of the job and early attrition is minimized.

Additionally, high-end VR simulations could include AI-powered avatars, real-time analytics, and branching narrative streams that respond to user input, providing more dynamism and depth to the assessment process. These systems are capable of listening for tone of voice, eye gaze, pause, and decision-making patterns, providing recruiters with a three-dimensional picture of every candidate. Haptic feedback, natural language processing, and voice recognition further increase the level of immersion, converting every simulation into an ethnographic data collector. This is especially useful for remote interviews, in which in-person contact is limited, and organizations are forced to use electronic tools to correctly assess talent.

5. DESIGN AND ARCHITECTURE OF VR INTERVIEW SYSTEMS

The success of a Virtual Reality (VR) interview simulation relies heavily on its system architecture and underlying design. A solid and carefully crafted VR system not only guarantees responsive and immersive user experiences but also easily integrates with current recruitment infrastructure. A systematic approach to designing VR systems ensures that virtual simulations simultaneously meet technical and strategic HR requirements, streamline candidate evaluation and boost engagement. At the core of any VR interview system is its technical configuration, which involves hardware as well as software elements. Hardware-wise, VR headsets like Oculus Quest 2, HTC Viv Pro, and Meta Quest are critical to provide a stereoscopic 3D display, offering users depth and a feeling of presence in the virtual setting. Motion controllers and tracking sensors enable users to execute gestures such as pointing, grabbing, or manipulating virtual tools, whereas body tracking transfers bodily movement into virtual action. These systems are usually accompanied by high-performance computing equipment in the form of VR-capable PCs or cloud-based streaming services that can render intricate environments in real-time with little latency. In more sophisticated uses, optional peripherals such as haptic gloves, omnidirectional treadmills, and VR vests can be employed in order to replicate touch, movement, and physical force, particularly for physically active roles or training simulations.

On the software front, robust VR development software like Unity or Unreal Engine is utilized in order to generate high-fidelity 3D environments, animate avatars, and control interactive components. These engines support scripting of simulation logic to facilitate dynamic branching scenarios that adjust based on the behavior of a candidate, fueled by artificial intelligence. Scenario management capabilities can manage the flow of interactions and tasks, and data analytics modules capture performance metrics such as eye movement, speech patterns, response time, gesture accuracy, and emotional indicators. All the data is safely stored and processed in the back-end to facilitate data-driven candidate assessment. For practical use, VR interview systems also need to integrate with current hiring ecosystems, including Application Tracking Systems (ATS), Human Resource Information Systems (HRIS), and video interviewing platforms. Real-time performance monitoring and feedback features enable HR teams to analyze candidate behavior, communicate findings, and share insights without switching between systems. Cloud-based solutions and APIs enable real-time data synchronization, reducing remote VR interviews to be efficient and scalable by geographical location.

One of the most important features of VR interview systems is their power to mimic human interaction and work environments in a realistic fashion, which depends on their intelligent utilization of avatars, voice interaction, and environmental realism. Avatars are AI-based virtual people imitating co-workers, supervisors, or customers. Avatars can produce natural facial expressions, body language, verbal communication, and emotional expressions, all of which enhance realistic interpersonal exchanges. Advanced avatars employ AI for real-time adaption based on candidate feedback, providing dynamic conversation and natural-sounding feedback. Voice interaction, driven by Natural Language Processing (NLP) and voice recognition technologies, enables candidates to converse naturally within simulations. This not only increases levels of realism but also facilitates communication skill assessment, decision-making based on dialogue, and emotional analysis through tone detection. It also fosters accessibility, enabling people with physical disabilities or limitations to engage fully in the simulation.

Moreover, environmental realism also plays a central part in the engagement of candidates and accuracy of behavior. Virtual environments should reflect genuine workplaces—e.g., with elaborate 3D models of offices, factory floors, or customer service countertops, ambient sound, interactive objects, and background dynamics.

For instance, a store simulation might include operating a virtual shop, dealing with computer-generated consumers, and resolving stock problems, while a technical interview could include fixing a virtual machine, handling system warnings, or reading computer reads. Such realism does not only enhance candidate performance but also provides recruiters with a useful insight into how people respond to pressure, handle multiple tasks, and solve real-life problems under authentic workplace conditions.

The Steps of Technical Architecture of VR Interviews shown in Figure 1

Figure 1. Technical architecture of VR-based interview systems, illustrating hardware and software components integrated with AI analytics and ATS system

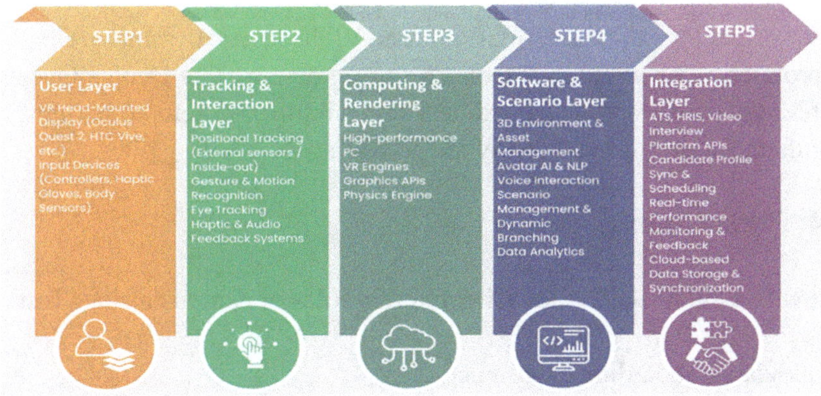

6. PRACTICAL IMPLEMENTATION STRATEGY FOR VR INTERVIEW SYSTEMS

While the technical and conceptual benefits of VR-based interviews are clear, successful adoption requires a structured, step-by-step implementation strategy. Many organizations fail to move beyond experimentation because they lack a concrete roadmap for integrating VR into existing HR systems. The following steps outline a practical and scalable approach:

Step 1: Define Objectives and Use Cases

Start by identifying what hiring goals VR should support. Are you focusing on evaluating soft skills, technical competencies, or role-specific decision-making? Clarify whether VR will be used for screening, interviewing, onboarding, or skill assessment.

Step 2: Select Technology Partners

Choose VR platforms and vendors that align with your use case (e.g., immersive assessments, AI integrations, analytics dashboards). Consider whether they offer:

- Pre-built role-specific modules
- Integration with existing ATS/HRIS
- Support for mobile and desktop users

Step 3: Infrastructure & Hardware Readiness

Decide on deployment: in-office (high-end VR headsets) or remote (cloud-based VR or browser-based solutions). Consider using devices like Oculus Quest, HTC Vive, or Meta Quest 3 based on candidate accessibility. For remote settings, ensure bandwidth and system compatibility are addressed.

Step 4: Pilot Testing

Start with a small-scale pilot using internal roles or campus hiring. Test:

- Candidate onboarding experience
- Performance data quality
- HR team usability and insights, Use the feedback to iterate.

Step 5: Integration with ATS/HR Tools

Ensure that the VR platform can export performance data into your Applicant Tracking System (ATS) or Human Resource Information System (HRIS). Use APIs for seamless data flow and candidate tracking.

Step 6: Train Recruiters and Candidates

Provide basic VR training for HR personnel. Offer tutorials or practice modules for candidates to reduce anxiety and ensure fairness. Train HR to interpret behavioral data, heat maps, and AI-generated reports effectively.

Step 7: Scale and Monitor

After a successful pilot, scale to more roles or departments. Continuously monitor usage, candidate feedback, bias levels, and system performance. Update modules regularly to reflect real-world changes and compliance needs.

A structured implementation strategy ensures that VR-based hiring is not just a tech experiment but a sustainable, inclusive, and measurable improvement in recruitment outcomes.

7. USE OF AI AND DATA ANALYSIS IN VR INTERVIEWS

The convergence of Data Analytics and Artificial Intelligence (AI) with Virtual Reality (VR) has made traditional recruitment processes intelligent, adaptive, and highly personalized evaluation tools. While VR simulates actual job environments, AI and analytics silently monitor, analyze, and interpret behavioral characteristics in real time—giving an insight much deeper than conventional interviews. One of the most revolutionary dimensions is AI-based behavioral analysis, scanning subtle and intangible human characteristics missed during systematic Q&A sessions. For instance, facial expression analysis uses computer vision to identify emotions such as confidence, nervousness, or excitement, which are critical indicators of emotional intelligence and stress tolerance. Likewise, voice tone and sentiment analysis, driven by Natural Language Processing (NLP), identifies the nuances in verbal communication—such as tone, pitch, and pacing—to evaluate clarity, assertiveness, and emotional state. AI also uses gaze tracking and attention mapping to identify where the candidate is looking, providing critical insights for jobs that demand sustained attention or attention to detail. Furthermore, body language analysis, through gesture and posture recognition, enables the system to deduce behavioral characteristics such as openness, nervousness, or assertiveness. Such behavioral characteristics are continuously monitored and analyzed through machine learning models trained on massive datasets, creating an aggregate psychological and performance profile for each candidate.

One aspect of VR-based interviews is the capability of real-time observation and data gathering without interfering with the candidate's natural behavior. Passive data collection makes the evaluation more objective and dismisses observer bias. Some of the most important metrics gathered in real-time are verbal responses (grammar, coherence, lexical choice), non-verbal responses (eye contact, gestures, facial expressions), and interaction metrics (clicking, dragging, object manipulation). Time-based metrics also measure the rate at which candidates respond to questions posed or complete tasks given, while scenario breaching logs measure decision paths in branching simulations that provide insight into cognitive strategies and problem-solving styles. All such inputs are stored in a central repository, encrypted for security. Advanced AI algorithms analyze this data in real-time, identifying anomalies and insights through recruiter dashboards. Real-time capability also makes possible adaptive simulations, where the system dynamically adjusts tasks based on performance. For instance, if a candidate shows high proficiency in customer service scenarios, the simulation may incorporate conflict-resolution tasks to evaluate leadership and coolness under pressure. This adaptive feature customizes the experience to the candidate's level of proficiency, making the assessment both more precise and more engaging.

8. ENHANCING CANDIDATE EXPERIENCE IN VR INTERVIEWS

While VR interview systems introduce cutting-edge technology and powerful analytics, their success also depends heavily on the experience of candidates using them. First-time VR users may experience anxiety, disorientation, or technical confusion, which can negatively affect performance—even when the candidate is otherwise highly capable. To ensure a fair and comfortable evaluation, organizations must design systems that are candidate-centric, inclusive, and intuitive.

1. Pre-Interview Orientation

Before the simulation begins, candidates should be offered a short interactive onboarding module that explains:

- How to use the VR headset or controls
- The nature of the simulation
- What kinds of behaviors or skills are being assessed

This helps reduce anxiety and prepares candidates for engagement.

2. Practice Environment

Offer a "practice run" or sandbox simulation, where candidates can familiarize themselves with navigation, interaction (e.g., voice input or gestures), and timing—without judgment or data logging.

3. User Interface Simplicity

Ensure that the interface is intuitive and minimal, with accessible design features for people with neurodiversity or motor disabilities (e.g., one-button controls, larger font, voice-guided instructions).

4. Feedback & Support

Provide candidates with basic feedback post-simulation or give them access to their behavioral heatmaps or response reports (non-score-based). Also, offer technical help via live chat, FAQs, or video guides.

5. Emotional Safety

Avoid overwhelming stimuli in high-pressure simulations. Simulations should gradually escalate difficulty, and scenarios involving conflict should include opt-out options or emotional debrief prompts.

6. Inclusive Hardware Options

Support candidates who don't own headsets by offering desktop or mobile versions of the VR interview. This ensures access regardless of geographic or economic limitations.

A well-designed candidate experience improves not only fairness but also employer brand perception and candidate satisfaction—factors that can directly influence offer acceptance and long-term retention.

9. SOFT SKILL AND BEHAVIOURAL EVALUATION THROUGH VR

In the modern workplace today, soft skills such as emotional intelligence, communication, leadership, and ethical judgment are more valuable than ever on a par with—or perhaps even more than—technical skills. These skills, however, are notoriously difficult to measure with traditional interviews, which are often impressionistic in nature and context-free. Virtual Reality (VR), particularly when supported by Artificial Intelligence (AI), provides a game-changer by placing candidates in interactive, realistic worlds where behavioral propensities may be observed and measured with precision. VR-based simulations can place candidates in high-fidelity representations of workplace situations, where recruiters can observe how candidates express emotional intelligence (EI) in the moment. High-arousal situations such as handling an irate customer or handling conflict within a team, for instance, enable AI to measure emotional awareness through proxy indicators such as facial expression, tone of voice, and path taken in response. Additionally, interpersonal simulations with AI avatars enable the measurement of empathy, listening skills, and rapport-building—skills which are particularly important in customer service, healthcare, and team-based environments.

In assessing leadership potential, VR enables interactive simulation of team leadership, crisis management, or decision-making in conditions of uncertainty. These situations entail commanding, delegating, and using strategic thinking, which provides a more realistic picture of leadership style and influence than questionnaires. Communication skill is assessed through immersive role-plays and virtual group discussions monitored by AI for verbal clarity, body language, and speech coherence. NLP methods analyze not just the literal meaning but also emotional impact, grammatical structure, and conversation dynamics, allowing close evaluation of communication skill.

One of the most powerful benefits of VR-based measurement of soft skills is its capability to track and measure non-verbal behavior—the subtle but powerful signals of interpersonal potential. Advanced AI-powered systems with eye tracking and motion sensors can track eye movement, setting whether a candidate is making good eye contact or showing signs of distraction. These measures are key to measuring confidence, attention, and honesty. Real-time facial expression analysis reads micro-expressions like smiles, frowns, or looks of confusion to gain insight into a candidate's control of emotions and honesty. Posture and movement analysis can read open, confident body language vs. nervous or defensive postures, unlocking deeper insights into personality predispositions, self-confidence, and approachability. Speech and voice modulation analysis is a further step, tracking changes in tone, pitch, rhythm, and pausing to measure emotional control, verbal fluency, and persuasive ability. These measures are critical in assessing confidence, attention, and honesty.

The Six Soft Skill & Behavioural Evaluation Through VR shown in Figure 2

Figure 2. Evaluation of soft skills and behavioral competencies using Virtual Reality systems powered by AI technologies such as Natural Language Processing (NLP), facial expression recognition, gaze tracking, and voice sentiment analysis. This enables dynamic, immersive measurement of emotional intelligence, communication, and leadership capabilities.

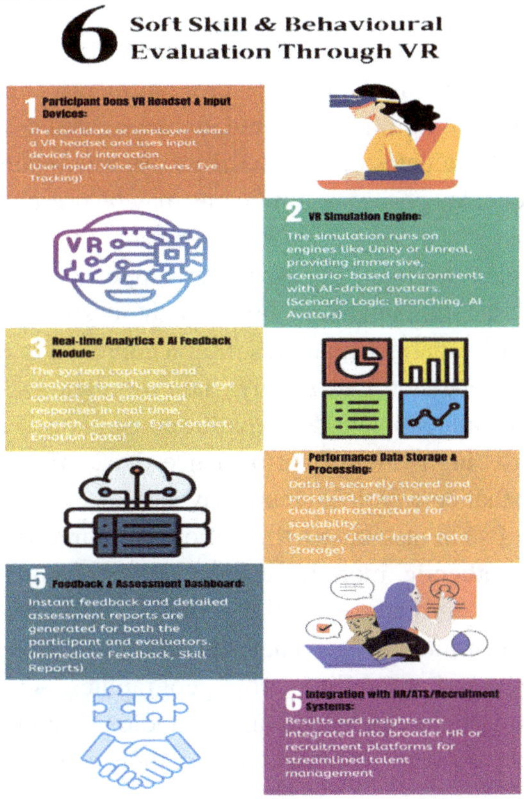

10. ROLE-SPECIFIC SKILL EVALUATION USING VIRTUAL REALITY

One of the most groundbreaking and impactful applications of Virtual Reality (VR) to date in recruitment is to tailor tests to the specifications of specific job roles with precision. Traditional interviews employ generic questions or hypothetical situations that say little about a candidate's hands-on competence. With VR, highly interactive, task-oriented simulations that replicate real job tasks are feasible, and recruiters can observe candidates actually perform role-related tasks inside a virtual environment that is very realistic. This is a supremely effective way of evaluating technical and functional skills in a systematic, objective, and scalable manner. Such simulations are more than theoretical knowledge and test how candidates apply their skills under real-world constraints, and deliver much better insights into their employability.

VR job simulations place the applicants in situations closely resembling their prospective work environment. A software programmer, for instance, may be required to debug a virtual program in an emulated integrated development environment (IDE), where AI evaluates coding precision, problem-solving rationale, and debugging speed. For sales positions, applicants may be presented with a pitch to a virtual customer, where the system evaluates persuasive communication, objection-handling, and presentation effect. For customer support positions, applicants can engage with simulated complainant/customers with questions, and the system can evaluate empathy, clarity, patience, and resolution approach in real-time. Logistics applicants could experience intricate supply chain simulations, specifying delivery timetables or inventory allocation under dynamic constraints. In all these situations, the simulation records high-fidelity performance data, offering quantitative and qualitative feedback that conventional tests may lack.

The advantages of such task-based simulations are three-fold. They render the recruitment process authentic, more interactive for the candidates and more valid for the recruiter. They introduce objectivity by measuring performance against quantifiable results, restraining bias. They introduce efficiency through modular standardization, reuse, and scalability across geographies. Above all, they enable in-depth competence assessment, more than the candidate says they know, and more importantly, how they solve problems, think on their feet, and carry out critical responsibilities.

A feature of VR recruitment platforms is that they are customizable, allowing organizations to create industry-specific modules that are tailored to different levels of experience and job roles. From hospital operating rooms and building sites to trading floors and classrooms, VR environments can be replicated to the point of realism to mimic real working conditions. Modularity in design allows customization in the following dimensions: environment, language and localization, job level, and scenario complexity. For instance, a healthcare simulation can place a candidate in a triage situation, with split-second instant judgment and accurate diagnosis, while an engineering module simulates a review of a product in an imaginary laboratory. Risk assessment exercises may be demonstrated to finance professionals, simulating risky portfolios in real time. For education, teaching candidates may be given a virtual classroom lesson, demonstrating instruction strategies and classroom management.

Manufacturing candidates may be tested in mock production lines where they must repair equipment, optimize workflow efficiency, or follow safety procedures.

With the use of AI-enabled technology, today's VR simulations can generate performance dashboards, auto-reports, and behavioral heat maps for all the applicants, giving recruiters in-depth analysis of strengths, weaknesses, and job-role fit. All this enables HR professionals to make informed, data-driven recruitment decisions and reduce time-to-hire. In the near future, with the use of wearable biometric sensors to measure heart rate, stress, or direction of view, the analysis of applicants' physiological and cognitive responses to high-stakes tasks can be further refined.

The Flow of Role-Specific Skill Evaluation Using Virtual Reality shown in Figure 3

Figure 3. Framework for evaluating job-specific competencies through immersive, task-based VR simulations across domains such as customer service, engineering, healthcare, and logistics. These scenarios use interactive environments and real-time feedback systems to assess technical proficiency, decision-making, and job readiness.

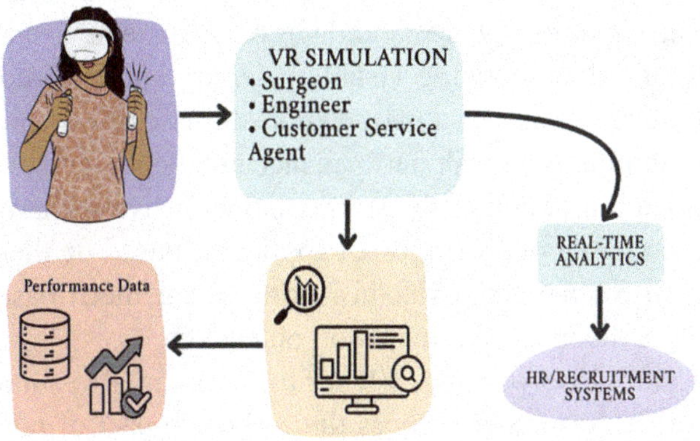

Overall, VR-based role-skilled assessment is a revolution in recruitment practice. It brings unprecedented realism, individualization, and fairness to the recruitment process, and improves predictive validity for future work performance. With these technologies becoming more accessible and advanced, VR-based assessments are poised to be a best practice in modern talent acquisition, especially in areas where precision, problem-solving, and situational performance are paramount.

11. BENEFITS OF VR-BASED INTERVIEW SIMULATIONS

The use of Virtual Reality (VR) for recruitment is a paradigm shift in how talent is evaluated and selected by organizations, providing a number of revolutionary benefits compared to conventional interviewing processes. Blending virtual environments with real-time analysis and AI-assisted assessment, VR-based interview simulations bring an unparalleled degree of objectivity, equity, scalability, and interaction into the employment process. Traditional interviews are usually subject to subjective factors—ranging from the biases of the interviewer to question delivery inconsistencies—that undermine the dependability of recruitment decisions. VR disqualifies much of this subjectivity through standardized, scenario-based simulations where all applicants undergo the same tasks and are evaluated on quantifiable performance indicators like decision accuracy, communication effectiveness, problem-solving approach, and task speed. Sophisticated AI algorithms perform automated scoring, using consistent evaluation standards for all candidates and creating data-intensive profiles that allow for accurate, apples-to-apples comparisons.

Reduction of unconscious bias is another vital benefit. Unconscious bias has always been a persistent issue with traditional hiring practices. Gender, racial, age, physical attractiveness, or educational biases tend to function below conscious awareness, quietly shaping results. VR solutions address this by facilitating anonymized or avatar-based participation, where candidates participate in virtual spaces through customizable avatars, thus reducing visual or demographic stereotyping. In more sophisticated platforms, blind evaluation procedures can be enforced, such that recruiters judge candidates on task performance and behavioral analytics alone. In addition, the application of culturally neutral and inclusive scenario designs assists in developing an unbiased platform for all applicants based on their background or geographic location. Such practices aid in a more ethical, merit-based hiring process that matches today's diversity and inclusion objectives.

On the other hand, incorporating VR for recruitment also supports sustainable business practices. It drastically reduces the carbon impact of physical interviews by curtailing travel, paper consumption, and dependency on physical infrastructure. This renders VR an ecologically sound option that aligns with wider Environmental, Social, and Governance (ESG) policies. As technology advances, the fusion of biometric monitoring, natural language understanding, and emotional sensing with VR systems will create even greater granularities of candidate assessment, allowing for richer insights into soft skills, stress tolerance, and flexibility. In short, VR interview simulations provide a breakthrough way to hire talent. They combine the power of technological creativity and psychological understanding to construct recruitment processes that are more equitable, quicker, more scalable, and highly immersive. As companies compete for the best talent in an interconnected digital economy, the use of VR in recruitment is not just something to consider—it is an evolving best practice for next-generation companies.

The following table 1 compares traditional interviews with VR-based systems. It outlines differences in bias control, candidate experience, and scalability. This highlights the practical benefits of adopting immersive technologies.

Table 1. Comparison of key features in traditional versus VR-based interview methods.

Feature	Traditional Interviews	VR-Based Interviews
Bias Control	Manual, prone to inconsistency	Standardized and AI-moderated assessments
Candidate Experience	Passive and high-pressure	Immersive, gamified, and engaging
Skill Evaluation	Verbal or paper-based	Real-world simulations and task interaction
Scalability	Requires physical presence	Remote access and large-scale deployment
Data Insights	Limited, qualitative	Rich behavioral data and real-time analytics

12. LIMITATIONS AND CHALLENGES OF VR-BASED INTERVIEW SIMULATIONS

Even with the revolutionary potential of Virtual Reality (VR) in hiring, its usage comes with a series of challenges that organizations need to overcome to facilitate effective, ethical, and inclusive use. Possibly the most pressing and outstanding among these is the high initial setup cost and technical sophistication involved in using VR-based recruitment systems. The equipment needed—equipping VR headsets such as Oculus Quest or HTC Vive, motion tracking equipment, haptic feedback equipment, and bespoke VR software—can be very costly, particularly for small and medium-sized businesses (SMEs) with limited budgets. It also requires successful operation usually involving the services of skilled technical personnel for the design, creation, and upkeep of these systems. Incubating VR platforms with current Human Resource Management Systems (HRMS), Applicant Tracking Systems (ATS), and AI-assisted evaluation engines can involve customized APIs and middleware, contributing to higher costs and compatibility challenges. In the absence of sufficient IT support and digital infrastructure, the rollout process could be slowed or discredited by technical problems, compromising the overall effectiveness of the initiative.

Discomfort and lack of familiarity with VR interfaces of candidates are also of significant concern. While technologically adept applicants will easily adapt, others might find it a challenging process. Dyscomfort due to extensive use of headsets, disorientation due to navigation confusion, or apprehension due to a novel digital environment can adversely affect performance—irrespective of the candidate's actual competence or potential for the job. In addition, VR-focused tests can unwittingly impose a bias toward candidates who are already familiar with such technology, thereby undermining the integrity of the assessment process. To counteract such risks, businesses ought to provide interactive tutorials, orientation modules, and guided practice environments to familiarize users prior to official evaluation commencing. Adding real-time technical support, either via live chat or on-call personnel, can help assuage anxiety and facilitate a smoother process.

In summary, as much as the use of VR technology in recruitment has the power to transform the way organizations assess talent, its successful implementation rides on an active approach toward addressing critical financial, technical, ethical, and access-related challenges. Only through meeting these limitations head-on can organizations maximize the advantages of VR while ensuring equity, inclusivity, and integrity in data within their recruitment processes. As the industry matures, ongoing research, regulation in alignment, and accessible innovation will be necessary to deliver on the full potential of immersive recruitment technologies.

13. GLOBAL ACCESS AND INCLUSION IN VR-BASED HIRING

As organizations adopt VR-based interview systems, it is essential to consider global accessibility, localization, and inclusive design. Without intentional adaptation, these systems risk excluding candidates from under-resourced regions, individuals with disabilities, and culturally diverse populations.

1. Localization for Cultural Relevance

VR simulations must reflect culturally appropriate scenarios. This includes:

- Local language voice-overs and instructions
- Context-sensitive simulations (e.g., workplace dynamics, dress code)
- Country-specific hiring norms or communication styles

For example, a leadership scenario in Japan may differ from one in Brazil based on social expectations and hierarchy.

2. Accessibility for People with Disabilities

Many candidates may have visual, auditory, motor, or cognitive impairments. VR hiring systems must:

- Support screen readers, large text, and alternative navigation (eye tracking, voice input)
- Offer haptic alternatives for audio/visual cues
- Ensure reduced-motion settings to prevent VR-induced nausea Compliance with WCAG 2.1 and accessibility laws (e.g., ADA, EN 301 549) should guide design.

3. Digital Equity for Low-Resource Settings

Not all candidates have access to high-end headsets or fast internet. To ensure inclusivity:

- Provide desktop or mobile-compatible versions of the VR simulation
- Enable cloud-streamed experiences with low bandwidth requirements
- Offer offline demos or practice simulations to rural applicants

4. Inclusive Design Principles

- Engage candidates from diverse backgrounds during usability testing
- Avoid scenarios that assume certain education levels, tech fluency, or physical capabilities
- Include multilingual instructions, especially for global graduate programs

Ensuring global usability and digital equity is not just a technical requirement but a moral imperative. Inclusive design expands your talent pool, protects your employer brand, and upholds fairness in hiring.

14. ETHICAL AND LEGAL IMPLICATIONS OF VR-BASED RECRUITMENT

With Virtual Reality (VR) technologies increasingly adopted in recruitment, organizations need to respond to an emerging list of ethical and legal obligations to guarantee equitable, compliant, and transparent hiring procedures. Even though VR-based interviews are poised to provide objective, immersive, and data-rich candidate assessments, they also pose major issues regarding fairness, bias, data protection, algorithmic responsibility, and legal obligations. At the heart of ethical recruitment is the notion of non-discrimination. VR simulations, while necessarily more standard than face-to-face interviews, need to be inclusively constructed such that they do not inadvertently discriminate against any particular group. This involves minimizing culturally loaded scenarios, preventing language assumption, and creating tasks that are contextually neutral and depict varying workplace settings. Furthermore, VR platforms need to support disabled candidates through provision of different formats or adaptive functionalities that assist visually impaired users, users with restricted mobility, neurodiverse users, or other users with special accessibility requirements. Equally so, is the stringent auditing of AI algorithms employed in VR platforms to guarantee that they do not reinforce past hiring discriminatory prejudices—e.g., biased towards some genders, ethnicities, or educational attainment—thus maintaining ethical recruitment standards and conformity with equal opportunity employment legislation.

Data privacy presents itself as another key legal area, especially in light of VR systems capturing broad behavioral and biometric data during simulations. Major global regulations, including the General Data Protection Regulation (GDPR) in the EU and the California Consumer Privacy Act (CCPA) in the USA, impose detailed frameworks for managing personal data in ethical and legal manners. Under GDPR, organizations have to get express consent from applicants prior to data collection, ensure they only take relevant data (data minimization), and offer rights to users to view, rectify, or delete their data. In addition, organizations need to have strict security practices such as encryption, secure storage, and transparent data management policies to avoid unauthorized access or misuses. Also, CCPA requires candidates to be notified regarding the types of information gathered and how they will be used. It also provides consumers with the right to opt out of selling data and safeguards them against discriminatory treatment for their data privacy preferences. Failure to abide by such legislation can lead not only to significant financial fines but also to long-lasting damage to reputation, which is why it is crucial that HR departments are knowledgeable in data privacy legislation and ethical methods.

The Steps of Ethical and Legal Implications of VR-Based Recruitment shown in Figure 4

Figure 4. Ethical and legal considerations in VR-based recruitment, including compliance with global data protection regulations such as GDPR and CCPA. The figure outlines data minimization, informed consent, algorithmic fairness, explainable AI (XAI), and accessibility principles as pillars of ethical design.

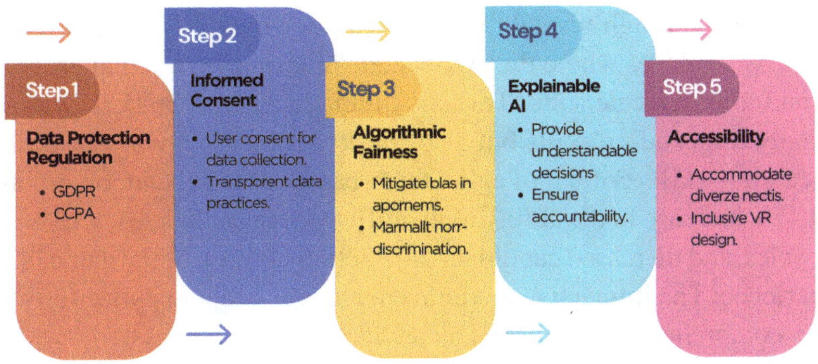

In summary, although VR-based hiring provides revolutionary benefits regarding standardization, participation, and data analysis, its legal and ethical environment is intricate and dynamic. Organizations have a responsibility to design their systems actively with ethical vision, compliance with law, transparency in algorithms, and candidate welfare. By incorporating fairness, accountability, and inclusivity into the very design of VR recruitment platforms, employers can responsibly leverage the potential of immersive technology while ensuring the rights and dignity of each candidate. A balanced strategy is not just a requirement of the law but a pillar of sustainable, equitable, and proactive talent acquisition.

15. CASE STUDIES AND INDUSTRY USE OF VR IN HIRING

The use of Virtual Reality (VR) in hiring is no longer a theoretical innovation—it is now a working reality in various industries. From high-tech companies to high-security defense departments, companies are increasingly using VR-based interview and evaluation systems to facilitate the hiring process, enhance accuracy, and enhance the candidate experience. These immersive simulations enable recruiters to assess technical and interpersonal abilities in a manner that is not possible with regular interviews, closing the gap between prospective talent and actual job performance. As the technology continues to evolve, VR is emerging as more than a flashy gadget—it is a strategic resource transforming the identification, engagement, and onboarding of talent.

In the technology industry, Firms such as Accenture have pioneered VR interview settings customized for software developers. As noted in industry showcases and recruitment blogs, these VR environments test real-time collaboration and problem-solving. Through virtual "coding rooms," candidates are put in cooperative, realistic workplaces where they write code in response to actual programming problems and communicate with AI avatars simulating team members. This arrangement not only tests coding skills but also checks problem-solving, flexibility, and communication—skills critical to agile, team-based settings. Outcomes have been notable: a 45% increase in the ability to identify leading candidates, a 25% decrease in hiring cycles, and increased candidate satisfaction because of the game like nature of the experience. The immersive medium encourages deeper connection and gives recruiters a comprehensive picture of a candidate's job-readiness.

In the healthcare profession, emotional intelligence and crisis management are as essential as clinical competencies. Johnson & Johnson has used VR simulations to evaluate nursing candidates in high-stress scenarios. While exact performance data is internally reported, simulations have been presented in recruitment webinars and healthcare training showcases. With realistic simulations of triage, ethical issues, and patient encounters, the candidates are judged on decision-making skills, empathy, and collaboration under stress. This method resulted in a 30% improvement in first-year employee retention and 60% better candidate understanding of job responsibilities prior to employment. Notably, the simulations also assist recruiters in picking up on characteristics commonly overlooked in resumes or regular interviews, including staying calm under pressure and moral judgment—vital for healthcare positions where lives are involved.

The retail industry has also witnessed mass VR use, especially for customer-facing positions. Walmart, in partnership with STRIVR Labs, created VR training and testing modules that immerse candidates in simulated stores, navigating situations such as navigating long lines, dealing with angry customers, and applying safety protocols. The modules have led to a 10% higher rate of successful first-round hires and a significant decrease in training expenses. By providing a behavior-oriented, standardized evaluation system to all sites, Walmart not only enhanced the consistency of hiring but also prepared candidates for the actual working conditions and pressures of the retail environment. Moreover, pre-employment exposure to job-simulation contexts improves transparency and minimizes early turnover.

In the defense industry, in which strategic planning and poise under pressure are crucial, VR has been utilized by the The U.S. Department of Defense has adopted VR to simulate battlefield command tasks. Though most use cases are internal, public defense technology briefings and military R&D reports have acknowledged the use of VR for recruitment screening. VR assessment centers now screen candidates for high-responsibility military positions by assessing spatial reasoning, mission planning, leadership decision-making, and operational execution in simulated battlefield environments. The outcomes have been dramatic: VR systems have been able to identify leaders with 40% more accuracy than conventional aptitude tests, as well as increase the talent pipeline through more diverse, skill-based assessments. The capability to simulate high-stakes scenarios with accuracy enables greater predictions of actual performance and readiness for dynamic, unpredictable missions.

The table 2 below summarizes real-world case studies of VR-based hiring. It highlights how companies across sectors apply VR to improve recruitment. Key outcomes and sources are included for comparison.

Table 2. Summary of real-world case studies showcasing the use of VR in hiring, with reported outcomes and organizational sources.

Industry	Company	Use Case	Outcome Highlights	Source
Technology	Accenture	VR coding simulations	+45% match rate	Accenture, 2023
Retail	Walmart + STRIVR	Customer service training	+10% hire success	Hetherington, 2017
Healthcare	J&J + Osso VR	Surgical/empathy simulations	+60% accuracy	XR Today, 2023

In summary, these actual case studies show that VR is changing recruitment from a reactive, resume-based method to an active, experience-based assessment system. With the technology becoming increasingly available and affordable, its uptake is anticipated to gain momentum across industries. Firms adopting VR-based hiring can look forward to more precise talent matching, high levels of engagement, lower hiring biases, and future-proofed workforce. The transition towards immersive, data-intensive recruitment processes not only adds to operational effectiveness but also resonates with the changed demands of a digital-native talent pool looking for impactful, transparent, and fair hiring processes.

16. FUTURE TRENDS IN VR INTERVIEW TECHNOLOGY

As Virtual Reality (VR) advances, its application in hiring is shifting from being an experimental fad to becoming a strategic necessity. Upcoming technologies like haptic feedback, biometric tracking, emotion detection, and the merging of augmented and mixed realities are set to redefine how organizations interview. Such technologies are not so much an improvement on current VR technologies—they are a paradigm shift in terms of the way human potential is measured, experienced, and known. Cloud-based VR platforms, meanwhile, are rendering the technology more accessible, scalable, and deployable at a global level, thereby

In addition to totally immersed VR, the combination of Augmented Reality (AR) and Mixed Reality (MR) is pushing the limits of virtual interviews. Whereas VR builds completely digital worlds, AR superimposes virtual objects on the physical world, enabling candidates to interact with immersive content in actual physical environments. In an interview scenario, this could include interacting with holographic coworkers, taking AR task instructions, or answering scenario-driven questions in live tests. Mixed Reality takes it a notch higher by merging physical and virtual objects that respond harmoniously. For example, a test-taker may work with actual devices that control virtual equipment, or perform group tasks in which one member is present and the other is an MR avatar. These features are particularly beneficial for jobs such as manufacturing, logistics, architecture, and field service engineering, in which physical reality in the real world mixes with digital operations. AR and MR also facilitate more collaborative, location-independent interviewing, allowing remote candidates and recruiters to coexist in shared hybrid spaces.

Ahead in the future, AI content and personalization will reshape how simulations are authored and delivered. Coming VR systems can design context-sensitive interview environments specific to individual resumes or job postings, creating naturalistic workplace challenges that are aligned with the actual job function of the candidate. We can also expect the growth of digital twins—virtual replicas that reflect a candidate's behavioral profile and physiological reactions over time, giving real-time, post-interview feedback that could be used to shape long-term talent development and internal mobility. Sophisticated machine learning algorithms will be applied more and more to forecast a candidate's on-the-job performance, probability of staying, and cultural fit based on detailed patterns from VR data. The deployment of 5G networks and edge computing will complement this ecosystem further, keeping latency to a bare minimum and allowing ultra-smooth, high-definition simulations in far-off or bandwidth-constrained areas. These technologies will also improve mobile VR performance, with high-quality tests able to be run even on low-power or portable devices.

The Road Map of Future Trends in VR Interview Technology shown in Figure 5

Figure 5. Roadmap of future trends in VR-based hiring technology, highlighting the integration of haptic feedback, biometric monitoring (e.g., heart rate, gaze), emotion detection AI, 5G connectivity, and mixed/augmented reality (MR/AR). These advancements enhance realism, personalization, and predictive capabilities in candidate assessment.

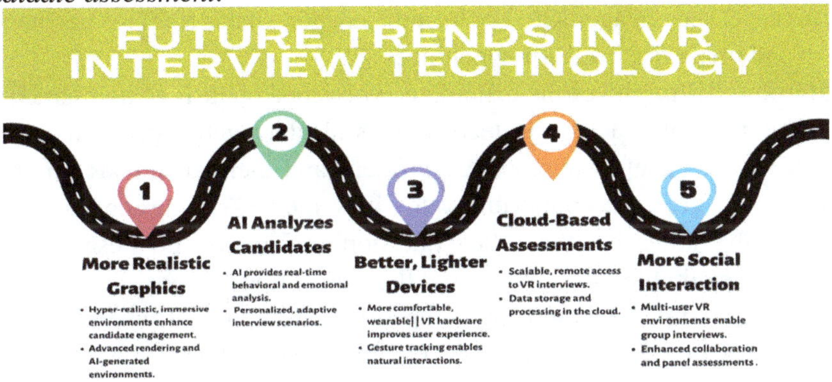

17. CONCLUSION

Virtual Reality (VR) has brought about a revolutionary age in hiring, transforming the process by which organizations discover, assess, and connect with would-be talent. Previously, interviews were based primarily on subjective judgments resulting from short, frequently shallow encounters—verbal answers, CVs, and limited behavioral observation. As useful as they have been, even these tools tend to miss much of a candidate's potential, emotional intelligence, and cultural fit. VR-based hiring transcends these restrictions by designing immersive, interactive simulations that replicate actual work challenges, providing a comprehensive picture of candidate performance in contextually appropriate settings.

In contrast to traditional testing, VR enables recruiters to put candidates into realistic situations that challenge a broad set of skills—spanning technical proficiency to teamwork, pressure decision-making, and ethics. Whether modeling an emergency response situation for medical professionals or a coordinated engineering project for technical recruits, VR can replicate the intricacies of a role within a controlled, quantifiable, and reproducible environment. These high-fidelity experiences provide a view into the way that candidates think, respond, and are able to adjust—allowing organizations to measure job readiness and role fit with unparalleled levels of depth and precision.

One of the strengths of VR in hiring is its capability to create rich behavioral data. When combined with Advanced Analytics and Artificial Intelligence (AI), VR platforms can monitor verbal as well as non-verbal signals—such as tone of speech, micro-expressions, gaze, posture, and physiological responses like heart rate or skin conductance. This allows for sophisticated assessment of emotional intelligence, stress tolerance, and engagement. For hiring managers, these findings become more objective and predictive recruitment choices.

In addition, VR improves the candidate experience by turning assessments into enjoyable, gamified interactions instead of stressful interrogations. Recruiters consistently state that they feel more relaxed, confident, and energized in VR simulations, especially when given the opportunity to show their skills through experiential problem-solving rather than theoretical questioning. Not only do these experiences facilitate more equitable assessments, but they also provide a positive, long-lasting impression of the employer brand. In a competitive labour market, where high-quality talent has choice between opportunities, offering a technology-led and open hiring experience is a business differentiator.

Regardless of its advantages, the large-scale adoption of VR in recruitment is moderated by problems which need to be addressed sensitively, and foremost among these is the initial investment in infrastructure. Advanced VR systems call for high-end hardware, including headsets and haptic devices, and strong software platforms that can provide scalable and secure simulations. Cost and technological constraints, in the form of cost and technological barriers, can be a deterrent to implementation for most organizations, particularly small and medium ones. There is a learning curve involved in using VR effectively both for recruiters and applicants. User training, support materials, and intuitive layout are key to ensuring usability and deriving maximum value from the system.

Accessibility and inclusion continue to be key concerns. Not everyone will have access to VR hardware or reliable internet connections—especially those from under-resourced or rural areas. To counteract this, organizations need to make VR experiences device-agnostic, with support for mobile devices, desktop platforms, or web-based solutions. Inclusive design also requires that individuals with disabilities be supported, making recruitment simulations flexible in the face of a range of physical and cognitive requirements. Accessibility is not a technical matter—its being a reflection of an organization's commitment to equitable hiring and equal opportunity.

The coupling of Augmented Reality (AR) and Mixed Reality (MR) extends the possibilities of immersive recruitment even further. AR can be applied to superimpose interactive questions, visual cues, or collaborative tools on top of a live interview, whereas MR enables the unproblematic interaction of physical tools and virtual components. These technologies are particularly suited for hybrid careers, field-based jobs, or collaborative office spaces, wherein real-world context and simulated digital elements need to coexist.

In the future, we can look forward to even more revolutionary innovations like AI-driven bespoke simulations from a candidate's profile, digital twins that simulate a candidate's behavioral patterns over a period of time, and predictive algorithms of performance that map simulation results to real-world performance. Augmented by 5G and edge computing, these platforms will be faster, more responsive, and ubiquitously accessible, opening doors to real-time global talent evaluation that is equitable and effective.

Overall, VR has become a foundation of future-proof recruitment, which bridges the divide between static assessments and dynamic, data-driven candidate judgments. It is a valuable means of minimizing bias, optimizing predictive validity, and offering customized, immersive hiring experiences. Through the use of VR, organizations not only enhance the purity and fairness of their hiring process but also place themselves at the center of digital transformation in recruitment. As technology advances, organizations that adopt immersive hiring now will be best positioned to attract, evaluate, and retain the best and brightest of the future workforce.

As hiring becomes more global, data-driven, and candidate-centered, the ability to simulate real-world scenarios through immersive technologies is no longer a luxury—it's a necessity. This chapter highlights why VR, when combined with thoughtful design and AI analytics, is not just a technological upgrade but a strategic enabler for ethical, scalable, and inclusive hiring. Future work should continue to explore long-term outcomes, cross-cultural effectiveness, and regulatory frameworks to ensure this transformation benefits both organizations and talent equally.

REFERENCES

Danielson, E. C., Smith, M. J., Ross, B., Sherwood, K., Smith, J. D., Atkins, M., & Jordan, N. (2024). Implementation preparation costs of virtual interview training in pre-employment transition services: A budget impact analysis. *Journal of Special Education Technology, 39*(1), 27–40. DOI: 10.1177/01626434231175372 PMID: 38975255

Izard, A., McEntee, E., & Maher, J. (2017). Comparing virtual reality and desktop interfaces for skill training and education. *Computers & Education, 113*, 50–62. DOI: 10.1371/journal.pone.0275119

Kandalaft, M. R., Didehbani, N., Krawczyk, D. C., Allen, T. T., & Chapman, S. B. (2013). Virtual reality social cognition training for young adults with high-functioning autism. *Journal of Autism and Developmental Disorders, 43*(1), 34–44. DOI: 10.1007/s10803-012-1544-6 PMID: 22570145

Kyaw, B. M., Saxena, N., Posadzki, P., Vseteckova, J., Nikolaou, C. K., George, P. P., Divakar, U., Masiello, I., Kononowicz, A. A., Zary, N., & Tudor Car, L. (2019). Virtual reality for health professions education: A systematic review and meta-analysis by the Digital Health Education Collaboration. *Medical Education, 53*(1), 3–25. DOI: 10.2196/12959 PMID: 30549096

Le, G. (2025). Augmented Reality in Higher Education: A Systematic Review and Meta-Analysis of the Literature from 2000 to 2023. *Education Sciences, 15*(6), 678. DOI: 10.3390/educsci15060678

Luo, X., Wang, Y., Lee, L.-H., Xing, Z., Jin, S., Dong, B., Hu, Y., Chen, Z., Yan, J., & Hui, P. (2024). Using a virtual reality interview simulator to explore factors influencing people's behavior. *Virtual Reality (Waltham Cross), 28*(1), 56. DOI: 10.1007/s10055-023-00934-5

Matthew, J. (2020). Virtual Reality Job Interview Training in Transition Services: Results of a Single-Arm, Noncontrolled Effectiveness-Implementation Hybrid Trial. *Journal of Special Education Technology, 36*(1), 016264342096009. DOI: 10.1177/0162643420960093 PMID: 38911489

Moro, C., Štromberga, Z., Raikos, A., & Stirling, A. (2017). The effectiveness of virtual and augmented reality in health sciences and medical anatomy. *Anatomical Sciences Education, 10*(6), 549–559. DOI: 10.1002/ase.1696 PMID: 28419750

Parham, B. D., & van Ryzin, M. J. (2024). Virtual job interview training: A dose–response to improve employment for transition-age youth with disabilities. *Career Development and Transition for Exceptional Individuals, 47*(2), 92–105. Advance online publication. DOI: 10.1177/21651434231160532 PMID: 38988658

Parong, J., & Mayer, R. E. (2018). Learning science in immersive virtual reality. *Journal of Educational Psychology, 110*(6), 785–797. DOI: 10.1037/edu0000241

Smith, M. J., & Fleming, M. F.. (2016). Virtual reality job interview training and 6-month employment outcomes for individuals with substance use disorders. *Journal of Vocational Rehabilitation, 44*(3), 323–331. DOI: 10.3233/JVR-160802 PMID: 31656389

Smith, M. J., Fleming, M. F., Wright, M. A., Jordan, N., Humm, L. B., Olsen, D., & Bell, M. D. (2015). Job offers to individuals with severe mental illness after participation in virtual reality job interview training. *Psychiatric Services (Washington, D.C.), 66*(11), 1173–1179. DOI: 10.1176/appi.ps.201400504 PMID: 26130002

Smith, M. J., & Ginger, E. J.. (2015). Virtual reality job interview training for individuals with schizophrenia seeking employment. *Schizophrenia Research, 166*(1-3), 86–91. DOI: 10.1016/j.schres.2015.05.022 PMID: 26032567

Smith, M. J., Parham, B. D., Mitchell, J., Blajeski, S., Harrington, M., Ross, B., Johnson, J., Brydon, D. M., Johnson, J. E., Cuddeback, G. S., Smith, J. D., Bell, M. D., Mcgeorge, R., Kaminski, K., Suganuma, A., & Kubiak, S. (2023). Virtual reality job interview training for adults receiving prison-based employment services: A randomized controlled feasibility and initial effectiveness trial. *Criminal Justice and Behavior, 50*(2), 272–293. DOI: 10.1177/00938548221081447 PMID: 38881730

Smith, M. J., Sherwood, K., Ross, B., Oulvey, E. A., Monahan, J. A., Sipovic, J. E., Atkins, M. S., Danielson, E. C., Jordan, N., & Smith, J. D. (2022). Scaling out virtual interview training for transition-age youth: A quasi-experimental hybrid effectiveness-implementation study. *Career Development and Transition for Exceptional Individuals, 45*(4), 213–227. DOI: 10.1177/21651434221081273 PMID: 38882261

Smith, M. J., & Wright, M. A.. (2015). Vocational outcomes for young adults with autism spectrum disorders six months after virtual reality job interview training. *Journal of Autism and Developmental Disorders, 45*(10), 3364–3369. DOI: 10.1007/s10803-015-2470-1 PMID: 25986176

Chapter 8
Shaping Tomorrow's Talent Strategies with Predictive Workforce Intelligence

Satya Subrahmanyam
https://orcid.org/0000-0003-0441-2742
Holy Spirit University of Kaslik, Lebanon

ABSTRACT

This chapter, Future Trends and Innovations in Data-Driven Workforce Analytics, examines how Artificial Intelligence (AI), Big Data, and advanced analytics are revolutionizing Human Resource Management (HRM). It traces the shift from traditional HR metrics to predictive and prescriptive analytics, showcasing how these tools enhance talent acquisition, retention, and employee engagement. The chapter highlights emerging innovations such as real-time analytics, Natural Language Processing, wearable tech, blockchain, and gamification. It also addresses the integration of workforce analytics into broader business strategies and critically explores ethical concerns including data privacy and algorithmic bias. Supported by real-world case studies, the chapter offers strategic guidance for building a future-ready, data-driven HR culture that aligns with organizational goals.

1. INTRODUCTION

The digital transformation of human capital management has ushered in a new era where data and algorithms increasingly shape recruitment strategies. Traditional intuition-based hiring is being replaced by data-informed decisions powered by

DOI: 10.4018/979-8-3373-6516-9.ch008

Artificial Intelligence (AI) and Big Data analytics. Workforce analytics now enables organizations to derive actionable insights from vast datasets, improving talent acquisition, employee retention, and overall HR efficiency. As enterprises strive to remain competitive, integrating AI-driven tools and predictive models has become essential in identifying, attracting, and managing top talent.

This chapter explores the foundational principles, emerging trends, and cutting-edge innovations transforming workforce analytics. Through real-world case studies and strategic insights, it highlights how technologies like natural language processing, cognitive profiling, and blockchain are reshaping the recruitment landscape. The chapter also examines the ethical and regulatory challenges involved, providing a roadmap for organizations to build agile, data-centric, and ethically responsible HR ecosystems in the evolving future of work.

1.1 Digital Transformation in Human Capital Management

The rapid advancement of digital technologies has significantly transformed the landscape of human capital management (HCM), reshaping how organizations attract, manage, and retain talent. Digital transformation in this domain is characterized by the integration of advanced data analytics, artificial intelligence (AI), and big data technologies into core human resources (HR) functions. These developments have empowered HR professionals with tools to make faster, more accurate, and more strategic decisions. Human capital management, once focused on administrative efficiency, is now evolving into a data-driven function that prioritizes strategic workforce planning, talent acquisition, employee engagement, and performance management. The integration of digital systems has enabled real-time tracking of HR metrics, predictive modeling for hiring and retention, and automation of repetitive HR tasks, resulting in enhanced productivity and effectiveness (Deloitte, 2020).

1.2 From Intuition-Based to Data-Informed Recruitment

Traditionally, recruitment decisions were often driven by subjective assessments, personal intuition, or anecdotal evidence. Hiring managers relied on interviews, résumés, and gut feelings to select candidates—a process prone to unconscious bias and inconsistency. With the rise of data analytics and AI in recruitment, organizations are moving towards a data-informed approach where hiring decisions are supported by empirical evidence and predictive insights. This paradigm shift allows HR departments to identify high-potential candidates more accurately, predict job performance, assess cultural fit, and even forecast attrition risk before a hiring decision is made. According to Subrahmanyam (2024), organizations that leverage data in their talent management processes are more likely to make better hiring decisions and experience improved business outcomes. Data-informed recruitment enables continuous refinement of hiring strategies based on feedback loops and performance data.

1.3 Importance of AI and Big Data in Workforce Analytics

AI and big data play a critical role in turning workforce analytics into a non-routine activity, which guides strategic decision making. Machine learning, natural language processing and neural networks, central aspects of AI, enable HR teams to analysis complex data and identify valuable trends in varied datasets. Here, one understands big data to comprise volume of information in addition to its diversity and velocity as well as aggregated datasets (e.g., applications & assessment), and unedited information (e.g., communications, interview records). By combining AI with big data, organizations can leverage predictive analytics to predict staffing needs, gaps in skills and develop more diverse efficient recruitment processes (Subrahmanyam, 2024).

Leading companies like IBM and Unilever have integrated AI-driven platforms into their recruitment workflows to screen candidates, evaluate video interviews, and identify talent with high potential. These technologies have led to measurable improvements in hiring efficiency, time-to-fill, and candidate satisfaction. AI tools can also help mitigate biases by applying consistent and objective criteria, provided the data used to train the algorithms is carefully curated. In this context, data-driven recruitment is not just about efficiency but also about fairness, compliance, and strategic alignment with organizational goals (Raisch & Krakowski, 2021).

1.4 Chapter Objectives and Structure

This chapter will discuss the key impact AI and big data is having on the recruitment strategies, with emphasis on how these technical tools are disrupting workplace-based analytics. The most significant emphasis is placed on the analysis of the manner in which new technologies and high-level analytical practices are changing the way companies approach the attraction and management of talent within contemporary organizations. Also, we will use case studies to show examples of how organizations successfully utilized big data and AI in recruitment as an incentive for the readers to put learned strategies into use. The chapter is organized into several key sections. Following this introduction, the next section outlines the conceptual foundations of workforce analytics, offering definitions, key components, and historical context. It then moves into a discussion on emerging trends, including predictive hiring, AI-powered candidate matching, and real-time dashboards. The chapter proceeds to explore groundbreaking innovations such as neuroparalytic, blockchain-based credentialing, and the use of digital twins in workforce modeling. A dedicated section will examine strategic implications for HR leaders, discussing how data analytics can drive business-aligned recruitment and talent development. Ethical challenges and considerations, including data privacy, algorithmic bias, and transparency, will also be addressed. The chapter concludes with a future outlook, emphasizing the evolving role of HR analytics and the competencies required to succeed in a data-rich environment.

2. FOUNDATIONS OF WORKFORCE ANALYTICS IN THE ERA OF BIG DATA

Workforce analytics, once limited to basic HR metrics, has evolved significantly with the advent of Big Data and AI technologies. It now encompasses descriptive, predictive, prescriptive, and diagnostic insights that inform strategic talent decisions. AI enhances the depth and speed of analysis, enabling organizations to uncover hidden patterns in employee behavior and performance. Google's Project Oxygen exemplifies this evolution, demonstrating how data-driven approaches can refine leadership development and optimize hiring processes.

2.1 Defining Workforce Analytics and Its Evolution

Workforce analytics refers to the systematic analysis of workforce-related data to optimize human resource (HR) practices and decision-making. Traditionally, workforce decisions were made based on intuition, prior experience, or broad organizational norms. As business environments have become more complex and competitive, the need for objective, data-driven insights into workforce dynamics have grown significantly. Workforce analytics emerged in the early 2000s, primarily as a tool for tracking employee data such as turnover, absenteeism, and compensation. Over time, its scope has expanded to encompass strategic domains like performance management, talent acquisition, employee engagement, and leadership development (Levenson, 2018).

The evolution of workforce analytics has been driven by technological advancements, including the advent of AI and big data. Initially, HR analytics was retrospective—summarizing historical events and offering insights on past workforce behavior. Today, it has matured into a predictive and prescriptive discipline that helps organizations forecast future trends, model various scenarios, and recommend actionable strategies. This transition has not only improved the accuracy of HR decision-making but has also elevated the strategic role of HR professionals within organizations.

2.2 Role of AI and Big Data in Amplifying HR Insights

The employment of Artificial Intelligence (AI) together with the use of big data tools has had significant impact on workforce analytics through the provision of never before speed and precision in working with large and complex data sets. The term 'big data' describes enormous, high-volume, and complex data consisting of both record types (employees' files, appraisals) and unstructured content (emails, social activities, and recordings). Using AI algorithms, this data enables organizations to detect patterns, generate meaningful insights, and automate important decision-making.

Natural language processing (NLP) tools can analyze sentiment in employee surveys or open-ended feedback, revealing underlying issues related to engagement or morale. Machine learning algorithms can forecast employee attrition based on behavioral patterns, while computer vision technologies are increasingly being used in video interviews to assess candidate attributes such as confidence, honesty, and cognitive ability (Margherita, 2021). AI also supports continuous learning within the HR function by updating its models as new data becomes available. This creates dynamic, real-time decision-making capabilities that are responsive to changing organizational and market conditions. The ability to integrate internal data (e.g., HRIS, ERP systems) with external sources (e.g., labor market trends, competitor benchmarking) enhances the predictive power of workforce analytics, positioning HR as a key driver of organizational strategy.

2.3 Types of Analytics: Descriptive, Predictive, Prescriptive, and Diagnostic

To understand the multifaceted nature of workforce analytics, it is essential to distinguish between its core types:

1. **Descriptive Analytics** responds to the inquiry "What transpired?" Making sense of performance and trend patterns from the past requires collecting relevant data from the past. Reports on diversity ratios, training attendance, and attrition rates from the previous year are just a few examples of how HR may employ descriptive analytics.
2. **Predictive Analytics** pays close attention to the question, "What is likely to happen?" It uses machine learning and statistical models to predict events from past data. The ability to foretell which applicants would be most valuable to a company is a typical application in the recruiting process.
3. **Prescriptive Analytics** addresses "What should we do?" It recommends specific actions based on predictive insights. An algorithm might suggest personalized

learning pathways for employees at risk of disengagement or recommend targeted retention strategies for high-potential staff.

4. **Diagnostic Analytics** explores "Why did it happen?" This type of analytics seeks to understand causal relationships and identify root causes of workforce issues. Diagnostic analysis might reveal that high turnover in a department is linked to ineffective leadership or a lack of career advancement opportunities (Van den Heuvel & Bondarouk, 2017).

These analytical frameworks work in concert to provide a comprehensive understanding of workforce dynamics, enabling HR leaders to move beyond reactive approaches and become proactive architects of organizational success.

2.4 Case Study: Google's Project Oxygen

A seminal example of effective workforce analytics is **Google's Project Oxygen**, which began in 2009 and has since become a benchmark for data-driven leadership development. The initiative was launched in response to a seemingly simple question: "Do managers matter?" At the time, Google's engineering-driven culture placed high value on technical expertise, sometimes to the exclusion of managerial skills. To determine whether managers had a measurable impact on team performance and how they could be more effective, Google turned to its abundant internal data. Using a combination of performance reviews, employee feedback, and interview data, Google's People Analytics team applied statistical techniques to analyze what differentiated high-performing managers from others. This descriptive and diagnostic analysis revealed that good managers consistently exhibited certain behaviors, including being a good coach, empowering the team without micromanaging, and expressing interest in team members' success and well-being.

The result of this analysis was the creation of a list of eight key behaviors of successful managers, which later expanded to ten. These findings became the foundation for Google's new management training programs, performance evaluation criteria, and leadership development initiatives (Garvin et al., 2013).

Project Oxygen illustrates the power of workforce analytics in transforming leadership culture through evidence-based practices. By applying descriptive and diagnostic analytics, Google not only validated the importance of effective management but also used predictive models to improve hiring and promotion decisions for managerial roles. The initiative led to measurable improvements in employee satisfaction, managerial effectiveness, and organizational performance.

In subsequent years, Google expanded its data-driven approach through initiatives like Project Aristotle, which examined the dynamics of effective teams, further demonstrating the strategic value of workforce analytics in shaping human capital outcomes. The foundations of workforce analytics lie in its ability to transform human resource practices from intuition-based decisions to evidence-informed strategies. With the integration of AI and big data, workforce analytics has evolved into a powerful tool that enables descriptive, diagnostic, predictive, and prescriptive insights. Organizations like Google have demonstrated the transformative impact of these capabilities, using workforce data not only to optimize hiring and leadership development but also to shape culture and strategy. As the availability and complexity of workforce data continue to grow, the role of analytics in human capital management will only become more central, demanding new competencies, ethical standards, and innovative approaches from HR professionals.

3. EMERGING TRENDS IN WORKFORCE ANALYTICS

The increasing difficulty for businesses to recruit, retain and retain the best talent against the backdrop of rapidly changing working environments is fuelling the greater use of workforce analytics. Fascinating advances in AI, big data, and digital tools are rewriting recruitment processes, enabling firms to have the ability to shift from passive reporting to proactive, strategic decision-making ventures. This section discusses the most recent advancements in workforce analytics and presents sample real-life scenarios that illustrate new ways in which workforce analytics can be used.

3.1 AI-Driven Candidate Matching and Resume Parsing

When it comes to artificial intelligence (AI), applicant matching, and resume parsing have been revolutionary in the recruiting industry. Machine learning (ML) and natural language processing (NLP) have improved HR systems' capacity to quickly and accurately analyze and rank a vast number of social media profiles, job descriptions, and resumes. NLP algorithms analyze unstructured data from resumes to identify skills, qualifications, and experience, converting them into structured formats that can be compared to job requirements. This significantly reduces manual screening time and ensures a more objective, consistent evaluation process (Black & van Esch, 2020). Machine learning models further refine this process by learning from recruiter behavior—understanding which candidate profiles lead to successful hires—and improving over time.

Case Study: LinkedIn Recruiter System Connect

LinkedIn's **Recruiter System Connect (RSC)** exemplifies the power of AI-driven candidate matching. RSC integrates directly with Applicant Tracking Systems (ATS), allowing recruiters to search LinkedIn's database of over 900 million profiles and receive AI-driven suggestions based on job descriptions and hiring history. LinkedIn's proprietary matching algorithms use NLP to understand job requirements and candidate qualifications, highlighting the most relevant prospects.

A key feature of RSC is "Spotlight," which filters candidates based on their engagement level—e.g., those who are open to new opportunities or have interacted with the company's brand. This has been shown to increase recruiter efficiency and reduce time-to-hire by 25% (LinkedIn Talent Solutions, 2021). By leveraging vast amounts of behavioral data and machine learning, LinkedIn has created a more dynamic, responsive recruitment system that aligns closely with organizational needs.

3.2 Predictive Hiring and Retention Models

Predictive analytics is another critical trend shaping the future of workforce analytics. By analyzing historical data—such as past performance, engagement metrics, and behavioral assessments—organizations can predict which candidates are most likely to succeed in specific roles or which employees may be at risk of leaving

These models use a combination of statistical techniques and machine learning to identify patterns that correlate with high performance or early attrition. Factors like personality traits, communication style, manager feedback, and even commute distance can be integrated into comprehensive predictive models (Van den Heuvel & Bondarouk, 2017). This not only improves hiring quality but also supports proactive retention strategies.

Case Study: IBM Watson Recruitment

IBM's Watson Recruitment platform utilizes AI to assess resumes and predict candidate success by analyzing historical hiring data. It evaluates factors such as skills relevance, prior job transitions, and educational background to rank applicants. It incorporates insights from current employees into similar roles, assessing cultural fit and long-term potential.

Watson also predicts attrition risks by evaluating behavioral patterns and engagement levels of new hires. For example, if a candidate's past tenures are short or they frequently change industries, the system may flag a higher likelihood of early turnover. This allows recruiters and HR teams to take preventive measures such as offering development opportunities or improved onboarding experience.

According to IBM (2018), companies using Watson Recruitment saw a 30% improvement in hiring efficiency and a 20% increase in candidate satisfaction. By aligning predictive hiring tools with strategic workforce planning, IBM has demonstrated how AI can optimize both recruitment outcomes and employee lifecycle management.

3.3 Real-Time Workforce Dashboards and Analytics Platforms

As workforce analytics become more integrated into organizational strategy, the need for real-time, accessible data has become essential. Workforce dashboards provide live, visual representations of key HR metrics, empowering recruiters, HR managers, and executives to make timely, informed decisions.

Modern analytics platforms offer customizable dashboards that track recruitment metrics such as applicant sources, time-to-fill, diversity statistics, and pipeline health. These platforms often incorporate AI to highlight anomalies, forecast trends, or suggest interventions. Real-time analytics not only improves transparency but also aligns recruitment efforts with broader business objectives.

Case Study: SAP SuccessFactors

SAP SuccessFactors is a leading example of a real-time workforce analytics platform. It offers HR professionals live dashboards that provide visibility into workforce demographics, skill gaps, hiring bottlenecks, and succession planning. Users can drill down into data segmented by department, geography, or job role, allowing for precise interventions. A major feature is the "Diversity and Inclusion" dashboard, which tracks representation across gender, ethnicity, and other categories. AI-driven insights flag areas where diversity hiring may be lagging and recommend targeted actions. In one instance, a multinational organization used SuccessFactors to identify a significant gender imbalance in engineering roles. The system suggested outreach to women's STEM networks, resulting in a 15% improvement in female hires within a year (SAP, 2022). By centralizing data and offering intuitive visual tools, SAP SuccessFactors helps organizations transform data into strategic assets for talent management and workforce development.

3.4 External Labor Market Intelligence Integration

Another significant trend is the integration of external labor market intelligence into workforce analytics. By incorporating macroeconomic indicators, demographic data, and industry benchmarks, organizations can develop more responsive and competitive recruitment strategies. This allows HR teams to understand talent availability, regional salary trends, emerging skills, and competitor activity. Labor market data can inform decisions such as where to open new offices, which roles to outsource, or how to structure compensation packages. It also supports long-term workforce planning by forecasting talent shortages and aligning internal training efforts with future skill demands.

Case Study: Burning Glass Technologies and Emsi

Burning Glass Technologies and Emsi are two analytics firms that specialize in labor market intelligence. They aggregate job postings, resume data, and employment statistics to offer granular insights into workforce trends. Their platforms enable recruiters and policymakers to identify in-demand skills, monitor regional talent flows, and benchmark hiring practices.

A healthcare provider used Burning Glass data to identify a growing demand for telehealth professionals in the Midwest. The platform showed a 45% year-over-year increase in job postings but a limited supply of qualified candidates. In response, the organization partnered with a local university to develop a telehealth certification program, effectively building its own talent pipeline (Emsi Burning Glass, 2021). By blending internal and external data, organizations can make smarter, market-aligned decisions that enhance their employer brand and strengthen workforce resilience.

The emergence of AI and big data has ushered in a new era of workforce analytics—one characterized by speed, precision, and strategic depth. From AI-driven resume parsing and candidate matching to predictive hiring models and real-time dashboards, technological innovation is reshaping how organizations identify, attract, and retain talent.

Real-world examples such as LinkedIn's Recruiter System Connect, IBM's Watson Recruitment, SAP SuccessFactors, and the labor market intelligence platforms of Burning Glass and Emsi demonstrate the practical and strategic value of these technologies. They not only enhance recruitment efficiency and accuracy but also enable organizations to align their workforce strategies with business goals and future market conditions. As workforce analytics continues to evolve, its success will depend on how well organizations balance technological innovation with ethical considerations, transparency, and inclusivity. Those that succeed will be better positioned to navigate the complexities of a digital labor market and build sustainable, data-informed talent strategies.

4. INNOVATIONS SHAPING THE FUTURE OF WORKFORCE ANALYTICS

The future of workforce analytics is being shaped by a new generation of digital innovations that extend far beyond traditional HR practices. As businesses adapt to an increasingly complex and competitive labor landscape, advanced technologies such as sentiment analysis, neuroanalytics, digital twin modeling, and blockchain are enabling more nuanced, predictive, and secure approaches to human resource management. These innovations are enhancing the strategic value of workforce analytics by offering insights into employee behavior, potential, and engagement, while also ensuring the authenticity and reliability of critical workforce data. This section explores these emerging technologies and their practical applications through real-world case studies.

4.1 Sentiment Analysis and NLP in Employee Feedback

When it comes to workforce analytics, one of the most potent uses of AI is sentiment analysis and Natural Language Processing (NLP) to make sense of unstructured employee input. Human resources departments have long used closed-ended questionnaires and reviewed open-text replies by hand to gauge employee engagement and morale. But these approaches don't always provide the whole picture of how employees really feel. NLP algorithms can analyze vast amounts of open-ended survey responses, performance reviews, and interview transcripts to detect themes, emotional tone, and linguistic patterns (Cao et al., 2020). Sentiment analysis enables organizations to track changes in morale, identify early signs of burnout, or detect disengagement, allowing timely intervention and policy adjustments.

Case Study: Unilever's HireVue AI Video Interviewing

Unilever's adoption of HireVue AI video interviewing demonstrates how sentiment analysis and NLP can be applied in talent acquisition. HireVue uses AI to evaluate video interviews based on candidates' facial expressions, tone of voice, and word choice. The platform incorporates NLP to parse the spoken content, assess communication style, and determine alignment with job competencies.

This method reduces unconscious bias and standardizes the assessment process across thousands of applicants. According to Unilever, the implementation of HireVue led to a 90% reduction in recruitment time and significantly increased candidate satisfaction (HireVue, 2020). It allowed recruiters to focus on high-potential candidates by filtering through large applicant pools efficiently and objectively. Such tools mark a significant departure from traditional recruitment by turning qualitative data into structured insights that contribute to better hiring outcomes and workforce planning.

4.2 Neuroanalytics and Cognitive Profiling

Neuroanalytics is an emerging field that applies cognitive science, neuroscience, and artificial intelligence to workforce analytics. By evaluating individuals' cognitive and emotional traits, organizations can forecast leadership potential, team fit, and long-term performance more effectively. Unlike traditional assessments, neuroanalytics aims to uncover subconscious behavioral patterns that influence decision-making, learning style, and interpersonal dynamics. Cognitive profiling through gamified assessments or biometric feedback mechanisms enables HR teams to move beyond resume-based evaluations and incorporate holistic, brain-based data in hiring and development strategies (Yuste et al., 2017).

Case Study: Pymetrics

Pymetrics is a neuroscience-based talent matching platform that uses a series of interactive, game-based exercises to assess cognitive and emotional attributes such as attention, risk tolerance, learning style, and memory. These attributes are then matched with ideal job profiles using machine learning algorithms.

Major companies like Accenture and Unilever have used Pymetrics to eliminate hiring biases and enhance talent prediction. For instance, Accenture integrated Pymetrics to assess thousands of early-career applicants, resulting in more diverse hiring and better job fit. According to Pymetrics (2021), candidates selected through their platform were 20% more likely to perform well and remain in their roles. By focusing on potential rather than pedigree, Pymetrics exemplifies how neuroanalytics can democratize hiring and enable more equitable, science-based workforce decisions.

4.3 Digital Twins and Scenario Planning for Talent Modeling

Digital twins—a concept originally used in manufacturing—are now being applied to HR as virtual replicas of workforce configurations. These digital models simulate organizational structures, employee movement, and skill evolution over time, allowing HR leaders to forecast future workforce needs, test different organizational scenarios, and prepare for multiple contingencies.

By integrating internal data (such as performance, skills, and attrition rates) with external labor market insights, digital twin systems support scenario planning for succession management, upskilling initiatives, and talent pipeline development (Chui et al., 2018).

Case Study: Accenture's Talent Futures Lab

Accenture's Talent Futures Lab has pioneered the use of digital twin technology for human capital planning. The platform creates a dynamic model of the organization, factoring in skills inventory, career pathways, mobility patterns, and retirement risks. It allows HR leaders to simulate different workforce scenarios—such as the impact of automation, shifts in business strategy, or expansion into new markets.

For example, when planning a digital transformation initiative, Accenture used its talent twin to assess which roles would be most impacted by automation and what reskilling pathways could be implemented. This proactive modeling helped reduce skill gaps and accelerate organizational readiness (Accenture, 2020). Digital twins in HR offer a forward-looking, systems-based approach to workforce strategy, shifting the paradigm from reactive planning to continuous optimization.

4.4 Blockchain in Credential Verification

In the era of remote work and global talent acquisition, verifying the authenticity of resumes, degrees, and certifications has become both a challenge and a necessity. Blockchain technology provides a decentralized and tamper-proof way of storing and sharing academic and professional credentials, ensuring trust and integrity in hiring processes.

With blockchain, candidates can own and control their credential data while providing employers with instant access to verified records. This not only reduces the time and cost of background checks but also minimizes the risk of credential fraud (Grech & Camilleri, 2017).

Case Study: Learning Machine + MIT

The collaboration between **Learning Machine** (now Hyland Credentials) and the Massachusetts Institute of Technology (MIT) marked a breakthrough in credential verification. In 2017, MIT issued blockchain-based digital diplomas to its graduates, allowing them to own, share, and verify their credentials instantly through a mobile app.

These digital certificates are stored on the Bitcoin blockchain, providing immutable proof of authenticity that can be accessed by employers or other institutions without involving intermediaries. The system also allows for revocation and re-issuance if errors are found, further enhancing reliability.

This innovation has since been adopted by institutions and employers worldwide, reducing verification time from weeks to minutes and streamlining recruitment in highly credential-sensitive industries like healthcare and finance (MIT News, 2017).

Workforce analytics is undergoing a profound transformation as it integrates emerging technologies that offer deeper, more nuanced insights into employee behavior, potential, and engagement. From sentiment analysis and neuroparalytic to digital twins and blockchain, each innovation addresses specific challenges in modern HR—ranging from bias reduction and skill forecasting to data security and process efficiency.

Unilever's use of HireVue AI, Pymetrics' neuroscience assessments, Accenture's digital twin simulations, and MIT's blockchain diplomas demonstrate the practical applications and strategic impact of these technologies. Together, they signal a shift toward a more intelligent, transparent, and proactive approach to human capital management. As these innovations continue to mature, their integration into mainstream HR practices will be key to building agile, data-driven organizations that can navigate the uncertainties of the future workforce landscape.

5. STRATEGIC IMPLICATIONS FOR RECRUITMENT AND TALENT MANAGEMENT

The value of workforce analytics in recruiting and talent management has come to the fore as HRM becomes responsive to change. With companies under pressure to source top talents and perform in optimal conditions simultaneously, it is critical that reliance on data-driven strategies is necessary to integrate HR strategy into organizational goals. With the transformation of raw workforce numbers into actionable insights, HR leaders can predict what talent will be needed, project performance, individualize recruitment strategies, and build their talent brand. This section discusses the strategic value of workforce analytics in recruitment and talent management, speaking to pragmatic practices, and the leading innovations with practical application.

5.1 Aligning Workforce Analytics with Broader Business Strategy

Strategic integration of workforce analytics with corporate goals enhances the capacity of HR to act not just as a support function but as a driver of organizational values. When workforce data is tied to business outcomes—such as customer satisfaction, innovation, or revenue growth—HR can forecast workforce needs aligned with market trends and strategic priorities (Levenson, 2018).

During a market expansion, predictive analytics can help identify talent gaps, forecast attrition risks, and suggest optimal sourcing strategies. Strategic workforce planning—anchored in analytics—enables organizations to anticipate and prepare for evolving skill demands rather than reactively hiring or reskilling. Advanced analytics can highlight links between workforce behaviors and business performance, aiding leaders in adjusting organizational structures and incentives to maximize impact (Subrahmanyam, 2025).

5.2 Building Data-Literate HR Teams and Investing in Analytics Capability

A significant barrier to leveraging workforce analytics is the lack of data literacy within HR functions. Building data-literate HR teams requires upskilling professionals to understand statistical reasoning, data visualization, and the application of analytical tools. This shift demands more than technical training—it necessitates a mindset change that embraces evidence-based decision-making and cross-functional collaboration with IT and data science teams (Minbaeva, 2018). Organizations must also invest in the right technologies, such as cloud-based Human Capital Management (HCM) systems, AI-enabled dashboards, and integrated analytics platforms. These tools facilitate real-time tracking of key performance indicators (KPIs), talent flows, and recruitment funnel metrics. Embedding data scientists within HR or creating hybrid roles (e.g., People Analytics Specialists) helps bridge the gap between technical expertise and HR domain knowledge (Van den Heuvel & Bondarouk, 2017).

5.3 Customizing Candidate Experiences Using Personalization Engines

The modern recruitment landscape is increasingly candidate-centric, and personalization is key to engaging top talent. Personalization engines, powered by AI and machine learning, tailor the candidate journey based on individual preferences, behaviors, and qualifications. This includes customizing job recommendations, email communications, interview scheduling, and onboarding processes. These technologies enhance candidate experience by providing timely and relevant content, reducing friction in application processes, and fostering a sense of individual recognition. According to Deloitte (2021), organizations that deliver personalized recruitment experiences report 30% higher candidate satisfaction and improved offer acceptance rates.

Case Study: Hilton Hotels – Personalization and AI in Recruitment

Hilton Hotels provides a compelling example of leveraging personalization and AI to transform its talent acquisition strategy. Facing high-volume recruitment for customer service roles, Hilton implemented AI-powered tools to automate resume screening and personalize candidate communications. By using AI to match candidates with the most suitable roles based on their skills and preferences, Hilton significantly reduced time-to-hire and increased applicant satisfaction. The AI system could also provide personalized feedback to candidates and recommend the next steps in the application process. According to internal metrics, Hilton saw a 40%

increase in qualified candidate conversion rates and a measurable improvement in candidate Net Promoter Scores (Hilton Careers, 2020).

This case highlights how AI-driven personalization not only enhances operational efficiency but also strengthens employer reputation by treating candidates as valued individuals rather than data points.

5.4 Enhancing Employer Branding Through Analytics-Driven Storytelling

Employer branding has traditionally relied on marketing-style communication, but workforce analytics introduces a more authentic and data-rich narrative. Analytics-driven storytelling enables organizations to showcase their culture, diversity, employee experience, and career development opportunities using real workforce data.

Data on internal mobility, training completion, and promotion rates can be used to highlight career growth opportunities. Diversity analytics can demonstrate commitment to inclusion with transparency, while sentiment analysis from employee feedback can reveal organizational strengths in leadership or work-life balance. This level of transparency builds credibility and appeals to a new generation of talent who values authenticity and data-backed claims. Platforms like LinkedIn, Glassdoor, and employer microsites are ideal venues for sharing these stories in digestible visual formats (LinkedIn Talent Solutions, 2021).

5.5 Leveraging Workforce Insights for Competitive Advantage in Talent Markets

In competitive talent markets, real-time workforce insights enable organizations to gain an edge by understanding where to find talent, how to engage them, and what incentives matter most. Labor market analytics—often derived from external data sources like job boards, social media, and economic indicators—can help HR teams with benchmark compensation, forecast demand for emerging roles, and identify untapped talent pools.

Internally, workforce analytics can be used to identify high-potential employees, anticipate flight risks, and personalize retention strategies. Predictive models can assess which interventions (e.g., promotions, job rotations, skill development) are most likely to retain top talent.

Corporates like Amazon and IBM have pioneered the use of such analytics to create agile talent pipelines and improve workforce responsiveness to business changes. In a study by Bersin (2020), organizations with advanced workforce analytics capabilities were twice as likely to outperform their peers in recruiting high-quality candidates and maintaining workforce stability.

Workforce analytics is no longer a niche capability but a strategic imperative for modern talent management. Its integration with recruitment and HR strategy enhances agility, precision, and personalization in acquiring and retaining talent. By aligning workforce insights with business strategy, building analytical capabilities, and using data to customize and humanize candidate experiences, organizations can strengthen their employer brand and achieve sustainable talent advantage.

The case of Hilton Hotels exemplifies how AI and personalization can transform recruitment outcomes, while the broader trends point to a future where data drives every stage of the talent lifecycle—from attraction to retention. As analytics maturity deepens, HR's role as a strategic partner will be solidified, supporting informed, evidence-based leadership in the dynamic world of work.

6. ETHICAL AND REGULATORY CONSIDERATIONS IN WORKFORCE ANALYTICS

The considerable adoption of the workforce of analytics and AI in recruitment and talent management can cause organizations to be faced with a set of challenging ethical and regulatory concerns. Such concerns are important and essential to guarantee continued success and credibility of HR driven by data. The issues of algorithmic bias, explainability, transparency, privacy of data, and adherence to regulations have a significant negative influence on the ability of organizations to ensure fairness, accountability and trust in the making of HR decisions. In this section, ethical and legal aspects are analyzed with an example of Amazon's problem with an AI recruitment tool for demonstrating the necessity of ethical AI in HR practices.

6.1 Addressing Bias and Discrimination in Algorithmic Hiring

Algorithmic prejudice is a major ethical worry when it comes to AI-driven hiring. It is possible that algorithms educated on past employment records would unintentionally uphold gender, racial, age, and socioeconomic biases. The model may perpetuate discriminatory behaviours if the training data is biassed or represents an uneven history (Binns, 2018).

In a firm that has a history of employing more males for technical positions, an AI model that is trained on those hiring choices might end up favouring male applicants and penalising characteristics that are often associated with women, such as women's colleges or certain career gaps. Apparent neutral variables may potentially introduce bias into algorithmic systems by standing in for sensitive qualities.

This creates ethical and legal concerns, especially when these biases are embedded in opaque models. Adopting fairness-aware algorithms, regularly auditing for bias, and including diverse stakeholders in model creation and review are ways organisations might tackle this issue. To lessen the influence of prejudice in AI decisions, researchers have used methods like fairness restrictions in ML models and differential effect analysis (Barocas et al., 2019).

6.2 Ensuring Explainability and Transparency of AI Decisions

Explainability—often referred to as "interpretable AI"—is essential for maintaining accountability in algorithmic hiring systems. HR professionals, job candidates, and regulators must understand the rationale behind AI-driven decisions such as why one candidate is shortlisted over another. Black-box models that provide predictions without intelligible explanations are ethically problematic and legally risky.

Explainability fosters transparency, enables error detection, and builds trust among stakeholders. Organizations are increasingly adopting explainable AI (XAI) techniques, such as LIME (Local Interpretable Model-Agnostic Explanations) and SHAP (SHapley Additive exPlanations), to make algorithmic decisions more transparent (Doshi-Velez & Kim, 2017).

Candidates have a right to understand why they were rejected, particularly in jurisdictions where AI is covered under discrimination or employment laws. Transparent AI not only helps organizations comply with regulations but also humanizes the hiring process.

6.3 Adhering to Data Privacy Regulations (e.g., GDPR, CCPA)

Workforce analytics and AI-enabled HR solutions collect a huge amount of personal data, from resumes and rating outcomes to social media activity, facial images, and keystroke habits. Privacy encompassed in AI acquisition, and storage and use must abide by statutory provisions such as GDPR and CCPA,_void from legal penalties and adherence to ethical acts. GDPR explains that sensitive personal data may only be processed with a clear approval of the individual and candidates are entitled to have their data accessed, modified or deleted. GDPR requires that organizations make the evaluation of risks regarding data protection, including algorithmic profiling, through DPIAs based on the guidance of Voigt and Von dem Bussche (2017).

CCPA provides California residents with the right to ask for data collection and restraining the sale of personal data and even removing it. The organizations that fail to comply stand to pay huge fines and run the risk of falling behind in terms of reputation. Corporates should set robust data governance policies, anonymize where possible and secure all stored information. Transparency during the collection and processing levels is essential to compliance and to maintain user trust.

Case Study: Amazon's AI Hiring Tool Controversy

The case of Amazon's 2018 AI recruitment algorithm, which was shut down because of gender bias, teaches caution about ethics in AI recruitment. Amazon developed an AI system for screening resumes with a view of expediting recruitment and reducing human bias. The system was based on the data from the 10-years archive of the resume submission received at Amazon, during the time male candidates were highly overrepresented in tech (Dastin, 2018). The system therefore skewed towards favoring male applicants and demoting resumes for mentioning "women's", as in the case of "women's chess club captain". Despite several rounds of changes, the same biases were retained by the algorithm. Eventually, the tool was abandoned.

This incident illustrates several key lessons:

- **Bias in training data can perpetuate systemic discrimination.**
- **Lack of transparency and explainability prevents early detection of bias.**
- **AI should not be seen as inherently objective**—its outputs are only as fair as its inputs and design.

Amazon's experience underscores the importance of rigorous model testing, interdisciplinary oversight, and continuous ethical review when deploying AI in HR.

6.4 Developing Frameworks for Responsible AI Use in HR

To mitigate the ethical and regulatory risks outlined above, organizations need structured frameworks for the responsible use of AI in HR. These frameworks should align with principles of fairness, accountability, transparency, and ethics (FATE). Key elements of such a framework include:

1. **Ethical AI Governance**: Establish cross-functional AI ethics committees involving HR, legal, IT, and external experts to review AI systems.
2. **Bias Auditing and Fairness Testing**: Conduct regular audits to detect disparate impacts on protected groups and adjust models accordingly.
3. **Explainability Protocols**: Use interpretable models or pair complex models with explanation tools to ensure decision transparency.
4. **Privacy Safeguards**: Enforce strict data protection measures, align with legal requirements (GDPR, CCPA), and adopt privacy-by-design principles.
5. **Informed Consent and Candidate Rights**: Clearly communicate to candidates how their data is used and respect their rights to access, correct, and delete data.
6. **Human-in-the-Loop (HITL)**: Ensure that automated decisions are reviewed by human recruiters, particularly in high-stakes employment decisions.

Organizations such as the IEEE and the European Commission have also published ethical AI guidelines that HR departments can adapt for workforce analytics. Proactive adoption of these standards not only mitigates risk but also builds trust with employees and the public.

The deployment of workforce analytics and AI in recruitment presents transformative opportunities, but it also introduces serious ethical and regulatory challenges. As seen in the Amazon AI case, unchecked algorithms can replicate and even amplify societal biases, undermining fairness and organizational integrity. To avoid such pitfalls, HR leaders must prioritize ethical AI design, ensure transparency, and rigorously comply with data privacy laws.

By developing comprehensive frameworks for responsible AI use, organizations can safeguard against bias and discrimination, respect individual privacy rights, and reinforce public trust. Ultimately, ethical and compliant use of workforce analytics is not just a legal obligation—it is a strategic necessity in building a future-ready, inclusive, and resilient workforce.

7. THE FUTURE OF WORKFORCE ANALYTICS

The domain of workforce analytics is undergoing rapid transformation, fueled by technological advancements and strategic reorientation toward data-driven decision-making. As organizations recognize the competitive advantage inherent in understanding employee behavior, performance, and engagement, they are investing more heavily in advanced tools and roles that can synthesize actionable insights from complex data sets. This evolution is reflected in key trends such as the rise of augmented analytics, low-code/no-code platforms, cross-functional collaboration, and the emergence of dedicated leadership roles like the Chief People Analytics Officer (CPAO). This section explores these developments and provides a real-world case study of Microsoft's workforce analytics transformation.

7.1 The Role of Augmented Analytics and Low-Code/No-Code Platforms

Augmented analytics—an approach that uses AI and machine learning to enhance data preparation, discovery, and sharing—represents the next frontier in workforce analytics. By automating routine tasks and highlighting patterns that might be missed by traditional analysis, augmented analytics empowers HR professionals to make faster, smarter decisions (Gartner, 2020). These systems can autonomously detect anomalies in workforce performance, recommend actions for employee retention, or predict leadership potential based on behavioral data.

Parallelly, low-code/no-code platforms are democratizing analytics by allowing non-technical HR professionals to build dashboards, run predictive models, and create visual reports without requiring extensive programming knowledge. This significantly reduces the dependency on IT departments and accelerates the time-to-insight. Tools like Microsoft Power Apps, Tableau, and Google Looker enable HR teams to construct bespoke solutions tailored to their unique organizational contexts (KPMG, 2021).

These technologies lower the barrier to entry, enhance agility, and support a more inclusive culture of data literacy within HR departments.

7.2 Emergence of the Chief People Analytics Officer (CPAO)

As data becomes central to talent strategy, organizations are formalizing leadership around workforce analytics through the appointment of Chief People Analytics Officers (CPAOs). The CPAO is responsible for aligning people's data with business strategy, ensuring ethical use of analytics, and fostering a data-driven culture within the HR function.

Unlike traditional HR roles, the CPAO straddles multiple domains—HR, data science, behavioral economics, and business strategy. They oversee the integration of data from disparate sources such as HRIS, performance management systems, employee surveys, and even external labor market data. Their remit often includes advising the C-suite on workforce risks, future skill requirements, diversity metrics, and employee sentiment trends (Minbaeva, 2020).

This strategic role is pivotal for converting raw employee data into predictive insights that inform leadership development, succession planning, and organizational design. As the demand for evidence-based HR intensifies, the CPAO will become a fixture in forward-looking enterprises.

7.3 Integration of Workforce Analytics into Enterprise-Wide BI Ecosystems

Traditionally, HR data has been siloed and analyzed in isolation. However, modern organizations are integrating workforce analytics into enterprise-wide business intelligence (BI) ecosystems, enabling a holistic view of how human capital influences financial and operational performance. This integration supports better strategic alignment and more robust scenario planning.

Combining workforce data with financial performance data can help organizations understand the ROI of training programs or the cost of attrition in key departments.

Integration with CRM systems can reveal how employee engagement correlates with customer satisfaction. When analytics are embedded within enterprise platforms like SAP, Oracle, or Microsoft Dynamics, HR can become an active participant in strategic forecasting and enterprise planning (Deloitte, 2022).

Case Study: Microsoft's People Analytics Transformation

Microsoft offers a compelling example of how large enterprises are leveraging workforce analytics to drive business outcomes. Faced with the challenge of improving employee engagement and retention in a rapidly evolving digital workplace, Microsoft undertook a comprehensive transformation of its people analytics capabilities.

The company established a People Analytics team embedded within HR but closely aligned with business units and IT. One of the key initiatives was the use of predictive analytics to identify early warning signs of employee disengagement and turnover. By analyzing data from email and calendar usage, collaboration patterns, employee surveys, and performance reviews, Microsoft was able to develop models that predicted attrition risk and suggested personalized interventions (Brynjolfsson & McElheran, 2021).

The organization invested in visualization tools and self-service analytics portals to democratize data access across leadership and HR business partners. This enabled managers to monitor team dynamics in real-time, identify potential burnout, and make proactive adjustments to workload and team structure.

Microsoft's success lay not only in technical execution but in its commitment to ethical data use and transparency. Employees were informed about how their data was being used, and privacy safeguards were prioritized. This case underscores the transformative potential of workforce analytics when embedded within a clear governance framework and aligned with business imperatives.

7.4 Trends in Cross-Functional Collaboration: HR + IT + Strategy

The future of workforce analytics is inherently cross-functional. No single department can deliver the full value of analytics in isolation. As a result, organizations are fostering collaboration between HR, IT, and strategic planning teams.

HR brings contextual understanding of people dynamics and organizational culture. IT contributes technical expertise in data integration, security, and platform management. The strategy team aligns analytics efforts with business goals and ensures executive sponsorship. This triad is essential for embedding analytics into core business processes, from budgeting and workforce planning to innovation and change management (Bersin, 2020).

Cross-functional collaboration ensures that ethical and compliance considerations are built into the design and deployment of analytics systems. As the workforce becomes more distributed and hybrid, such collaboration will be critical in developing new frameworks for digital employee experience and performance management.

Workforce analytics is no longer a peripheral HR function—it is a strategic asset that shapes how organizations attract, engage, and retain talent. With the advent of augmented analytics, low-code platforms, and integrated BI ecosystems, the tools available to HR professionals are more powerful and accessible than ever. The emergence of the Chief People Analytics Officer and the increasing alignment of HR with IT and strategy departments reflect the growing recognition of people data as a cornerstone of business success.

The case of Microsoft illustrates how predictive analytics, when implemented thoughtfully and ethically, can transform employee experience and drive retention. Looking ahead, organizations that invest in data literacy, foster cross-functional partnerships, and embed analytics into their decision-making will be best positioned to navigate the complexities of the modern workforce and sustain a competitive edge.

8. CONCLUSION

The landscape of workforce analytics is rapidly evolving, shaped by groundbreaking innovations and strategic imperatives that are redefining recruitment and talent management. Key trends such as sentiment analysis and natural language processing (NLP), neuroparalytic, blockchain credentialing, and digital twin simulations are transforming how organizations understand, evaluate, and engage talent. These tools are not only enabling deeper insights into employee potential and organizational needs but are also making recruitment processes more predictive, personalized, and proactive.

The strategic value of adopting workforce analytics lies in its capacity to align hiring practices with broader business objectives. Organizations leveraging analytics can forecast talent needs, enhance candidate experiences, and build resilient talent pipelines. Through platforms like Pymetrics and Microsoft's people's analytics framework, companies are demonstrating how data can drive more equitable, informed, and efficient hiring decisions. The emergence of roles like the Chief People Analytics Officer reflects a deeper integration of analytics into core business strategy, underscoring its critical role in navigating the complexities of the modern workplace.

The promise of analytics comes along with significant requirements on ethics and compliance. The controversy around AI usage by Amazon for its hiring shows the risks of wild algorithmic bias, and calls for algorithmic fairness, transparency and explainability in AI driven HR technology. Companies should be responsible in their usage of AI, adhere to data privacy laws such as GDPR and CCPA, and work on building inclusive and ethical technology solutions.

In future, there is no doubt that the need for change is time sensitive: Companies need to develop recruitment systems that they can be trusted, evidence–based, and flexible. Critical steps are developing teamwork between HR, IT, and strategy, developing HR for working with data, and accountability with defined oversight for AI in hiring. The use of low code/no code technology and augmented analytics enhances the accessibility and comprehensibility of valuable data to stakeholders.

Eventually, preparing for the data-centric future of work demands not only technological adoption but also a cultural shift toward evidence-based decision-making and continuous learning. Organizations that act now to integrate workforce analytics thoughtfully and ethically will not only enhance their recruitment effectiveness but also gain a sustainable competitive edge in attracting and retaining top talent in an increasingly dynamic global labor market.

REFERENCES

Bouhsaien, L., & Azmani, A. (2024, Oct). Challenges and Strategies in Recruitment: Insights from Digital Transformation. In *The Proceedings of the International Conference on Smart City Applications* (pp. 328-340). Cham: Springer Nature Switzerland. DOI: 10.1007/978-3-031-88653-9_33

Grech, A., & Camilleri, A. F. (2017). *Blockchain in education. Joint Research Centre (JRC)*. Science for Policy Report., DOI: 10.2760/60649

Lawande, N. (2024). Exploring the trends of artificial intelligence in recruitment: A bibliometric study. *Int. J. Supply Oper. Manag. Online First*, (May). DOI: 10.22034/ijsom.2024.110284.3016

Margherita, A., & Heikkilä, M. (2021). Business continuity in the COVID-19 emergency: A framework of actions undertaken by world-leading companies. *Business Horizons*, *64*(5), 683–693. DOI: 10.1016/j.bushor.2021.02.020 PMID: 33558777

Minbaeva, D. (2018). Building credible human capital analytics for organizational competitive advantage. *Human Resource Management*, *57*(3), 701–713. DOI: 10.1002/hrm.21848

Ore, O., & Sposato, M. (2022). Opportunities and risks of artificial intelligence in recruitment and selection. *The International Journal of Organizational Analysis*, *30*(6), 1771–1782. DOI: 10.1108/IJOA-07-2020-2291

Raisch, S., & Krakowski, S. (2021). Artificial intelligence and management: The automation–augmentation paradox. *Academy of Management Review*, *46*(1), 192–210. DOI: 10.5465/amr.2018.0072

Shaddiq, S. (2023). Khuzaini, Irpan, M.: Governance of human resources management in the digital era. *J. Bus. Manag. Stud.*, *5*(3), 80–96. DOI: 10.32996/jbms.2023.5.3.8

Van den Heuvel, S., & Bondarouk, T. (2017). The rise (and fall?) of HR analytics: A study into the future application, value, structure, and system support. *Journal of Organizational Effectiveness: People and Performance*, *4*(2), 157–178. DOI: 10.1108/JOEPP-03-2017-0022

Yuste, R., Goering, S., Bi, G., Carmena, J. M., Carter, A., Fins, J. J., & Wolpaw, J. (2017). Four ethical priorities for neurotechnologies and AI. *Nature*, *551*(7679), 159–163. DOI: 10.1038/551159a PMID: 29120438

Zou, J., & Schiebinger, L. (2018). AI can be sexist and racist—It's time to make it fair. *Nature*, *559*(7714), 324–326. DOI: 10.1038/d41586-018-05707-8 PMID: 30018439

REFERENCES

Compilation of References

Abaddi, S. (2025). Factors and moderators influencing artificial intelligence adoption by Jordanian MSMEs. *Management & Sustainability: An Arab Review*, *4*(1), 47–73. DOI: 10.1108/MSAR-10-2023-0049

Abbaschian, B. J., Elmaghraby, A., & Sierra-Sosa, D. (2021). Deep Learning Techniques for Speech Emotion Recognition, from Databases to Models. *Sensors (Basel)*, *21*(4), 1249. DOI: 10.3390/s21041249 PMID: 33578714

Abdelhay, S., AlTalay, M. S. R., Selim, N., Altamimi, A. A., Hassan, D., Elbannany, M., & Marie, A. (2025). The impact of generative AI (ChatGPT) on recruitment efficiency and candidate quality: The mediating role of process automation level and the moderating role of organizational size. *Frontiers in Human Dynamics*, *6*, 1487671. DOI: 10.3389/fhumd.2024.1487671

Abdul-Karim, M., Aguilar, J., Ahlen, S., Alam, S., Allen, L., Prieto, C. A., Alves, O., Anand, A., Andrade, U., Armengaud, E., Aviles, A., Bailey, S., Baltay, C., Bansal, P., Bault, A., Behera, J., BenZvi, S., Bianchi, D., Blake, C., . . . Zou, H. (2025). *DESI DR2 Results II: Measurements of Baryon Acoustic Oscillations and Cosmological Constraints* (arXiv:2503.14738). arXiv. https://arxiv.org/abs/2503.14738

Abraham, S., Paripoornam, R., & Sharma, G. (2025). The role of artificial intelligence in recruitment and talent acquisition—An empirical study. *Journal of Informatics Education and Research*, *5*(1).

Acharya, S., Das, S., & Kitmo, D. (2024). Adaptive Learning and Self-Organization in Swarm Robotics. In *Bio-inspired Swarm Robotics and Control: Algorithms, Mechanisms, and Strategies* (pp. 116–139). IGI Global Scientific Publishing. https://www.igi-global.com/gateway/chapter/345311

Adam, A. K. (2020). Modern challenges of human resource management practice in job placement and recruitment within organisations in the African continent. *Journal of Human Resource Management*, *8*(2), 69–75. DOI: 10.11648/j.jhrm.201200802.14

Agarwal, P., & Sinha, J. (2024). Digitizing talent acquisition: A comprehensive analysis of e-recruitment practices and trends.

Ahmed, M. I., Spooner, B., Isherwood, J., Lane, M., Orrock, E., & Dennison, A. (2023). A Systematic Review of the Barriers to the Implementation of Artificial Intelligence in Healthcare. *Cureus*, *15*(10), e46454. DOI: 10.7759/cureus.46454 PMID: 37927664

Ajunwa, I. (2019). The paradox of automation as anti-bias intervention. *Cardozo Law Review*, *41*, 1671.

Akinrinola, O., Ugochukwu, C., Ofodile, O., & Okoye, C. (2024). Navigating and reviewing ethical dilemmas in AI development: Strategies for transparency, fairness, and accountability. GSC Advanced Research and Reviews, 18(3), 050–058.

Alalwan, A. A., Dwivedi, Y. K., Rana, N. P., & Williams, M. D. (2016). Consumer adoption of mobile banking in Jordan: Examining the role of usefulness, ease of use, perceived risk, and self-efficacy. *Journal of Enterprise Information Management*, *29*(1), 118–139. DOI: 10.1108/JEIM-04-2015-0035

Albassam, W. A. (2023). The power of artificial intelligence in recruitment: An analytical review of current AI-based recruitment strategies. *International Journal of Professional Business Review*, *8*(6), e02089. DOI: 10.26668/businessreview/2023.v8i6.2089

Albassam, W. A. (2023). The power of artificial intelligence in recruitment: An analytical review of current AI-based recruitment strategies. International Journal of Professional Business Review: Int. *J. Prof. Bus. Rev.*, *8*(6), 4.

Aljohani, A., Rana, O., & Perera, C. (2025). Self-adaptive Federated Learning in Internet of Things Systems: A Review. *ACM Comput. Surv.*, *57*(10), 252:1-252:36. https://dl.acm.org/doi/10.1145/3725527

Al-Quraishi, T., Al-Quraishi, N., Alnabulsi, H., Al-Qarishey, H., & Ali, A. H. (2024). Big Data Predictive Analytics for Personalized Medicine: Perspectives and Challenges. *Applied Data Science and Analysis*, *2024*, 32–38. DOI: 10.58496/ADSA/2024/004

Alshdaifat, E., Hussein, F., Alshdaifat, D., El-Salhi, S. M. F. S., & Alsarhan, A. (2021). The Effect of Preprocessing Techniques, Applied to Numeric Features, on Classification Algorithms' Performance. *Data*, *6*(2), 11. DOI: 10.3390/data6020011

Artha, B., Kurniyati, N. N., & Ratnawati, E. T. R. (2024). Artificial Intelligence: A New Paradigm in Human Resource Management. Jurnal Penelitian Pendidikan IPA, 10(SpecialIssue), 372-376.

B, S., Meeradevi, M., S, S., Alex, S. A., Kanavalli, A., S, R., & G, S. (2024). Machine learning model for emotion detection and recognition using an enhanced Convolutional Neural Network. Journal of Integrated Science and Technology, 12(4).

Badouch, M. Boutaounte, M. (2025). Smart E-commerce Recommendations with Semantic AI. Fusion: Practice and Applications, (), 264-271. DOI: 10.54216/FPA.170120

Badouch, M., & Boutaounte, M. (2024). Design and implementation of a hotel recommendation system using deep learning. In Advances in marketing, customer relationship management, and e-services book series (pp. 388–408). DOI: 10.4018/979-8-3693-3172-9.ch019

Badouch, M., Boulmane, E. S., Mahmoud, H., Zioudi, O., & Boutaounte, M. (2024, December). Smart Tourism: How AI is Reimagining the Travel Experience. In International Conference on Electrical Systems and Smart Technologies (pp. 187-198). Cham: Springer Nature Switzerland.

Badouch, M., Boutaounte, M., Mahmoud, H., & Elmobark, N. (2025a). AI-Powered Smart Tourism Reimagining Travel. In Advances in computational intelligence and robotics book series (pp. 431–464).

Badouch, M., Boulmane, Es., Mahmoud, H., Zioudi, O., & Boutaounte, M. (2025b). Smart Tourism: How AI is Reimagining the Travel Experience. In Aboudrar, I., Ilahi Bakhsh, F., Nayyar, A., & Ouachtouk, I. (Eds.), *Innovative Technologies on Electrical Power Systems for Smart Cities Infrastructure. ICESST 2024. Sustainable Civil Infrastructures*. Springer. DOI: 10.1007/978-3-031-86705-7_18

Badouch, M., & Boutaounte, M. (2025). Smart E-commerce Recommendations with Semantic AI. Fusion. *Practice and Applications*, *17*(1), 264–271.

Badouch, M., Boutaounte, M., Zioudi, O., & Mahmoud, H. (2025). The Future of Travel: A Review of Chatbot Recommender Systems in E-Tourism and Smart Tourism. In *International Conference on Electrical Systems and Smart Technologies* (pp. 103-115). Springer, Cham. DOI: 10.1007/978-3-031-86705-7_10

Bag, S., Dhamija, P., Pretorius, J. H. C., Chowdhury, A. H., & Giannakis, M. (2022). Sustainable electronic human resource management systems and firm performance: An empirical study. *International Journal of Manpower*, *43*(1), 32–51. DOI: 10.1108/IJM-02-2021-0099

Ballesteros, J. A., Ramírez, V. G. M., Moreira, F., Pelaez, C. A., & Solano, A. (2024). Facial emotion recognition through artificial intelligence. *Frontiers of Computer Science*, 6.

Bates, T., Cobo, C., Mariño, O., & Wheeler, S. (2020). Can artificial intelligence transform higher education? *International Journal of Educational Technology in Higher Education, 17*(1), 42. Advance online publication. DOI: 10.1186/s41239-020-00218-x

Benedict, C., Hahn, A. L., Diefenbach, M. A., & Ford, J. S. (2019). Recruitment via social media: Advantages and potential biases. *Digital Health, 5*, 2055207619867223. DOI: 10.1177/2055207619867223 PMID: 31431827

Bernhardt, M., Lungren, M. P., Glocker, B., Alvarez-Valle, J., Bannur, S., Tanno, R., Tezcan, K. C., Castro, D. C., Monteiro, M., Oktay, O., Schwaighofer, A., & Nori, A. (2022). Active label cleaning for improved dataset quality under resource constraints. *Nature Communications, 13*(1), 1161. DOI: 10.1038/s41467-022-28818-3 PMID: 35246539

Bessen, J. E. (2018). AI and jobs: The role of demand. In Agrawal, A., Gans, J., & Goldfarb, A. (Eds.), *The economics of artificial intelligence: An agenda* (pp. 291–307). National Bureau of Economic Research., DOI: 10.2139/ssrn.3078715

Bhangale, K., & Kothandaraman, M. (2023). Speech Emotion Recognition Based on Multiple Acoustic Features and Deep Convolutional Neural Network. *Electronics (Basel), 12*(4), 839. DOI: 10.3390/electronics12040839

Bharti, S. K., Shukla, P. K., Mahmoud, A., Varadhaganapathy, S., Bouye, M., Gupta, R. K., & Hingaa, S. K. (2022). Text-Based Emotion Recognition Using Deep Learning Approach. Computational Intelligence and Neuroscience, 2022(45–60), 1–8.

Biased Performance Results of Commercial AI Products (2019 Jan) in Proceedings of the 2019 AAAI/ACM Conference on AI, Ethics, and Society, Honolulu HI USA: ACM, pp. 429–435. DOI: 10.1145/3306618.3314244

Black, J. S., & van Esch, P. (2020). AI-enabled recruiting: What is it and how should a manager use it? *Business Horizons, 63*(2), 215–226. DOI: 10.1016/j.bushor.2019.12.001

Bouhsaien, L., & Azmani, A. (2024, Oct). Challenges and Strategies in Recruitment: Insights from Digital Transformation. In *The Proceedings of the International Conference on Smart City Applications* (pp. 328-340). Cham: Springer Nature Switzerland. DOI: 10.1007/978-3-031-88653-9_33

Breaugh, J. A. (2013). Employee recruitment. *Annual Review of Psychology, 64*(1), 389–416. DOI: 10.1146/annurev-psych-113011-143757 PMID: 23121331

Bulut, O., & Beiting-Parrish, M. (2024). The Rise of Artificial Intelligence in Educational Measurement: Opportunities and Ethical Challenges. *Chinese/English Journal of Educational Measurement and Evaluation*, *5*(3). DOI: 10.59863/MIQL7785

Burrell, D. N., Springs, D., Jones, A. J., Muller, S. R., Wright, J. B., Richardson, K., Burton, S. L., Huff, A. J., Brown-Jackson, K. L., & Nobles, C. (2023). The Managerial Ethical and Operational Challenges of Hospital Cybersecurity (pp. 444–458). igi global.

Bursell, M., & Roumbanis, L. (2024). After the algorithms: A study of meta-algorithmic judgments and diversity in the hiring process at a large multisite company. *Big Data & Society*, *11*(1), 20539517231221758. DOI: 10.1177/20539517231221758

Carrico, C., Matusovich, H. M., & Paretti, M. C. (2019). A qualitative analysis of career choice pathways of college-oriented rural central Appalachian high school students. *Journal of Career Development*, *46*(2), 94–111. DOI: 10.1177/0894845317725603

Chamorro-Premuzic, T., Akhtar, R., Winsborough, D., & Sherman, R. A. (2017). The datafication of talent: How technology is advancing the science of human potential at work. *Current Opinion in Behavioral Sciences*, *18*, 13–16. DOI: 10.1016/j.cobeha.2017.04.007

Chamorro-Premuzic, T., Winsborough, D., Sherman, R. A., & Hogan, R. (2016). New talent signals: Shiny new objects or a brave new world? *Industrial and Organizational Psychology: Perspectives on Science and Practice*, *9*(3), 621–640. DOI: 10.1017/iop.2016.6

Chapman, D. S., & Gödöllei, A. F. (2017). E-recruiting: Using technology to attract job applicants. In *The Wiley Blackwell Handbook of the Psychology of the Internet at Work* (pp. 211–230). Wiley.

Chapman, D. S., Uggerslev, K. L., Carroll, S. A., Piasentin, K. A., & Jones, D. A. (2005). Applicant attraction to organizations and job choice: A meta-analytic review of the correlates of recruiting outcomes. *The Journal of Applied Psychology*, *90*(5), 928–944. DOI: 10.1037/0021-9010.90.5.928 PMID: 16162065

Chassignol, M., Khoroshavin, A., Klimova, A., & Bilyatdinova, A. (2022). AI-driven skill mapping via e-learning engagement patterns. *Computers in Human Behavior*, *128*, 107075. DOI: 10.1016/j.chb.2021.107075

Chaudhari, A., Krishna, A., Travieso-González, C. M., & Bhatt, C. (2023). Facial Emotion Recognition with Inter-Modality-Attention-Transformer-Based Self-Supervised Learning. *Electronics (Basel)*, *12*(2), 288. DOI: 10.3390/electronics12020288

Chen, H., Ma, Q., Lin, Z., & Yan, J. (2021). Hierarchy-aware Label Semantics Matching Network for Hierarchical Text Classification. In Zong, C., Xia, F., Li, W., & Navigli, R. (Eds.), *Proceedings of the 59th Annual Meeting of the Association for Computational Linguistics and the 11th International Joint Conference on Natural Language Processing (*Volume 1*: Long Papers)* (pp. 4370–4379). Association for Computational Linguistics. DOI: 10.18653/v1/2021.acl-long.337

Chien, W.-S., & Lee, C.-C. (2023). Achieving Fair Speech Emotion Recognition via Perceptual Fairness. 17, 1–5.

Chiu, T. K. F., Xia, Q., Zhou, X., Chai, C. S., & Cheng, M. (2023). Systematic literature review on opportunities, challenges, and future research recommendations of artificial intelligence in education. *Computers and Education: Artificial Intelligence*, *4*, 100118. DOI: 10.1016/j.caeai.2022.100118

Choi, G. W., Kim, S. H., Lee, D., & Moon, J. (2024). Utilizing generative AI for instructional design: Exploring strengths, weaknesses, opportunities, and threats. *TechTrends*, *68*(4), 832–844. DOI: 10.1007/s11528-024-00967-w

Chowdary, M. K., Hemanth, D. J., & Anitha, J. (2022). Emotion Recognition from EEG Signals Using Recurrent Neural Networks. *Electronics (Basel)*, *11*(15), 2387. DOI: 10.3390/electronics11152387

Chowdary, M. K., Nguyen, T. N., & Hemanth, D. J. (2021). Deep learning-based facial emotion recognition for human–computer interaction applications. *Neural Computing & Applications*, *35*(32), 23311–23328. DOI: 10.1007/s00521-021-06012-8

Cowan, K., Javornik, A., & Jiang, P. (2021). Privacy concerns when using augmented reality face filters? Explaining why and when use avoidance occurs. *Psychology and Marketing*, *38*(10), 1799–1813. DOI: 10.1002/mar.21576

Craig, S. L., Goulden, A., Eaton, A. D., & Mcinroy, L. B. (2021). Engaging the Senses in Qualitative Research via Multimodal Coding: Triangulating Transcript, Audio, and Video Data in a Study With Sexual and Gender Minority Youth. *International Journal of Qualitative Methods*, *20*, 160940692110136. DOI: 10.1177/16094069211013659

Crompton, H., & Burke, D. (2023). Artificial intelligence in higher education: The state of the field. *International Journal of Educational Technology in Higher Education*, *20*(1), 22. DOI: 10.1186/s41239-023-00392-8

Crompton, H., & Burke, D. (2024). The educational affordances and challenges of ChatGPT: State of the field. *TechTrends*, *68*(2), 380–392. DOI: 10.1007/s11528-024-00939-0

Dada, E. G., Joseph, S. B., Oluwagbemi, O. O., Emebo, O., & Oyewola, D. O. (2023). Facial Emotion Recognition and Classification Using the Convolutional Neural Network-10 (CNN-10). *Applied Computational Intelligence and Soft Computing, 2023*, 1–19. DOI: 10.1155/2023/2457898

Danielson, E. C., Smith, M. J., Ross, B., Sherwood, K., Smith, J. D., Atkins, M., & Jordan, N. (2024). Implementation preparation costs of virtual interview training in pre-employment transition services: A budget impact analysis. *Journal of Special Education Technology*, *39*(1), 27–40. DOI: 10.1177/01626434231175372 PMID: 38975255

Daugherty, P. R., & Wilson, H. J. (2018). *Human + machine: Reimagining work in the age of AI*. Harvard Business Review Press. https://dl.acm.org/doi/10.5555/3235249

Davis, F. D. (1989). Perceived usefulness, perceived ease of use, and user acceptance of information technology. *Management Information Systems Quarterly*, *13*(3), 319–340. DOI: 10.2307/249008

Delcker, J., Heil, J., Ifenthaler, D., Seufert, S., & Spirgi, L. (2024). First-year students' AI competence as a predictor for intended and de facto use of AI tools for supporting learning processes in higher education. *International Journal of Educational Technology in Higher Education*, *21*(1), 13. DOI: 10.1186/s41239-024-00452-7

Demopoulos, N. (2025). *From Chaos to Order: A Stochastic Approach to Self Organizing Systems* (2025021719). *Preprints*. DOI: 10.20944/preprints202502.1719.v1

Depuru, S., Nandam, A., Sivanantham, S., Amala, K., Akshaya, V., & Saktivel, M. (2022). Convolutional Neural Network based Human Emotion Recognition System: A Deep Learning Approach. 1–4.

Deshmukh, A., & Raut, A. (2025). Applying BERT-based NLP for automated resume screening and candidate ranking. *Annals of Data Science*, *12*(2), 591–603. DOI: 10.1007/s40745-024-00524-5

Dhamija, P. (2012). E-recruitment: A roadmap towards e-human resource management. *Research World*, *3*(3), 33.

Dogani, J., Namvar, R., & Khunjush, F. (2023). Auto-scaling techniques in container-based cloud and edge/fog computing: Taxonomy and survey. *Computer Communications*, *209*, 120–150. DOI: 10.1016/j.comcom.2023.06.010

Dolka, H. (2021). *M, A. X. V., & Juliet, S.* Speech Emotion Recognition Using ANN on MFCC Features.

Du, J. (2024). Exploring gender bias and algorithm transparency: Ethical considerations of AI in HRM. *Journal of Theory and Practice of Management Science.*

Dwivedi, Y. K., Hughes, L., Ismagilova, E., Aarts, G., Coombs, C., Crick, T., Duan, Y., ... (2021). Artificial intelligence (AI): Multidisciplinary perspectives on emerging challenges, opportunities, and agenda for research, practice, and policy. *International Journal of Information Management, 57*, 101994. El Khoury (Ed.), *Anticipating future business trends: Navigating artificial intelligence innovations* (Vol. 535, pp. 1–14). Springer, Cham.

Ebrahim, S. S., & Rajab, H. A. (2025). The Future of HR: The Role of AI-Powered Recruitment in Shaping the Modern Workforce. *OAlib, 12*(1), 1–22. DOI: 10.4236/oalib.1112770

Fan, F. X., Tan, C., Wattenhofer, R., & Ong, Y.-S. (2025). *Position Paper: Rethinking Privacy in RL for Sequential Decision-making in the Age of LLMs* (arXiv:2504.11511). arXiv. https://doi.org//arXiv.2504.11511DOI: 10.2139/ssrn.5219045

Farooq, M., Raja, F. R., Baloch, N. K., Zikria, Y. B., Hussain, F., & Yu, H. (2020). Impact of Feature Selection Algorithm on Speech Emotion Recognition Using Deep Convolutional Neural Network. *Sensors (Basel), 20*(21), 6008. DOI: 10.3390/s20216008 PMID: 33113907

Fenech, R., Baguant, P., & Ivanov, D. (2019). The changing role of human resource management in an era of digital transformation. *Journal of Management Information & Decision Sciences, 22*(2).

Funabashi, M. (2024). Synecoculture experiments: Human augmentation of ecosystems and Planetary Health. *Science Talks, 12*, 100405. DOI: 10.1016/j.sctalk.2024.100405

Gelinas, D., Sadreddin, A., & Vahidov, R. (2022). Artificial intelligence in human resources management: A review and research agenda. *Pacific Asia Journal of the Association for Information Systems, 14*(6), 1–42. DOI: 10.17705/1pais.14601

Gerczuk, M., Ottl, S., Amiriparian, S., & Schuller, B. W. (2023). EmoNet: A Transfer Learning Framework for Multi-Corpus Speech Emotion Recognition. *IEEE Transactions on Affective Computing, 14*(2), 1472–1487. DOI: 10.1109/TAFFC.2021.3135152

Ghadekar, P., Shaligram, Y., Shimpi, V., Shingade, O., Singh, S., & Thakur, S. (2024). Simultaneous Localization and Mapping using object detection and Reinforcement Learning for automated Robot. *2024 IEEE Calcutta Conference (CALCON)*, 1–5. https://doi.org/DOI: 10.1109/CALCON63337.2024.10914203

Gheibi, O., & Weyns, D. (2024). Dealing with Drift of Adaptation Spaces in Learning-based Self-Adaptive Systems Using Lifelong Self-Adaptation. *ACM Transactions on Autonomous and Adaptive Systems*, *19*(1), 1–57. DOI: 10.1145/3636428

Ghosh, R., & Scott, J. E. (2023). The adoption of artificial intelligence in human resources management: A systematic literature review. *Journal of Business Research*, *150*, 1–15. DOI: 10.1016/j.jjimei.2023.100208

Gilch, P. M., & Sieweke, J. (2021). Recruiting digital talent: The strategic role of recruitment in organisations' digital transformation. *German Journal of Human Resource Management*, *35*(1), 53–82. DOI: 10.1177/2397002220952734

Gizi Gulomkodirova, M. S. (2024). A STUDY ON VARIOUS E-RECRUITMENT TOOLS AND ITS EFFECTIVENESS FOR RECRUITMENT. QO 'QON UNIVERSITETI XABARNOMASI, 10, 32-34.

Gkintoni, E., Aroutzidis, A., Antonopoulou, H., & Halkiopoulos, C. (2025). From Neural Networks to Emotional Networks: A Systematic Review of EEG-Based Emotion Recognition in Cognitive Neuroscience and Real-World Applications. *Brain Sciences*, *15*(3), 220. DOI: 10.3390/brainsci15030220 PMID: 40149742

Goda, S., Hayashi, Y., & Saito, Y. (2024). A Best-of-Both Approach to Improve Match Predictions and Reciprocal Recommendations for Job Search. arXiv preprint arXiv:2409.10992.

Golpayegani, F., Chen, N., Afraz, N., Gyamfi, E., Malekjafarian, A., Schäfer, D., & Krupitzer, C. (2024). Adaptation in Edge Computing: A Review on Design Principles and Research Challenges. *ACM Transactions on Autonomous and Adaptive Systems*, *19*(3), 1–43. DOI: 10.1145/3664200

Graham, M. E., Kennavane, E., & Wears, K. H. (2008). Diversity management content in introductory human resource management textbooks. *Academy of Management Learning & Education*, *7*(3), 429–433. DOI: 10.5465/amle.2008.37029277

Grech, A., & Camilleri, A. F. (2017). *Blockchain in education. Joint Research Centre (JRC)*. Science for Policy Report., DOI: 10.2760/60649

Gunawan, T. S., Rosnelly, R., Kartiwi, M., Riza, B. S., Haryanto, E. V., Ashraf, A., & Janin, Z. (2020). Development of video-based emotion recognition using deep learning with Google Colab. *Telkomnika*, *18*(5), 2463. DOI: 10.12928/telkomnika.v18i5.16717

Gupta, N. (2023). Artificial Intelligence Ethics and Fairness: A study to address bias and fairness issues in AI systems, and the ethical implications of AI applications. *Revista Review Index Journal of Multidisciplinary*, *3*(2), 24–35. DOI: 10.31305/rrijm2023.v03.n02.004

Han, C., Yang, T., Sun, X., & Cui, Z. (2025). Secure Hierarchical Federated Learning for Large-Scale AI Models: Poisoning Attack Defense and Privacy Preservation in AIoT. *Electronics (Basel)*, *14*(8), 8. DOI: 10.3390/electronics14081611

Hasan, H. E., Jaber, D., Khabour, O. F., & Alzoubi, K. H. (2024). Ethical considerations and concerns in the implementation of AI in pharmacy practice: A cross-sectional study. *BMC Medical Ethics*, *25*(1), 55. DOI: 10.1186/s12910-024-01062-8 PMID: 38750441

Hickman, L., Ng, V., Saef, R., Woo, S. E., Bosch, N., & Tay, L. (2021). Developing and evaluating language-based machine learning algorithms for inferring applicant personality in video interviews. *Human Resource Management Journal*, *34*(2), 255–274. DOI: 10.1111/1748-8583.12356

Horodyski, P. (2023). Applicants' perception of artificial intelligence in the recruitment process. *Computers in Human Behavior Reports*, *11*, 100303. DOI: 10.1016/j.chbr.2023.100303

Hung, L. P., & Alias, S. (2023). Beyond Sentiment Analysis: A Review of Recent Trends in Text Based Sentiment Analysis and Emotion Detection. *Journal of Advanced Computational Intelligence and Intelligent Informatics*, *27*(1), 84–95. DOI: 10.20965/jaciii.2023.p0084

Hu, Q. (2023). Unilever's Practice on AI-based Recruitment. Highlights in Business. *Economics and Management*, *16*, 256–263.

Idoko, I., Manuel, H., Igbede, M., Ukaegbu, C., Akpa, F., & Adeoye, T. (2024). Big data and AI in employment: The dual challenge of workforce replacement and protecting customer privacy in biometric data usage. Global Journal of Engineering and Technology Advances, 19(2), 089–106.

Islam, M., Rahman, M. M., Taher, M. A., Quaosar, G. M., & Uddin, M. A. (2024). Using artificial intelligence for hiring talents in a moderated mechanism. *Future Business Journal*, *10*(1), 1–16. DOI: 10.1186/s43093-024-00303-x

Izard, A., McEntee, E., & Maher, J. (2017). Comparing virtual reality and desktop interfaces for skill training and education. *Computers & Education*, *113*, 50–62. DOI: 10.1371/journal.pone.0275119

Jaiswal, A., Deb, S., & Krishnama Raju, A. (2020, Jun 1). Facial Emotion Detection Using Deep Learning.

Jatoba, M. N., Ferreira, J. J., Fernandes, P. O., & Teixeira, J. P. (2023). Intelligent human resources for the adoption of artificial intelligence: A systematic literature review. *Journal of Organizational Change Management, 36*(7), 1099–1124. DOI: 10.1108/JOCM-03-2022-0075

Jiang, J., Ye, S., Wang, W., Xu, J., & Luo, X. (2020). Learning Effective Representations for Person-Job Fit by Feature Fusion. 2549–2556.

Jiang, P., Zhao, L., Xu, X., Tao, H., & Zou, C. (2022). Convolutional-Recurrent Neural Networks With Multiple Attention Mechanisms for Speech Emotion Recognition. *IEEE Transactions on Cognitive and Developmental Systems, 14*(4), 1564–1573. DOI: 10.1109/TCDS.2021.3123979

Jiang, Z., Seyedi, S., Griner, E., Abbasi, A., Rad, A. B., Kwon, H., Cotes, R. O., & Clifford, G. D. (2024). Multimodal Mental Health Digital Biomarker Analysis From Remote Interviews Using Facial, Vocal, Linguistic, and Cardiovascular Patterns. *IEEE Journal of Biomedical and Health Informatics, 28*(3), 1680–1691. DOI: 10.1109/JBHI.2024.3352075 PMID: 38198249

Jin, D., Wang, L., Zhang, H., Zheng, Y., Ding, W., Xia, F., & Pan, S. (2023). A survey on fairness-aware recommender systems. *Information Fusion, 100*, 101906. DOI: 10.1016/j.inffus.2023.101906

Johar, N. A., Kew, S. N., Tasir, Z., & Koh, E. (2023). Learning analytics on student engagement to enhance students' learning performance: A systematic review. *Sustainability (Basel), 15*(10), 7849. DOI: 10.3390/su15107849

Johnson, R. D., Lukaszewski, K. M., & Stone, D. L. (2016). The evolution of the field of human resource information systems: Co-evolution of technology and HR processes. *Communications of the Association for Information Systems, 38*(1), 28. DOI: 10.17705/1CAIS.03828

Kakuba, S., Han, D. S., & Poulose, A. (2022). Attention-Based Multi-Learning Approach for Speech Emotion Recognition With Dilated Convolution. *IEEE Access : Practical Innovations, Open Solutions, 10*, 122302–122313. DOI: 10.1109/ACCESS.2022.3223705

Kandalaft, M. R., Didehbani, N., Krawczyk, D. C., Allen, T. T., & Chapman, S. B. (2013). Virtual reality social cognition training for young adults with high-functioning autism. *Journal of Autism and Developmental Disorders, 43*(1), 34–44. DOI: 10.1007/s10803-012-1544-6 PMID: 22570145

Kanjanawattana, S., Kittichaiwatthana, P., Praneetpholkrang, P., & Srivisut, K. (2023). Deep Learning-Based Emotion Recognition through Facial Expressions. Journal of Image and Graphics, 140–145.

Kardakis, S., Perikos, I., Hatzilygeroudis, I., & Grivokostopoulou, F. (2021). Examining Attention Mechanisms in Deep Learning Models for Sentiment Analysis. *Applied Sciences (Basel, Switzerland), 11*(9), 3883. DOI: 10.3390/app11093883

Kathuria, A., Singla, R. K., & Gupta, A. (2020). A Review of Tools and Techniques for Preprocessing of Textual Data (pp. 407–422). springer singapore.

Kazim, E., Koshiyama, A. S., Hilliard, A., & Polle, R. (2021). Systematizing Audit in Algorithmic Recruitment. *Journal of Intelligence, 9*(3), 46. DOI: 10.3390/jintelligence9030046 PMID: 34564294

Kim, J.-Y., & Heo, W. (2022). Artificial intelligence video interviewing for employment: Perspectives from applicants, companies, developers, and academicians. *Information Technology & People, 35*(3), 861–878. DOI: 10.1108/ITP-04-2019-0173

Kitsiou, A., Pantelelis, M., Mazarakis, P.-A., Mavroeidi, A. G., Simou, S., Tzortzaki, E., Stavridis, S., Koutzamanis, G., & Kalloniatis, C. (2025). Self-Adaptive Privacy in Cloud Computing Environments: Developing an Integrated Framework and a Beta Tool for Social Media Platforms. *Electronics (Basel), 14*(7), 1412. DOI: 10.3390/electronics14071412

Kothari, P., Mehta, P., Patil, S., & Hole, V. (2024). InterviewEase: AI-powered interview assistance.

Kumar, P., Iwamura, M., Roy, P. P., Jain, S., & Raman, B. (2021). End-to-end Triplet Loss based Emotion Embedding System for Speech Emotion Recognition. 13, 8766–8773.

Kumari, S. (2023). Job Recommendation System Using NLP. *International Journal for Research in Applied Science and Engineering Technology, 11*(5), 2721–2728. DOI: 10.22214/ijraset.2023.52183

Kyaw, B. M., Saxena, N., Posadzki, P., Vseteckova, J., Nikolaou, C. K., George, P. P., Divakar, U., Masiello, I., Kononowicz, A. A., Zary, N., & Tudor Car, L. (2019). Virtual reality for health professions education: A systematic review and meta-analysis by the Digital Health Education Collaboration. *Medical Education, 53*(1), 3–25. DOI: 10.2196/12959 PMID: 30549096

Lamjid, A., Ennejjai, I., Anass, A., Soumia, Z., & Mabrouki, J. (2024). Enhancing the hiring process: A predictive system for soft skills assessment. Data and Metadata, 3.

Lawande, N. (2024). Exploring the trends of artificial intelligence in recruitment: A bibliometric study. *Int. J. Supply Oper. Manag. Online First*, (May). DOI: 10.22034/ijsom.2024.110284.3016

Le, G. (2025). Augmented Reality in Higher Education: A Systematic Review and Meta-Analysis of the Literature from 2000 to 2023. *Education Sciences*, *15*(6), 678. DOI: 10.3390/educsci15060678

Leutner, F., Akhtar, R., & Chamorro-Premuzic, T. (2022). Talent and the Data Science Revolution. In The Future of Recruitment: Using the New Science of Talent Analytics to Get Your Hiring Right (pp. 17-50). Emerald Publishing Limited. DOI: 10.1108/978-1-83867-559-220221002

Li, C., Chen, B., Cummins, N., Schuller, B. W., & Zhao, Z. (2021). Hierarchical Attention-Based Temporal Convolutional Networks for Eeg-Based Emotion Recognition. 1240–1244.

Li, E., Li, D., Li, C., Wang, S., Hao, Q., & Wu, X. (2020). SUSTech POINTS: A Portable 3D Point Cloud Interactive Annotation Platform System. abs 1903 11027, 1108–1115.

Li, J., Zhang, M., Li, N., Weyns, D., Jin, Z., & Tei, K. (2024). Generative AI for Self-Adaptive Systems: State of the Art and Research Roadmap. *ACM Trans. Auton. Adapt. Syst.*, *19*(3), 13:1-13:60. DOI: 10.1145/3686803

Lian, H., Zong, Y., Zhao, Y., Li, S., Lu, C., & Tang, C. (2023). A Survey of Deep Learning-Based Multimodal Emotion Recognition: Speech, Text, and Face. *Entropy (Basel, Switzerland)*, *25*(10), 1440. DOI: 10.3390/e25101440 PMID: 37895561

Li, M., Liu, X., Li, X., Huang, X., Xu, H., & Song, Z. (2021). Facial Expression Recognition with Identity and Emotion Joint Learning. *IEEE Transactions on Affective Computing*, *12*(2), 544–550. DOI: 10.1109/TAFFC.2018.2880201

Liu, Q., Yang, M., Mohammadi, K., Song, D., Bi, J., & Wang, G. (2022). Machine Learning Crop Yield Models Based on Meteorological Features and Comparison with a Process-Based Model. *Artificial Intelligence for the Earth Systems*, *1*(4). DOI: 10.1175/AIES-D-22-0002.1

Li, W., Zeng, G., Chen, X., Cui, Y., Guo, G., Cao, D., Ma, Y., & Li, G. (2023). A Spontaneous Driver Emotion Facial Expression (DEFE) Dataset for Intelligent Vehicles: Emotions Triggered by Video-Audio Clips in Driving Scenarios. *IEEE Transactions on Affective Computing*, *14*(1), 747–760. DOI: 10.1109/TAFFC.2021.3063387

Li, Y., Chan, J., Peko, G., & Sundaram, D. (2023). Mixed emotion extraction analysis and visualisation of social media text. *Data & Knowledge Engineering, 148*, 102220. DOI: 10.1016/j.datak.2023.102220

Lopez, E., Grassucci, E., Comminiello, D., & Chiarantano, E. (2023, Jun 4). Hypercomplex Multimodal Emotion Recognition from EEG and Peripheral Physiological Signals.

Luo, X., Wang, Y., Lee, L.-H., Xing, Z., Jin, S., Dong, B., Hu, Y., Chen, Z., Yan, J., & Hui, P. (2024). Using a virtual reality interview simulator to explore factors influencing people's behavior. *Virtual Reality (Waltham Cross), 28*(1), 56. DOI: 10.1007/s10055-023-00934-5

Lu, W., Zhang, X., Xia, L., Ma, H., & Tan, T.-P. (2024). Domain adaptation spatial feature perception neural network for cross-subject EEG emotion recognition. *Frontiers in Human Neuroscience, 18*, 18. DOI: 10.3389/fnhum.2024.1471634 PMID: 39741785

M.r.m., V., & Ramesh, P. (2022). Analysis on quality of learning in e-Learning platforms. Advances in Engineering Software (Barking, London, England: 1992), 172(103168), 103168. DOI: 10.1016/j.advengsoft.2022.103168

Macchion, L., Danese, P., & Vinelli, A. (2015). Redefining supply network strategies to face changing environments. A study from the fashion and luxury industry. Operations management research, 8, 15-31.

Macher, T.-H., Schütz, R., Yildiz, A., Beermann, A., & Leese, F. (2023). Evaluating five primer pairs for environmental DNA metabarcoding of Central European fish species based on mock communities. *Metabarcoding and Metagenomics, 7*, e103856. DOI: 10.3897/mbmg.7.103856

Mahmoud, H., Zioudi, O., Boulmane, E.-S., Badouch, M., & Boutaounte, M. (2025). Recommendation system in the educational context: Experience in Morocco. In Benabid, A., El Imadi, I., & Chemsi, G. (Eds.), *Personalized learning through adaptive systems and intelligent tutoring* (pp. 167–188). IGI Global., DOI: 10.4018/979-8-3373-0740-4.ch006

Mahmud Sujon, K., Binti Hassan, R., Choi, K., Abdus Samad, M., Tusnia Towshi, Z., & Othman, M. A. (2024). When to Use Standardization and Normalization: Empirical Evidence From Machine Learning Models and XAI. *IEEE Access : Practical Innovations, Open Solutions, 12*, 135300–135314. DOI: 10.1109/ACCESS.2024.3462434

Mai, J., Cao, K., & Wei, T. (2025). Personalized Federated Learning with State-Adaptive IoT Device Scheduling in Mobile Edge Computing. *IEEE Transactions on Computer-Aided Design of Integrated Circuits and Systems*, 1–1. DOI: 10.1109/TCAD.2025.3560221

Maji, B., Swain, M., Guha, R., & Routray, A. (2023). Multimodal Emotion Recognition Based on Deep Temporal Features Using Cross-Modal Transformer and Self-Attention. 1–5.

Makhmudov, F., Kultimuratov, A., & Cho, Y.-I. (2024). Enhancing Multimodal Emotion Recognition through Attention Mechanisms in BERT and CNN Architectures. mdpi ag.

Margherita, A., & Heikkilä, M. (2021). Business continuity in the COVID-19 emergency: A framework of actions undertaken by world-leading companies. *Business Horizons*, *64*(5), 683–693. DOI: 10.1016/j.bushor.2021.02.020 PMID: 33558777

Martín-Raugh, M. P., Randall, J. G., Kell, H. J., Banfi, J. T., & Anguiano-Carrasco, C. (2022). Speaking without words: A meta-analysis of over 70 years of research on the power of nonverbal cues in job interviews. *Journal of Organizational Behavior*, *44*(1), 132–156. DOI: 10.1002/job.2670

Mashayekhi, Y., Li, N., Kang, B., Lijffijt, J., & De Bie, T. (2024). A challenge-based survey of e-recruitment recommendation systems. *ACM Computing Surveys*, *56*(10), 1–33. DOI: 10.1145/3659942

Matthew, J. (2020). Virtual Reality Job Interview Training in Transition Services: Results of a Single-Arm, Noncontrolled Effectiveness-Implementation Hybrid Trial. *Journal of Special Education Technology*, *36*(1), 016264342096009. DOI: 10.1177/0162643420960093 PMID: 38911489

Minbaeva, D. (2018). Building credible human capital analytics for organizational competitive advantage. *Human Resource Management*, *57*(3), 701–713. DOI: 10.1002/hrm.21848

Mislevy, R. J., Yan, D., Gobert, J., & Sao Pedro, M. (2020). Automated scoring in intelligent tutoring systems. In *Handbook of automated scoring* (pp. 403–422). Chapman and Hall/CRC. DOI: 10.1201/9781351264808-22

Mohapatra, R. B., & Li, K.-C. (Eds.). (2021). *Advances in Intelligent Systems and Computing* (Vol. 1199, pp. 353–365). Springer Singapore., DOI: 10.1007/978-981-15-6353-9_32

Moro, C., Štromberga, Z., Raikos, A., & Stirling, A. (2017). The effectiveness of virtual and augmented reality in health sciences and medical anatomy. *Anatomical Sciences Education, 10*(6), 549–559. DOI: 10.1002/ase.1696 PMID: 28419750

Muaad, A. Y., Chola, C., Benifa, J. V. B., Guru, D. S., Gumaei, A. H., Davanagere, H. J., Al-Antari, M. A., & Alsalman, H. (2022). Arabic Document Classification: Performance Investigation of Preprocessing and Representation Techniques. *Mathematical Problems in Engineering, 2022*, 1–16. DOI: 10.1155/2022/3720358

Nikolaou, I. (2014). Social networking web sites in job search and employee recruitment. *International Journal of Selection and Assessment, 22*(2), 179–189. DOI: 10.1111/ijsa.12067

Nwokwu, T. C. (2020). Delay in Recruitment: Evidence from a Developing Country. NWOKWU, TC (2020). Delay in Recruitment: Evidence from a Developing Country. *International Journal of Business and Economic Affairs, 5*(1), 9–22. DOI: 10.24088/IJBEA-2020-51002

Ogunseyi, T. B., Avoussoukpo, C. B., & Jiang, Y. (2023). A systematic review of privacy techniques in recommendation systems. *International Journal of Information Security, 22*(6), 1651–1664. DOI: 10.1007/s10207-023-00710-1

Omar, M., & Burrell, D. N. (2023). Organizational Dynamics and Bias in Artificial Intelligence (AI) Recruitment Algorithms (pp. 269–290). igi global.

Ong, K. L., Lim, H. S., Lim, K. M., & Lee, C. P. (2023). Speech emotion recognition with light gradient boosting decision trees machine. [IJECE]. *International Journal of Electrical and Computer Engineering, 13*(4), 4020. DOI: 10.11591/ijece.v13i4.pp4020-4028

Ore, O., & Sposato, M. (2022). Opportunities and risks of artificial intelligence in recruitment and selection. *The International Journal of Organizational Analysis, 30*(6), 1771–1782. DOI: 10.1108/IJOA-07-2020-2291

Padilla, R., Dias, T. L. B., Passos, W. L., Netto, S. L., & Da Silva, E. A. B. (2021). A Comparative Analysis of Object Detection Metrics with a Companion Open-Source Toolkit. *Electronics (Basel), 10*(3), 279. DOI: 10.3390/electronics10030279

Palakurti, N. R. (2025). Ethical Considerations of AI and ML in Insurance Risk Management: Addressing Bias and Ensuring Fairness. International Journal of Multidisciplinary Research in Science, Engineering and Technology, 08(01).

Parasa, S. K. (2024). Impact of AI in recruitment and talent acquisition. *Human Resource and Leadership Journal, 9*(1), 45–60.

Parham, B. D., & van Ryzin, M. J. (2024). Virtual job interview training: A dose–response to improve employment for transition-age youth with disabilities. *Career Development and Transition for Exceptional Individuals*, *47*(2), 92–105. Advance online publication. DOI: 10.1177/21651434231160532 PMID: 38988658

Parong, J., & Mayer, R. E. (2018). Learning science in immersive virtual reality. *Journal of Educational Psychology*, *110*(6), 785–797. DOI: 10.1037/edu0000241

Parra-Ullauri, J., García-Domínguez, A., Bencomo, N., & Garcia-Paucar, L. (2022). History-aware explanations: Towards enabling human-in-the-loop in self-adaptive systems. *Proceedings of the 25th International Conference on Model Driven Engineering Languages and Systems: Companion Proceedings*, 286–295. DOI: 10.1145/3550356.3561538

Pastor, M. A., Lleida, E., Miguel, A., Ribas, D., & Ortega, A. (2023). Cross-Corpus Training Strategy for Speech Emotion Recognition Using Self-Supervised Representations. *Applied Sciences (Basel, Switzerland)*, *13*(16), 9062. DOI: 10.3390/app13169062

Pepino, L., Ferrer, L., & Riera, P. (2021, Aug 30). Emotion Recognition from Speech Using wav2vec 2.0 Embeddings.

Pereira, V., Hadjielias, E., Christofi, M., & Vrontis, D. (2023). A systematic literature review on the impact of artificial intelligence on workplace outcomes: A multi-process perspective. *Human Resource Management Review*, *33*(1), 100857. DOI: 10.1016/j.hrmr.2021.100857

Philip, B., Mathew, G. A., Sebastian, R. T., Eshwari, B., Roopa, M. B., & Mathews, S. B. (2024). Strategizing talent acquisition for fostering future workforce success: Addressing millennial turnover and hiring challenges in a rapidly evolving business landscape. In R.

Picoral, A., Reppen, R., & Staples, S. (2021). Automated annotation of learner English. *International Journal of Learner Corpus Research*, *7*(1), 17–52. DOI: 10.1075/ijlcr.20003.pic

Pisica, A. I., Edu, T., Zaharia, R. M., & Zaharia, R. (2023). Implementing artificial intelligence in higher education: Pros and cons from the perspectives of academics. *Societies (Basel, Switzerland)*, *13*(5), 118. DOI: 10.3390/soc13050118

Portillo, A. E., & Mancera-Valencia, F. J. (2021). The processes of recruitment and selection of personnel: Between objectivity and subjectivity. *International Journal of Social Sciences Perspectives*, *9*(1), 1–8. DOI: 10.33094/7.2017.2021.91.1.8

Pourkhodabakhsh, N., Mamoudan, M. M., & Bozorgi-Amiri, A. (2023). Effective machine learning, Meta-heuristic algorithms and multi-criteria decision making to minimizing human resource turnover. *Applied Intelligence*, *53*(12), 16309–16331. DOI: 10.1007/s10489-022-04294-6 PMID: 36531972

Pratama, M. P., Sampelolo, R., & Lura, H. (2023). Revolutionizing education: harnessing the power of artificial intelligence for personalized learning. *Klasikal: Journal of education, language teaching and science*, *5*(2), 350-357. DOI: 10.52208/klasikal.v5i2.877

Qiu, L., & Zhao, L. (2019). Opportunities and challenges of artificial intelligence to human resource management. *Academic Journal of Humanities & Social Sciences*, *2*, 144–153. https://francis-press.com/papers/349

Raghavan, M., Barocas, S., Kleinberg, J., & Levy, K. (2020, January). Mitigating bias in algorithmic hiring: Evaluating claims and practices. In *Proceedings of the 2020 conference on fairness, accountability, and transparency* (pp. 469-481). DOI: 10.1145/3351095.3372828

Rai, R. S., & Selnes, F. (2019). Conceptualizing task-technology fit and the effect on adoption–A case study of a digital textbook service. *Information & Management*, *56*(8), 103161. DOI: 10.1016/j.im.2019.04.004

Raisch, S., & Krakowski, S. (2021). Artificial intelligence and management: The automation–augmentation paradox. *Academy of Management Review*, *46*(1), 192–210. DOI: 10.5465/amr.2018.0072

Raji, I. D., & Buolamwini, J. (2019, Jan). Actionable auditing: Investigating the impact of publicly naming biased performance results of commercial ai products. In Proceedings of the 2019 AAAI/ACM Conference on AI, Ethics, and Society (pp. 429-435).

Rivera, M., Kumar, S., Qiu, L., & Petrucci, T. (2021). Are Traditional Performance Reviews Outdated? An Empirical Analysis on Continuous, Real-Time Feedback in the Workplace. *Information Systems Research*, *32*(2), 517–540. DOI: 10.1287/isre.2020.0979

Robert, L. P., Pierce, C., Morris, L., Kim, S., & Alahmad, R. (2020). Designing fair AI for managing employees in organizations: A review, critique, and design agenda. *arXiv preprint arXiv:2002.09054*. https://arxiv.org/abs/2002.09054

Rodgers, W., Murray, J. M., Stefanidis, A., Degbey, W. Y., & Tarba, S. Y. (2023). An artificial intelligence algorithmic approach to ethical decision-making in human resource management processes. *Human Resource Management Review, 33*(1), 100925. DOI: 10.1016/j.hrmr.2022.100925

Rogers, E. M. (1995). Diffusion of Innovations: Modifications of a Model for Telecommunications. In Stoetzer, M. W., & Mahler, A. (Eds.), *Die Diffusion von Innovationen in der Telekommunikation. Schriftenreihe des Wissenschaftlichen Instituts für Kommunikationsdienste* (Vol. 17). Springer. DOI: 10.1007/978-3-642-79868-9_2

Romano, J. D., Moore, J. H., Goldberg, D. J., Chakraborty, P., Le, T. T., Ray, N. L., Himmelstein, D., La Cava, W., Fu, W., & Gregg, J. T. (2021). PMLB v1.0: An open-source dataset collection for benchmarking machine learning methods. *Bioinformatics (Oxford, England), 38*(3), 878–880. DOI: 10.1093/bioinformatics/btab727 PMID: 34677586

Romero Garces, A. (2022). *On Managing Knowledge for MAPE-K Loops in Self-Adaptive Robotics Using a Graph-Based Runtime Model.* Alejandro. https://www.mdpi.com/2076-3417/12/17/8583

Saad, M. F. M., Nugro, A. W. L., Thinakaran, R., & Baijed, M. (2021, December). A review of artificial intelligence based platform in human resource recruitment process. In 2021 6th IEEE International Conference on Recent Advances and Innovations in Engineering (ICRAIE) (Vol. 6, pp. 1-5). IEEE.

Saif, N., Khan, S. U., Shaheen, I., ALotaibi, F. A., Alnfiai, M. M., & Arif, M. (2024). Chat-GPT; validating technology acceptance model (TAM) in education sector via ubiquitous learning mechanism. *Computers in Human Behavior, 154*, 108097. DOI: 10.1016/j.chb.2023.108097

Salekshahrezaee, Z., Leevy, J. L., & Khoshgoftaar, T. M. (2023). The effect of feature extraction and data sampling on credit card fraud detection. *Journal of Big Data, 10*(1), 6. DOI: 10.1186/s40537-023-00684-w

Santomartino, S. M., Zech, J. R., Hall, K., Jeudy, J., Parekh, V., & Yi, P. H. (2024). Evaluating the Performance and Bias of Natural Language Processing Tools in Labeling Chest Radiograph Reports. *Radiology, 313*(1), e232746. DOI: 10.1148/radiol.232746 PMID: 39436298

Saouabe, A., Oualla, H., Mazar, M., & Messadia, M. (2024, Dec). Evolution of Human Resources Management Methods: From Traditional Approaches to Generative Artificial Intelligence. In *2024 International Conference on Decision Aid Sciences and Applications (DASA)* (pp. 1-5). IEEE. DOI: 10.1109/DASA63652.2024.10836655

Sathyaseelan, D. D., & Siva, D. S. (2024). Role of Artificial Intelligence in Reshaping the Human Resource Practices. *Educational Administration: Theory And Practice, 30*(4), 354–359.

Saumard, M. (2023). Enhancing Speech Emotions Recognition Using Multivariate Functional Data Analysis. *Big Data and Cognitive Computing, 7*(3), 146. DOI: 10.3390/bdcc7030146

Shaddiq, S. (2023). Khuzaini, Irpan, M.: Governance of human resources management in the digital era. *J. Bus. Manag. Stud., 5*(3), 80–96. DOI: 10.32996/jbms.2023.5.3.8

Shuford, J. (2024). Exploring Ethical Dimensions in AI: Navigating Bias and Fairness in the Field. Journal of Artificial Intelligence General Science (JAIGS) ISSN:3006-4023, 103–124.

Smelyakov, K., Hurova, Y., & Osiievskyi, S. (2023). Analysis of the effectiveness of using machine learning algorithms to make hiring decisions. *Proceedings of CEUR Workshop*, 1613, 0073.

Smith, M. J., & Fleming, M. F.. (2016). Virtual reality job interview training and 6-month employment outcomes for individuals with substance use disorders. *Journal of Vocational Rehabilitation, 44*(3), 323–331. DOI: 10.3233/JVR-160802 PMID: 31656389

Smith, M. J., Fleming, M. F., Wright, M. A., Jordan, N., Humm, L. B., Olsen, D., & Bell, M. D. (2015). Job offers to individuals with severe mental illness after participation in virtual reality job interview training. *Psychiatric Services (Washington, D.C.), 66*(11), 1173–1179. DOI: 10.1176/appi.ps.201400504 PMID: 26130002

Smith, M. J., & Ginger, E. J.. (2015). Virtual reality job interview training for individuals with schizophrenia seeking employment. *Schizophrenia Research, 166*(1-3), 86–91. DOI: 10.1016/j.schres.2015.05.022 PMID: 26032567

Smith, M. J., Parham, B. D., Mitchell, J., Blajeski, S., Harrington, M., Ross, B., Johnson, J., Brydon, D. M., Johnson, J. E., Cuddeback, G. S., Smith, J. D., Bell, M. D., Mcgeorge, R., Kaminski, K., Suganuma, A., & Kubiak, S. (2023). Virtual reality job interview training for adults receiving prison-based employment services: A randomized controlled feasibility and initial effectiveness trial. *Criminal Justice and Behavior, 50*(2), 272–293. DOI: 10.1177/00938548221081447 PMID: 38881730

Smith, M. J., Sherwood, K., Ross, B., Oulvey, E. A., Monahan, J. A., Sipovic, J. E., Atkins, M. S., Danielson, E. C., Jordan, N., & Smith, J. D. (2022). Scaling out virtual interview training for transition-age youth: A quasi-experimental hybrid effectiveness-implementation study. *Career Development and Transition for Exceptional Individuals*, *45*(4), 213–227. DOI: 10.1177/21651434221081273 PMID: 38882261

Smith, M. J., & Wright, M. A.. (2015). Vocational outcomes for young adults with autism spectrum disorders six months after virtual reality job interview training. *Journal of Autism and Developmental Disorders*, *45*(10), 3364–3369. DOI: 10.1007/s10803-015-2470-1 PMID: 25986176

Speed, F., & Kulichyova, A. (2021). The role of talent intermediaries in accessing and developing refugee talent pools. *Journal of Organizational Effectiveness: People and Performance*, *8*(4), 407–426. DOI: 10.1108/JOEPP-01-2021-0023

StaticData_IDX. (n.d.). https://www.idx.co.id/StaticData/NewsAndAnnouncement/ANNOUNCEMENTSTOCK/From_EREP/202503/9a1083775c_cbda72f34a.pdf

Staubitz, J., Renz, J., Meinel, C., & Teusner, R. (2022). Using MOOC analytics to evaluate digital learning behaviors and predict professional competencies. *IEEE Transactions on Learning Technologies*, *15*(2), 210–223. DOI: 10.1109/TLT.2022.3160012

Stone, D. L., Deadrick, D. L., Lukaszewski, K. M., & Johnson, R. (2015). The influence of technology on the future of human resource management. *Human Resource Management Review*, *25*(2), 216–231. DOI: 10.1016/j.hrmr.2015.01.002

Suen, H.-Y., & Hung, K.-E. (2023). Comparing job applicant deception in asynchronous vs synchronous video interviews, with and without AI-assisted assessments. *Information Technology & People*, *38*(2), 963–983. DOI: 10.1108/ITP-02-2023-0189

Sühr, T., Hilgard, S., & Lakkaraju, H. (2021). Does Fair Ranking Improve Minority Outcomes? Understanding the Interplay of Human and Algorithmic Biases in Online Hiring. 989–999.

Tambe, P., Cappelli, P., & Yakubovich, V. (2019). Artificial intelligence in human resources management: Challenges and a path forward. *California Management Review*, *61*(4), 15–42. DOI: 10.1177/0008125619867910

Ullah, R., Ullah, I., Khurshaid, T., Shah, W. A., Alibakhshikenari, M., Anjam, F., Asif, M., Ali, S. M., Shah, S., & Wuttisittikulkij, L. (2023). Speech Emotion Recognition Using Convolution Neural Networks and Multi-Head Convolutional Transformer. *Sensors (Basel)*, *23*(13), 6212. DOI: 10.3390/s23136212 PMID: 37448062

UNESCO. (2022). *AI and education: Guidance for policymakers*. United Nations Educational, Scientific and Cultural Organization. https://unesdoc.unesco.org/ark:/48223/pf0000376709

Unver, M. B. (2023). Governing fiduciary relationships or building up a governance model for trust in AI? Review of healthcare as a socio-technical system. *International Review of Law Computers & Technology, 37*(2), 198–226. DOI: 10.1080/13600869.2023.2192569

Upadhyay, A. K., & Khandelwal, K. (2018). Applying artificial intelligence: Implications for recruitment. *Strategic HR Review, 17*(5), 255–258. DOI: 10.1108/SHR-07-2018-0051

Van den Heuvel, S., & Bondarouk, T. (2017). The rise (and fall?) of HR analytics: A study into the future application, value, structure, and system support. *Journal of Organizational Effectiveness: People and Performance, 4*(2), 157–178. DOI: 10.1108/JOEPP-03-2017-0022

Van Esch, P., Black, J. S., & Ferolie, J. (2019). Marketing AI recruitment: The next phase in job application and selection. *Computers in Human Behavior, 90*, 215–222. DOI: 10.1016/j.chb.2018.09.009

Van Hoye, G., & Lievens, F. (2009). Tapping the grapevine: A closer look at word-of-mouth as a recruitment source. *The Journal of Applied Psychology, 94*(2), 341–352. DOI: 10.1037/a0014066 PMID: 19271794

Vedapradha, R., Hariharan, R., Praveenraj, D. D., Sudha, E., & Ashok, J. (2023). Talent acquisition—Artificial intelligence to manage recruitment. *E3S Web of Conferences, 376*, 05001.

Venkatesh, V., Morris, M. G., Davis, G. B., & Davis, F. D. (2003). User acceptance of information technology: Toward a unified view. *Management Information Systems Quarterly, 27*(3), 425–478. DOI: 10.2307/30036540

Voigt, P., & Von dem Bussche, A. (2017). The eu general data protection regulation (gdpr). A practical guide, 1st ed., Cham: Springer International Publishing, 10(3152676), 10-5555.

Volynets, S., Saarimäki, H., Nummenmaa, L., & Smirnov, D. (2020). Statistical pattern recognition reveals shared neural signatures for displaying and recognizing specific facial expressions. *Social Cognitive and Affective Neuroscience, 15*(8), 803–813. DOI: 10.1093/scan/nsaa110 PMID: 33007782

Wahyuningrum, S. R. (2022, Oct). *Analisis Penilaian Mahasiswa Terhadap Strategi Pembelaran Dosen Institut Agama Islam Periode Transisi Normal.* AICIS, UIN MATARAM. http://repository.iainmadura.ac.id/795/

Wahyuningrum, S. R., & Damayanti, M. C. O. (2024). *Self-Management: Peningkatan Konsentrasi Belajar Siswa SMPN 1 Galis* (SSRN Scholarly Paper 4932267). Social Science Research Network. DOI: 10.2139/ssrn.4932267

Wahyuningrum, S. R., & Fitriyah. (2023). Pengaruh Penggunaan Gadget Terhadap Pola Belajar Siswa di SMPN 4 Pamekasan. *DA'WA: Jurnal Bimbingan Penyuluhan & Konseling Islam, 2*(2). https://doi.org/DOI: 10.36420/dawa.v2i2.217

Wahyuningrum, S. R., & Fransiska, M. (2023). Pengaruh Efikasi Diri dan Kemandirian terhadap Pilihan Karier Siswa. *Edu Consilium : Jurnal Bimbingan dan Konseling Pendidikan Islam, 4*(1), Article 1. DOI: 10.19105/ec.v4i1.7713

Wahyuningrum, S. R., Putro, P. W., & Wulandari, D. R.Pera Wibowo PutroDian Ratri Wulandari. (2024). Analisis Potensi Ekonomi terhadap PAD Sektor Pariwisata Kabupaten Tulungagung di Masa Transisi Covid-19. *IQTISHADIA Jurnal Ekonomi & Perbankan Syariah, 11*(1), 1. DOI: 10.19105/iqtishadia.v11i1.10475

Wang, X., Qu, H., Wang, Y., Yang, M., Jin, Z., & He, J. (2022). M2Lens: Visualizing and Explaining Multimodal Models for Sentiment Analysis. *IEEE Transactions on Visualization and Computer Graphics, 28*(1), 802–812. DOI: 10.1109/TVCG.2021.3114794 PMID: 34587037

Wang, Y., Liang, Y., Huang, Y., & Qin, G. (2025). An automated data stream analysis framework for Internet of Vehicles based on online ensemble learning and two-dimensional fractal dimension. *The Journal of Supercomputing, 81*(5), 744. DOI: 10.1007/s11227-025-07227-5

Wang, Y., Yang, C., Lan, S., Zhu, L., & Zhang, Y. (2024). End-Edge-Cloud Collaborative Computing for Deep Learning: A Comprehensive Survey. *IEEE Communications Surveys and Tutorials, 26*(4), 2647–2683. DOI: 10.1109/COMST.2024.3393230

Wani, T. M., Mansor, H., Kartiwi, M., Gunawan, T. S., Qadri, S. A. A., & Ismail, N. (2020). Speech Emotion Recognition using Convolution Neural Networks and Deep Stride Convolutional Neural Networks. 1–6.

Weyns, D., Gerostathopoulos, I., Abbas, N., Andersson, J., Biffl, S., Brada, P., Bures, T., Di Salle, A., Lago, P., Musil, A., Musil, J., & Pelliccione, P. (2022). Preliminary results of a survey on the use of self-adaptation in industry. *Proceedings of the 17th Symposium on Software Engineering for Adaptive and Self-Managing Systems*, 70–76. DOI: 10.1145/3524844.3528077

Xu, L., Wang, K., Jung, T.-P., Xu, M., Ma, Z., & Ming, D. (2021). Enhancing transfer performance across datasets for brain-computer interfaces using a combination of alignment strategies and adaptive batch normalization. Journal of Neural Engineering, 18(4), 0460e5.

Yanamala, K. K. R. (2023). Transparency, privacy, and accountability in AI-enhanced HR processes. *Journal of Advanced Computing Systems*, *3*(3), 10–18. DOI: 10.69987/JACS.2023.30302

Yang, C., Zhao, W. X., Zhang, T., Hou, Y., Song, Y., & Wen, J.-R. (2022). Modeling Two-Way Selection Preference for Person-Job Fit.

Yassine, T. K., & Said, A. (2024). Predictive Hiring and AI: Elevating Recruitment with Optimized Neural Networks and Gradient Descent. *International Journal of Intelligent Information Systems*, *13*(6), 117–127. DOI: 10.11648/j.ijiis.20241306.11

Yuste, R., Goering, S., Bi, G., Carmena, J. M., Carter, A., Fins, J. J., & Wolpaw, J. (2017). Four ethical priorities for neurotechnologies and AI. *Nature*, *551*(7679), 159–163. DOI: 10.1038/551159a PMID: 29120438

Zbib, R., Lacasa, L. A., Retyk, F., Poves, R., Aizpuru, J., Fabregat, H., & García-Casademont, E. (2022). Learning job titles similarity from noisy skill labels. arXiv preprint arXiv:2207.00494.

Zhang, T., & Tan, Z. (2023). Deep Emotion Recognition using Facial, Speech and Textual Cues: A Survey. institute of electrical electronics engineers.

Zhang, Y., Rahman, S., & Hossain, M. Z. (2021). DeepVANet: A Deep End-to-End Network for Multi-modal Emotion Recognition (pp. 227–237). springer.

Zhang, H., Han, H., & Huang, H. (2020). Attention-Based Convolution Skip Bidirectional Long Short-Term Memory Network for Speech Emotion Recognition. *IEEE Access : Practical Innovations, Open Solutions*, *9*, 5332–5342. DOI: 10.1109/ACCESS.2020.3047395

Zhang, K., Li, Y., Wang, Z., Wang, J., & Li, X. (2021). Feature Fusion for Multimodal Emotion Recognition Based on Deep Canonical Correlation Analysis. *IEEE Signal Processing Letters*, *28*, 1898–1902. DOI: 10.1109/LSP.2021.3112314

Zhang, X., Wang, M.-J., & Guo, X.-D. (2020). Multi-modal Emotion Recognition Based on Deep Learning in Speech. *Video and Text.*, *30*, 328–333.

Zhang, Z., Zhang, S., Ni, D., Wei, Z., Yang, K., Jin, S., Huang, G., Liang, Z., Zhang, L., Li, L., Ding, H., Zhang, Z., & Wang, J. (2024). Multimodal Sensing for Depression Risk Detection: Integrating Audio, Video, and Text Data. *Sensors (Basel), 24*(12), 3714. DOI: 10.3390/s24123714 PMID: 38931497

Zhou, L., Cui, W., & Yang, F. (2024). Spatiotemporal variations and driving forces analysis of ecosystem water conservation in coastal areas of China. *Ecological Indicators, 162*, 112019. DOI: 10.1016/j.ecolind.2024.112019

Zioudi, O., Mahmoud, H., Badouch, M., Boulmane, E., & Boutaounte, M. (2025). AI-powered predictions transforming the future of brand management. In Aboudrar, I., Ilahi Bakhsh, F., Nayyar, A., & Ouachtouk, I. (Eds.), *Innovative technologies on electrical power systems for smart cities infrastructure* (pp. 177–186). Springer Nature Switzerland., DOI: 10.1007/978-3-031-86705-7_17

Zottoli, M. A., & Wanous, J. P. (2000). Recruitment source research: Current status and future directions. *Human Resource Management Review, 10*(4), 353–382. DOI: 10.1016/S1053-4822(00)00032-2

Zou, J., & Schiebinger, L. (2018). AI can be sexist and racist—It's time to make it fair. *Nature, 559*(7714), 324–326. DOI: 10.1038/d41586-018-05707-8 PMID: 30018439

About the Contributors

Mohamed Badouch combines eight years of industrial expertise in IT development with a rich academic approach. Currently a doctoral student in Artificial Intelligence at Ibn Zohr University in Agadir, he has a solid background in software and web development and holds executive responsibilities in project management and maintenance. Holding a master's degree in information systems engineering from Cadi Ayyad University (2017), he is passionate about technological innovation. He explores artificial intelligence and machine learning, notably by designing personalized recommendation solutions for tourism and e-commerce. An active member of UNESCO's Inclusive Policy Lab and a visiting lecturer at Abdelmalek Essaâdi University, he inspires with his ethical commitment and his ability to harness new technologies to address contemporary challenges.

Mehdi Boutaounte is a Moroccan computer science researcher and professor at the National School of Business and Management (ENCG) in Dakhla, affiliated with Ibn Zohr University. His research focuses on artificial intelligence, particularly in the development of personalized recommendation systems for tourism and hospitality. He has published several works on machine learning techniques for travel suggestions and hotel recommendation systems, including deep learning-based models that analyze user preferences and content such as images and reviews. Dr. Boutaounte is recognized in academic rankings within Morocco and actively contributes to research in smart tourism, computer vision, and hybrid AI systems.PhD

***

Abd. Ghofur, M.Pd is a distinguished academic with an exceptional educational background, holding doctoral degrees from two prestigious universities in East Java, Indonesia. He earned his Doctorate in Language and Literature Education from Universitas Negeri Surabaya and a Doctorate in Sociology from another leading university in the region. With over two decades of teaching experience at the Faculty of Education, he currently serves as a dedicated lecturer at IAIN Madura, an esteemed Islamic university in Indonesia. His commitment to academia is evident in his active engagement in teaching, research, and fostering innovative educational practices, particularly in digital learning. In addition to his role as an educator, He has established himself as a prolific researcher with a significant body of work available on platforms like ResearchGate and Google Scholar. He is deeply involved in scholarly publishing, serving as Editor-in-Chief of a Sinta 2-accredited journal in the field of language and literature, which is equivalent to Quartile 2 standards. His expertise extends to peer reviewing for various academic journals published in Indonesia and internationally, further showcasing his commitment to advancing global scholarship. Beyond his editorial and research responsibilities, he holds the position of Deputy Dean for Academic Affairs at IAIN Madura, where he plays a pivotal role in shaping academic strategies and policies. He is also active on the international stage, contributing as a resource person and participant in numerous global events. Currently, he serves as the President of the International Education Share to Care Volunteers (IES2CV), an organization dedicated to education, research, and community service initiatives. His unwavering dedication to education and his leadership in promoting knowledge-sharing initiatives continue to inspire and impact communities locally and globally.

Rituraj Jain is currently working in the Department of Information Technology, Marwadi University, Rajkot, Gujarat, India. He has published many papers in International Journals and Conferences. He has published 4 books. He is an Oracle Database SQL Certified Expert. He is also associated with professional bodies like the Indian Society of Technical Education (ISTE), Computer Science Teachers Association (CSTA), Academy & Industry Research Collaboration Center (AIRCC), International Association of Computer Science and Information Technology (IACSIT), International Association of Engineers (IAENG). His research interests include Cloud Computing, Machine Learning, Deep Learning, Fuzzy Logic, IoT, Genetic Algorithms, Big Data and Software Engineering.

ShinyK.V. is Currently working as an Assistant Professor in the Department of Computer Science and Engineering at Bharath Institute of Higher Education and Research, Chennai-600073 India. She has published more than 3 Scopus indexed Journals and 1 Book Chapter. Her research area includes Disaster Management, Artificial Intelligence, Machine Learning,and Cyber Security.

Hasna Mahmoud is a PhD researcher in Computer Science at the Faculty of Sciences University Ibn Zohr:. I graduated with a Master's degree in Big Data and

Artificial Intelligence from the Faculty of Taroudant in 2023. My research centers on advancements in Artificial Intelligence.

S. Ninisha Nels is Currently working as an Assistant Professor in the Department of Computer Science and Engineering at Noorul Islam Centre for Higher Education, Kumaracoil, Thakalai, India. She has published 4 Scopus indexed Journals and 2 Book Chapter. Her research area includes Disaster Management, Artificial Intelligence, Machine Learning,and Cyber Security.

Mathusoothana S Kumar R. received his Bachelor's degree in Electronics and Communication Engineering from National Engineering College, Kovilpatti in 1994. He received Master's degree in Computer Science and Engineering from Arulmigu Kalasalingam College of Engineering, Srivilliputtur, Krishnankoil in 1998. He received Ph.D in Information and communication engineering from Anna University, Chennai in 2014. He is currently working as Professor & Head, in the Department of Information Technology, Noorul Islam Centre for Higher Education, Kumaracoil. His research area includes Image processing, Information Coding Techniques, Database Management Systems, Data Mining, and Multimedia. Published a patent, thirty papers in International Journals and three papers in National Journals. Published a text book "Information Theory and Coding" during 2004. He is a Life member of ISTE and Faculty Advisor of Student Chapter IET

Divya S.V. M.E, Ph.D., is currently working as a Professor at the Department of Computer Science & Engineering in V.S.B College of Engineering Technical Campus, Coimbatore, TamilNadu, India . She has the teaching experience of more than 16 years and had published more than 20 research papers in SCI/Scopus indexed journals, 2 Patents and 2 text books. She had published more than 15 papers in National/International Conferences.She received her B.Tech Degree in Information Technology from Jayamatha Engineering College, Aralvoimozhi and M.E Degree in Computer Science and Engineering from Mepco Schlenk Engineering College, Sivakasi in 2005 and 2007 respectively. She received her Ph.D in Computer Science and Engineering at Noorul Islam Centre for Higher Education in 2017 under the area of Cloud Computing and guiding four research scholars. Her research area includes Wireless Communications, Cloud Computing, Big Data and Cyber Security. Acted a s reviewer in many journals and IEEE conferences. She is a Life member of ISTE

Saptarshi Kumar Sarkar is an Assistant Professor at Brainware University. With a dedication to academic excellence, he brings a wealth of knowledge and experience to his students. His research interests include AI, ML and Social Networking, contributing significantly to advancements in his field.

Anupama Sen, an Assistant Professor at Brainware University, is committed to academic excellence. She brings extensive knowledge and experience to her students, with research interests spanning artificial intelligence (AI), machine learning (ML), and social networking. Her contributions have significantly advanced these fields.

L. Shalini is currently working as an Assistant Professor in the Department of Computer Science & Engineering at Bharath Institute of Higher Education and Research, Chennai-600073. Her Research Area includes Data Mining, Artificial Intelligence, Cloud Computing, IoT and Web Technology.

Satya Subrahmanyam is a distinguished academic leader, researcher, and institutional strategist with over 27 years of experience in higher education, leadership, and research management. He holds two PhDs and a Postdoctoral qualification from the Polytechnic Institute of Leiria, Portugal. Currently serving as Professor and Dean (Research) at Holy Spirit University of Kaslik (USEK), Lebanon, he spearheads research initiatives that enhance academic excellence and institutional reputation. He played a pivotal role in the development of the Catholic University in Erbil, Kurdistan, where he established new departments, led research programs, and collaborated on international educational projects. As a founding member and Managing Partner of Vignan Institute of Technology and Management, India, he contributed to its transformation into a premier institution. With expertise in AI-driven business strategies, HR analytics, and leadership in technology adoption, he has published extensively, guided PhD research, and led training programs in corporate and academic settings.

M. Sudhan is currently pursuing his B.Tech Artificial Intelligence and Data Science at V.S.B College of Engineering Technical Campus, Coimbatore. He has published one patent and journal. His area of interest includes, Artificial Intelligence, Cloud Computing and Cyber Security

R. Sukesh is currently pursuing his B.Tech Artificial Intelligence and Data Science at V.S.B College of Engineering Technical Campus, Coimbatore, His Research Area includes Data Ware Housing, Cloud Computing, IoT and Web Technology.

P. Venkadesh M.E, Ph.D., is currently working as a Professor in the Department of Artificial Intelligence & Data Science in V.S.B College of Engineering Technical Campus, Coimbatore, TamilNadu, India . He received his M.E Degree in Computer Science & Engineering from Sathyabama University, Chennai, TamilNadu, India in 2007. He completed his Ph.D at Noorul Islam Centre for Higher Education in 2017 under the area of Network Security . He is guiding five research scholars and three scholars received their Ph.D degree under his guidance. His research area includes Network Security, Image Processing, Wireless Communications and Cloud Computing. He has a teaching experience of more than 22 years and had published more than 30 research papers in SCI/Scopus indexed journals . He has published more than 30 Patents and two patents were granted. He has published more than 5 text books, 5 SCOPUS indexed Book Chapters He is a life member of ISTE

Sri Rizqi Wahyuningrum, Born in Probolinggo-Indonesia, June 13, 1991. Wahyu, his nickname, is a lecturer in Statistics at the State Islamic Institute of Madura starting in 2019. Wahyu received a Bachelor of Science in Statistics (2013) from the Faculty of Mathematics and Natural Sciences, Sepuluh Nopember Institute of Technology, Surabaya (ITS), and a Master of Science in Statistics (2014) from the Faculty of Mathematics and Natural Sciences, Sepuluh Nopember Institute of Technology, Surabaya (ITS). Before working in the world of education as an educator, Wahyu had worked as an analyst at one of the Indonesian Ministries, a permanent employee at one of the BUMN Companies (PT BNI [Persero], Tbk.). Wahyu had written an article published in a Scopus-indexed journal in 2016 with the title GSTARX-GLS model for spatio-temporal data forecasting. In addition, Wahyu is active in writing articles, journal editor (Jurnal Edu Consilium, NUANSA, and KARSA) in the IAIN Madura environment, and the Cognitive journal, as well as the director of the ISBN book publishing center, UIN Madura Press. She has written several books, which have ISBNs, especially in the field of statistics.

Index

N

P

R

S

T

V

W

www.ingramcontent.com/pod-product-compliance
Lightning Source LLC
LaVergne TN
LVHW080855300926
849162LV00003B/423